WOLVERINE
ORIGINS & ENDINGS

WRITER: DANIEL WAY
BREAKDOWNS: JAVIER SALTARES
FINISHES: MARK TEXEIRA
COLORS: J.D. SMITH
LETTERS: VIRTUAL CALLIGRAPHY'S RANDY GENTILE
COVER ARTISTS: JOE QUESADA & RICHARD ISANOVE
AND KAARE ANDREWS

ASSISTANT EDITOR: MICHAEL O'CONNOR
EDITOR: AXEL ALONSO

COLLECTION EDITOR: JENNIFER GRÜNWALD
ASSISTANT EDITOR: MICHAEL SHORT
ASSOCIATE EDITOR: MARK D. BEAZLEY
SENIOR EDITOR, SPECIAL PROJECTS: JEFF YOUNGQUIST
VICE PRESIDENT OF SALES: DAVID GABRIEL
PRODUCTION: JERRY KALINOWSKI
BOOK DESIGNER: JEOF VITA
VICE PRESIDENT OF CREATIVE: TOM MARVELLI

EDITOR IN CHIEF: JOE QUESADA
PUBLISHER: DAN BUCKLEY

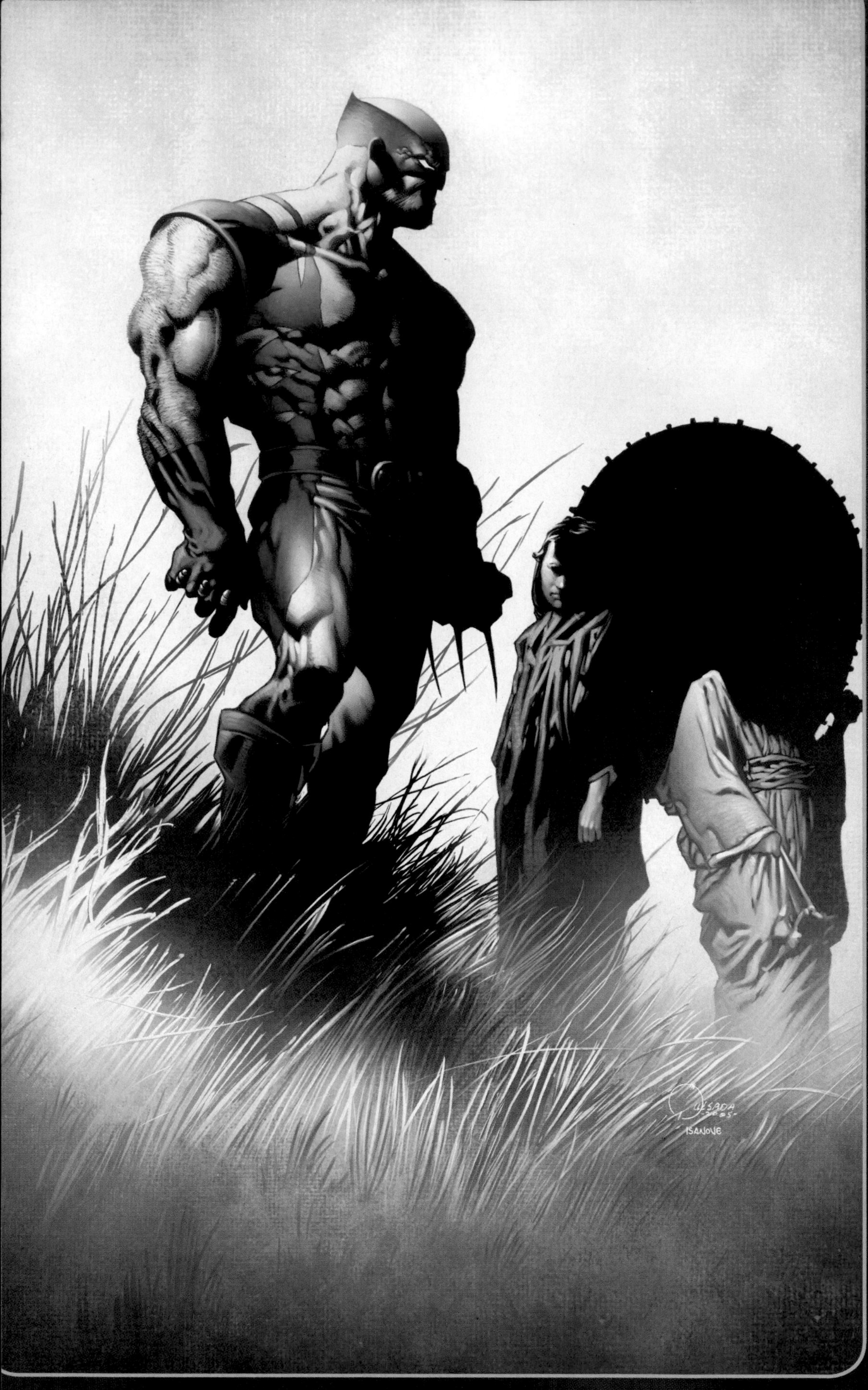

ISSUE #36

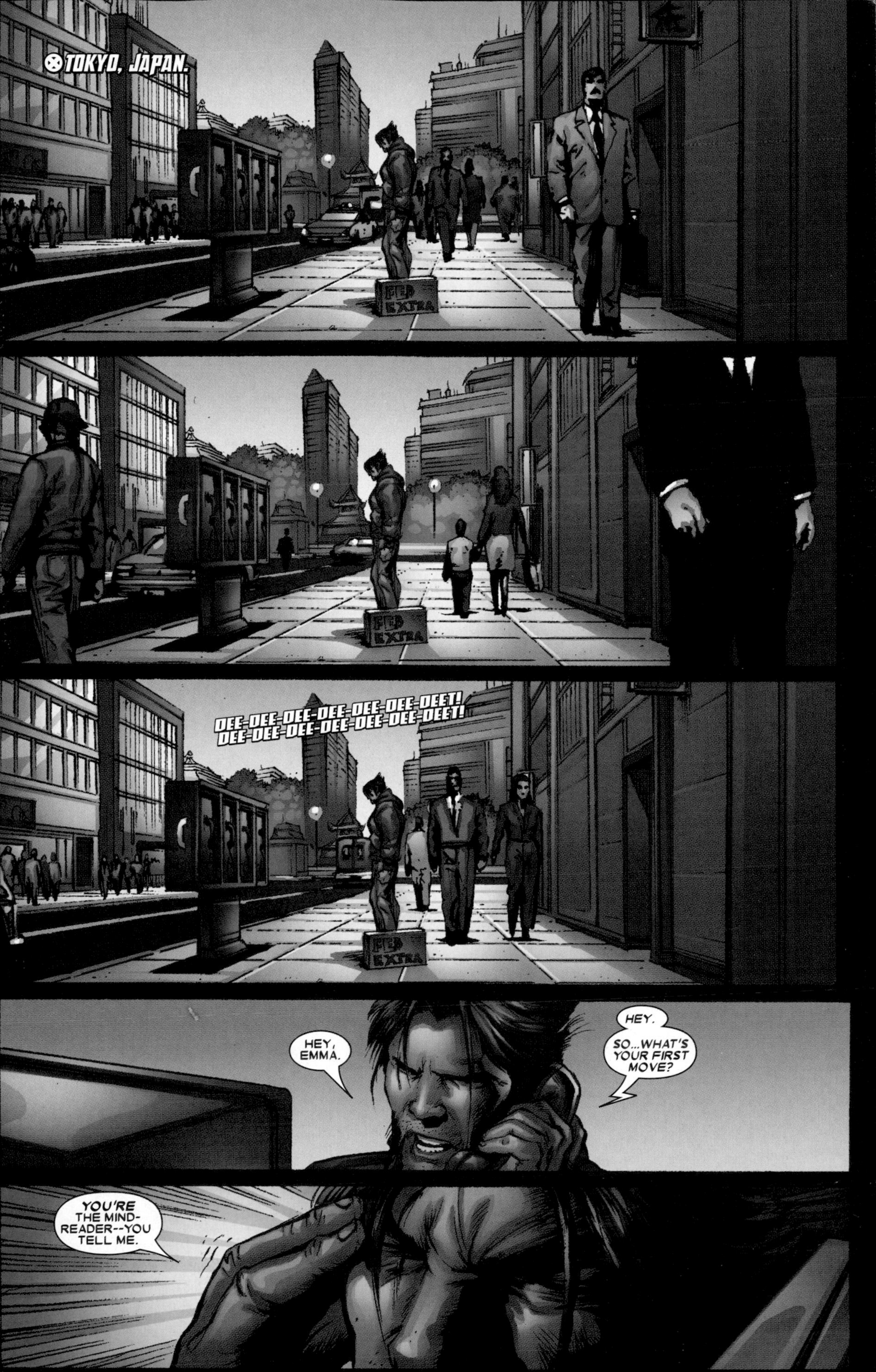
TOKYO, JAPAN.
FED EXTRA
DEE-DEE-DEE-DEE-DEE-DEE-DEET!
DEE-DEE-DEE-DEE-DEE-DEE-DEET!
HEY, EMMA.
HEY.
SO...WHAT'S YOUR FIRST MOVE?
YOU'RE THE MIND-READER--YOU TELL ME.

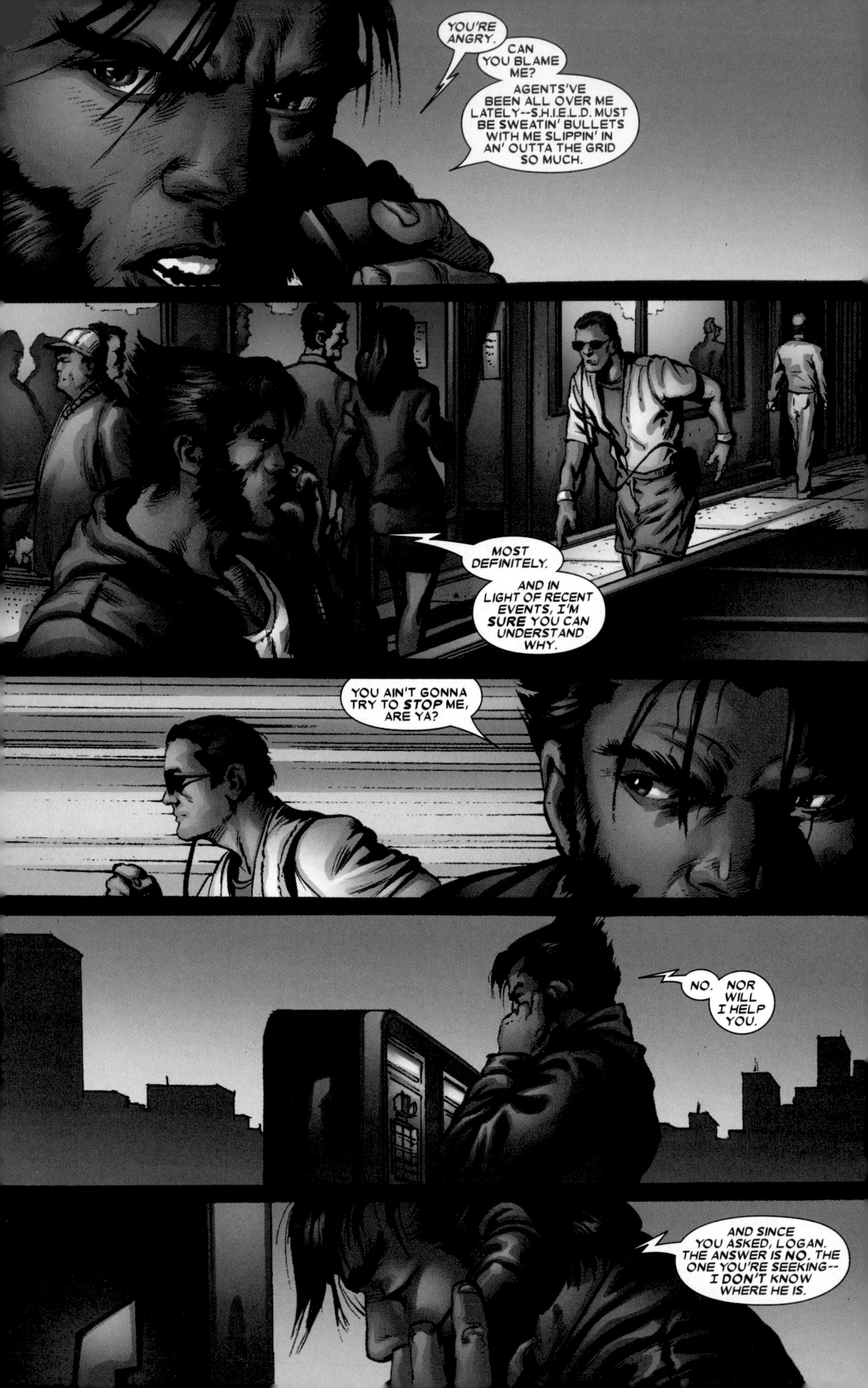
YOU'RE ANGRY.
CAN YOU BLAME ME?
AGENTS'VE BEEN ALL OVER ME LATELY--S.H.I.E.L.D. MUST BE SWEATIN' BULLETS WITH ME SLIPPIN' IN AN' OUTTA THE GRID SO MUCH.
MOST DEFINITELY.
AND IN LIGHT OF RECENT EVENTS, I'M **SURE** YOU CAN UNDERSTAND WHY.
YOU AIN'T GONNA TRY TO ***STOP*** ME, ARE YA?
NO. NOR WILL I HELP YOU.
AND SINCE YOU ASKED, LOGAN. THE ANSWER IS **NO**. THE ONE YOU'RE SEEKING-- ***I DON'T*** KNOW WHERE HE IS.

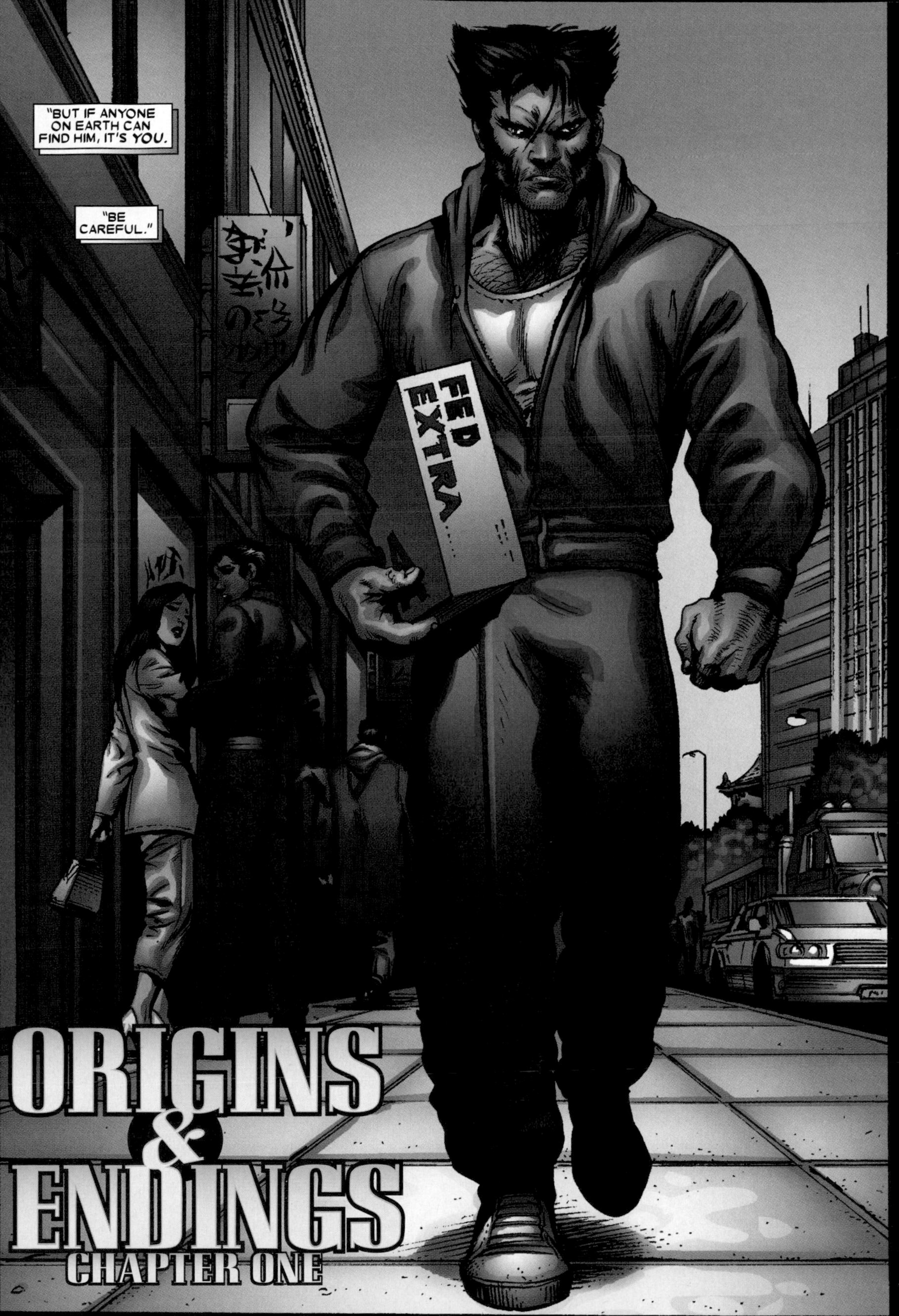
"BUT IF ANYONE ON EARTH CAN FIND HIM, IT'S *YOU*.
"BE CAREFUL."
FED EXTRA
ORIGINS & ENDINGS
CHAPTER ONE

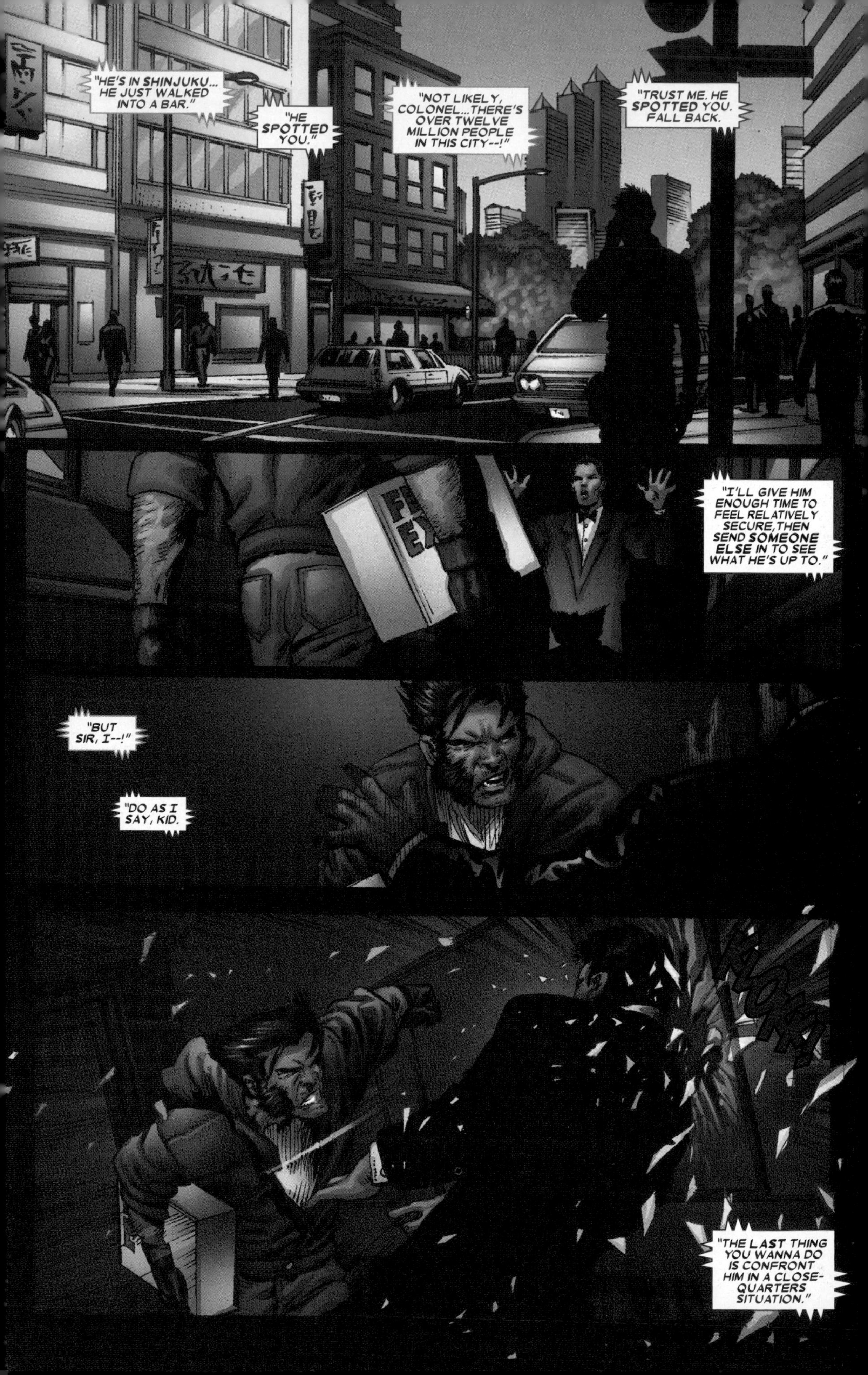
"HE'S IN SHINJUKU... HE JUST WALKED INTO A BAR."
"HE SPOTTED YOU."
"NOT LIKELY, COLONEL...THERE'S OVER TWELVE MILLION PEOPLE IN THIS CITY--!"
"TRUST ME. HE SPOTTED YOU. FALL BACK.
"I'LL GIVE HIM ENOUGH TIME TO FEEL RELATIVELY SECURE, THEN SEND SOMEONE ELSE IN TO SEE WHAT HE'S UP TO."
"BUT SIR, I--!"
"DO AS I SAY, KID.
KLOKK!
"THE LAST THING YOU WANNA DO IS CONFRONT HIM IN A CLOSE-QUARTERS SITUATION."

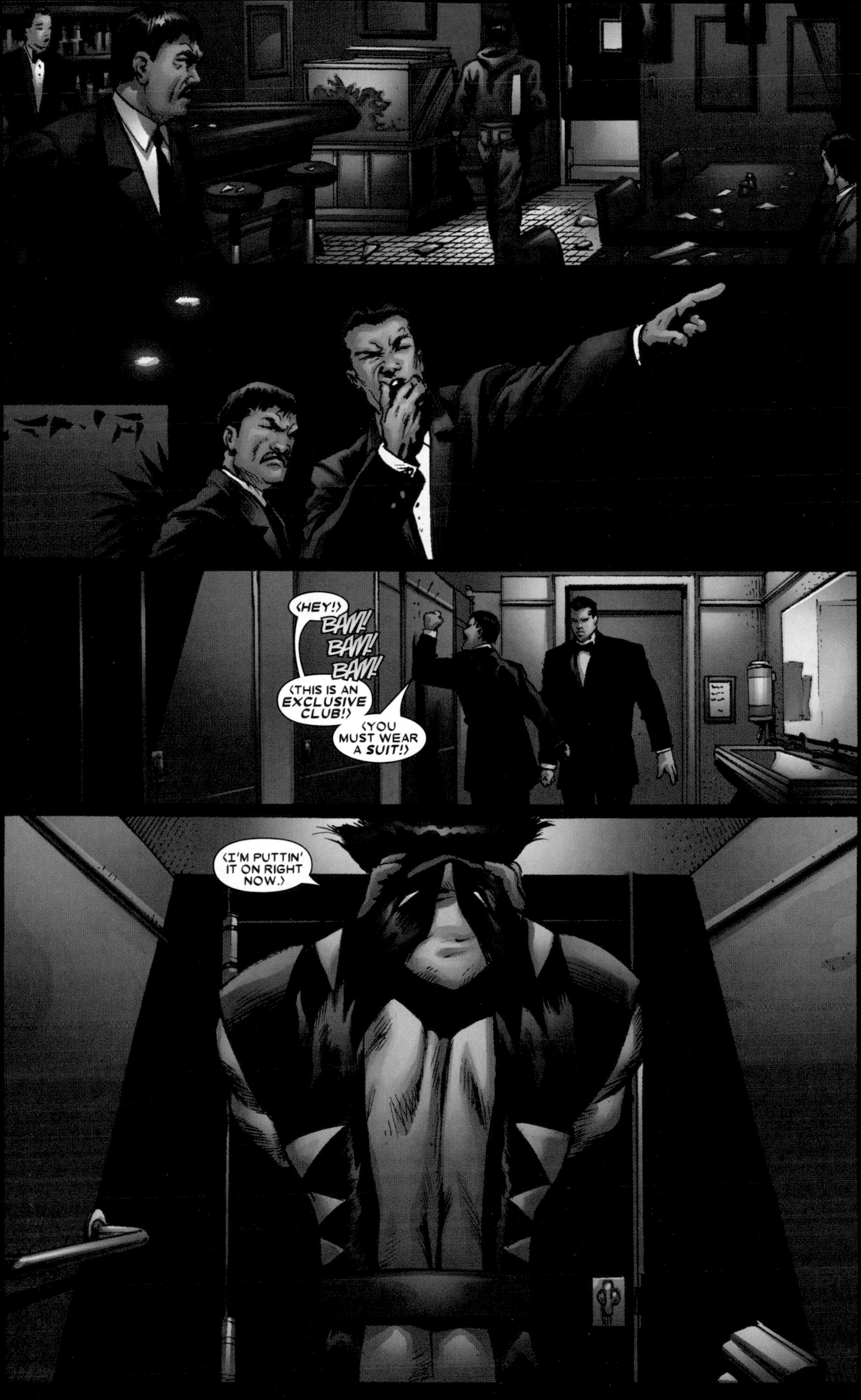
‹HEY!›
BAM!
BAM!
BAM!
‹THIS IS AN EXCLUSIVE CLUB!›
‹YOU MUST WEAR A SUIT!›
‹I'M PUTTIN' IT ON RIGHT NOW.›

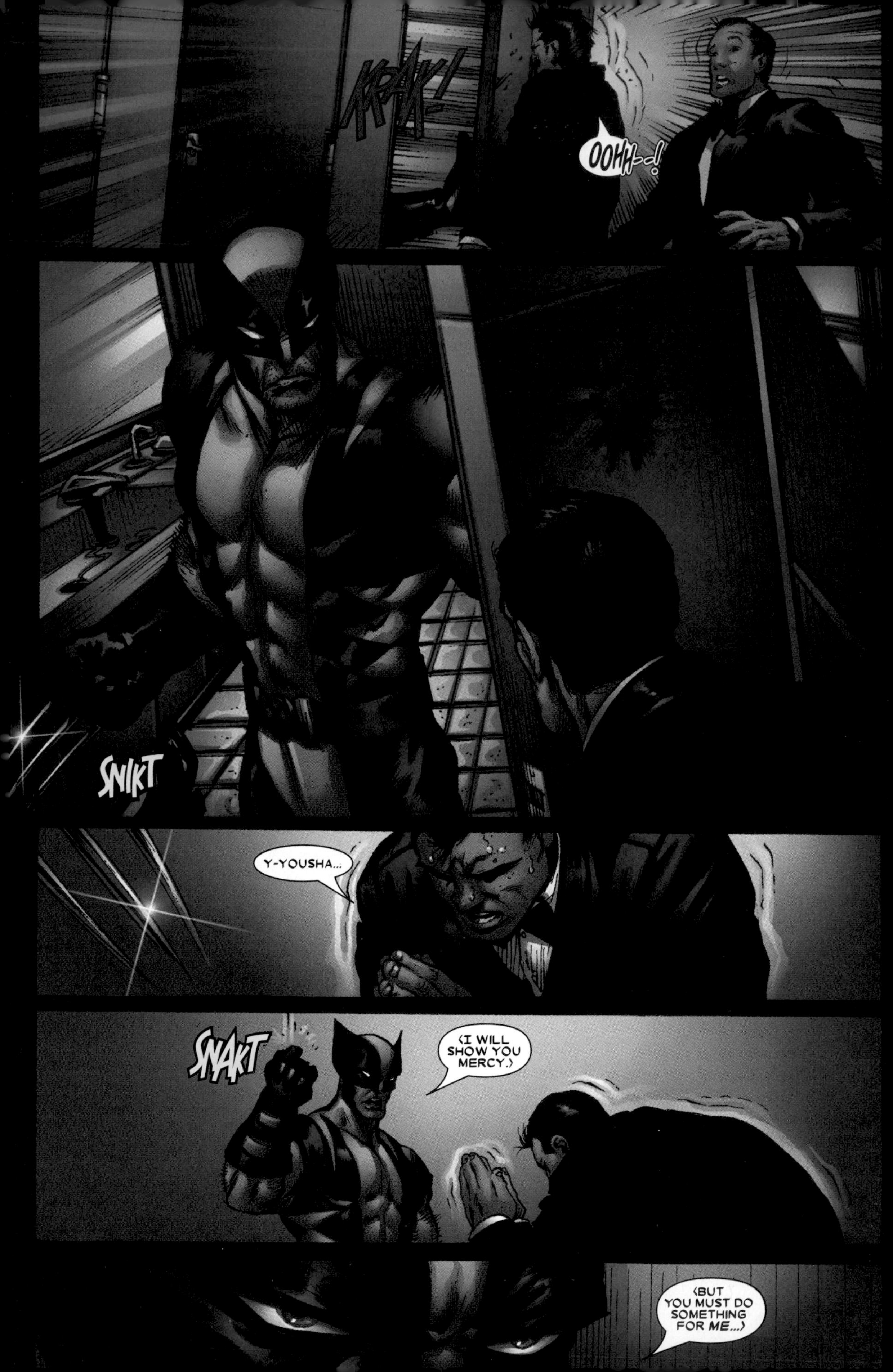
KRAK!
OOHH--!
SNIKT
Y-YOUSHA...
SNAKT
‹I WILL SHOW YOU MERCY.›
‹BUT YOU MUST DO SOMETHING FOR ME...›

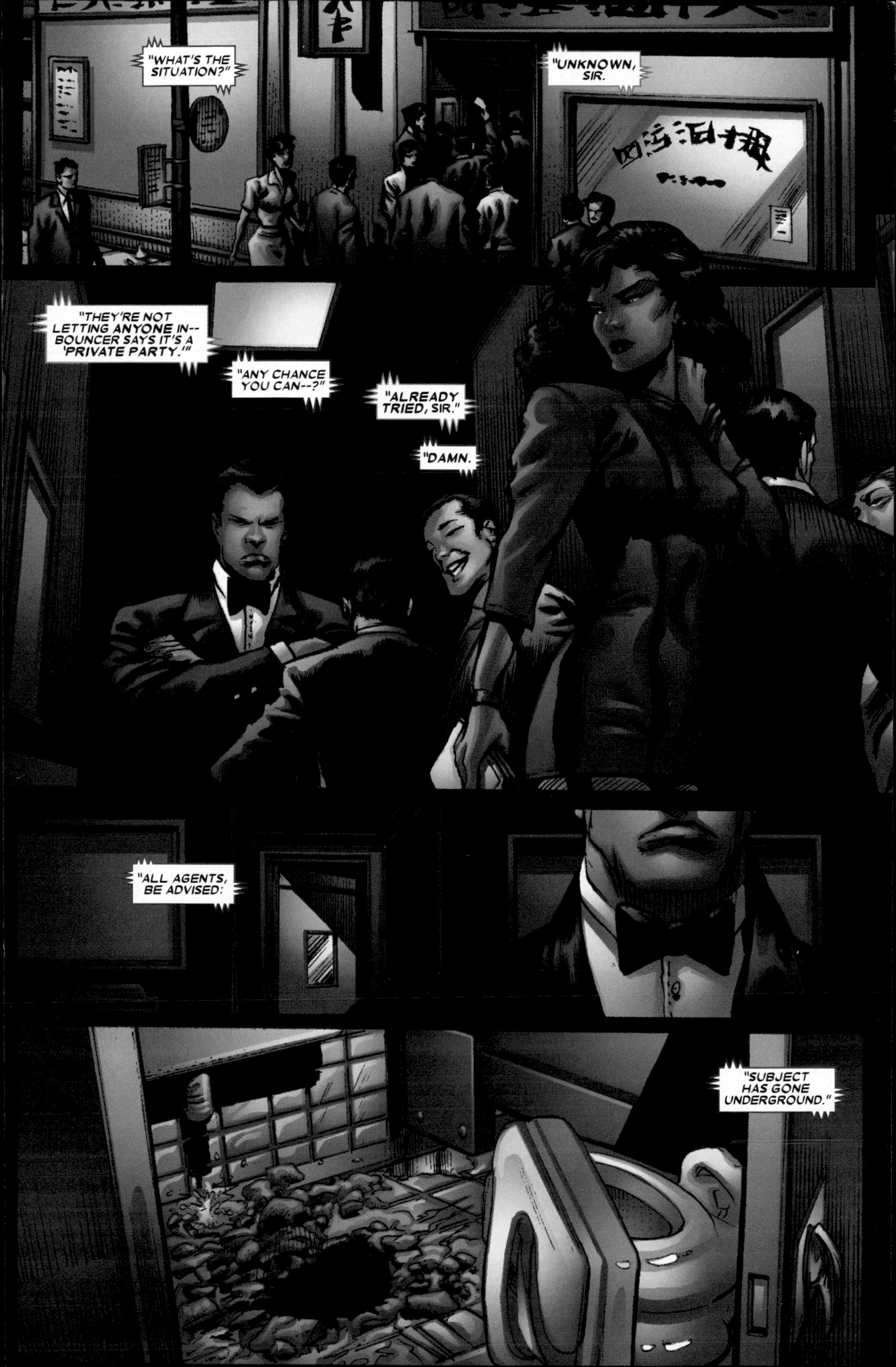
"WHAT'S THE SITUATION?"
"UNKNOWN, SIR.
"THEY'RE NOT LETTING ANYONE IN-- BOUNCER SAYS IT'S A 'PRIVATE PARTY.'"
"ANY CHANCE YOU CAN--?"
"ALREADY TRIED, SIR."
"DAMN.
"ALL AGENTS, BE ADVISED:
"SUBJECT HAS GONE UNDERGROUND."

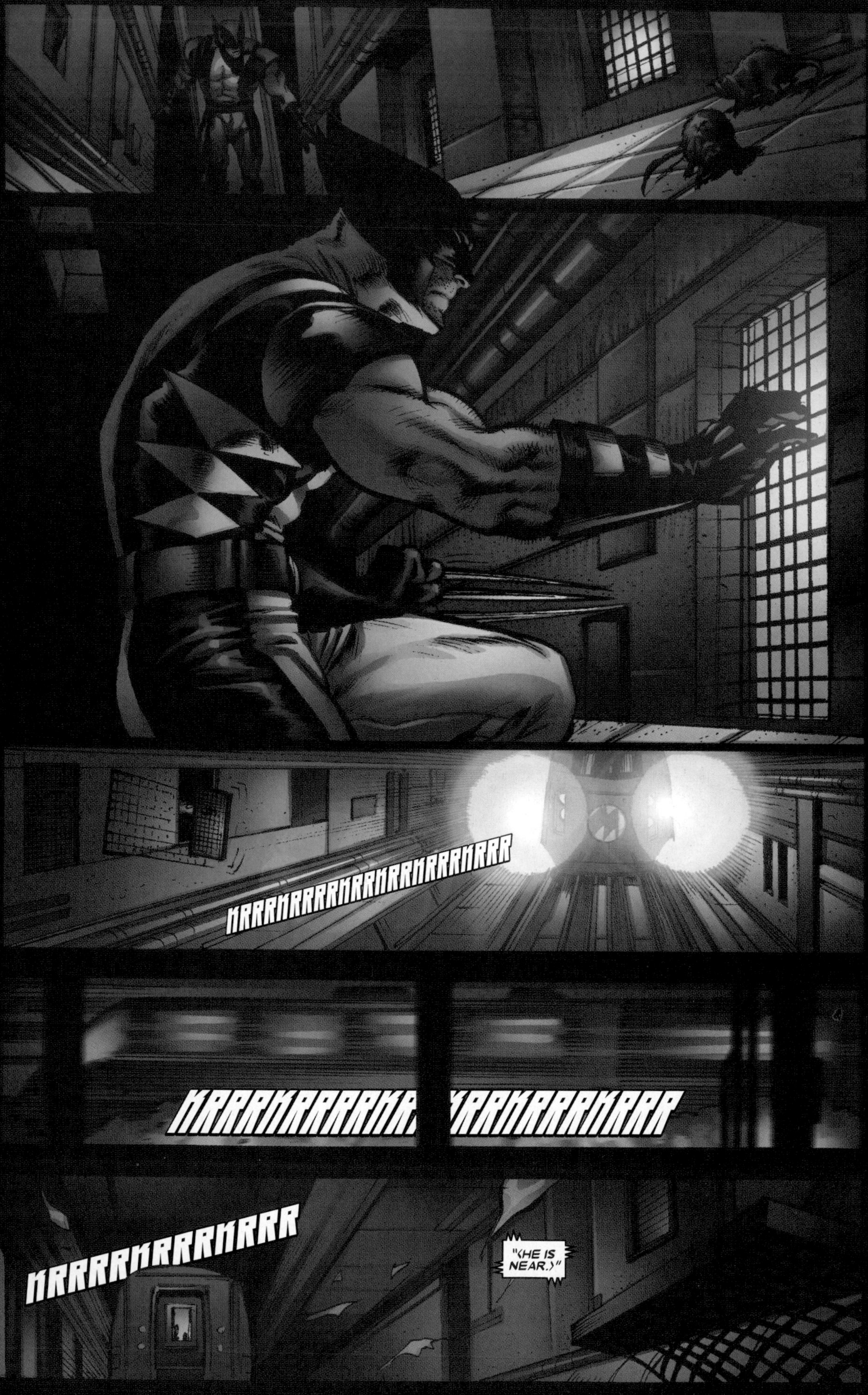
KRRRKRRRRKRRKRRKRRRKRRR
KRRRKRRRRKR
RRKRRRKRRR
KRRRRKRRRKRRR
"‹HE IS NEAR.›"

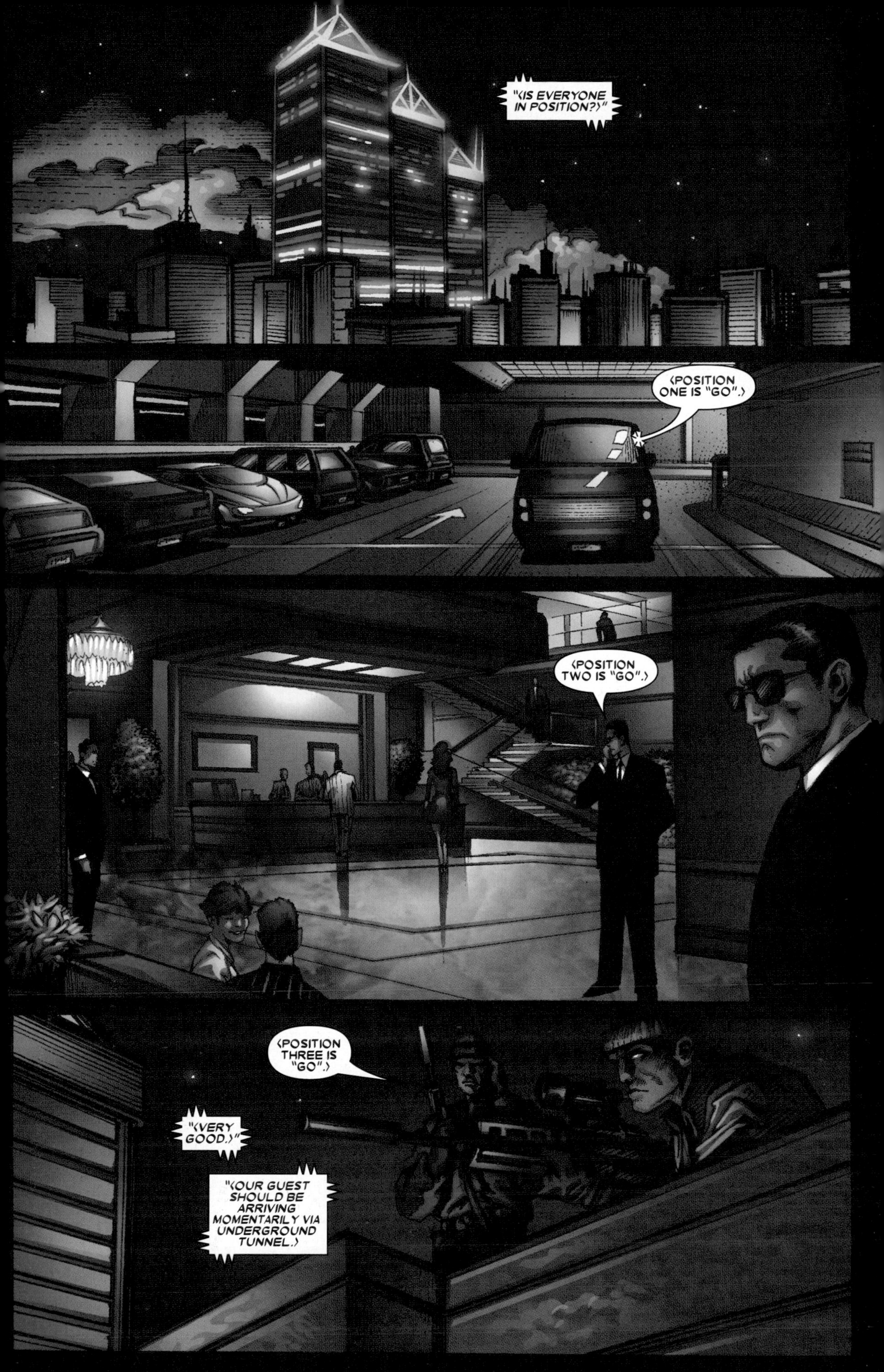
"⟨IS EVERYONE IN POSITION?⟩"
⟨POSITION ONE IS "GO".⟩
⟨POSITION TWO IS "GO".⟩
⟨POSITION THREE IS "GO".⟩
"⟨VERY GOOD.⟩"
"⟨OUR GUEST SHOULD BE ARRIVING MOMENTARILY VIA UNDERGROUND TUNNEL.⟩"

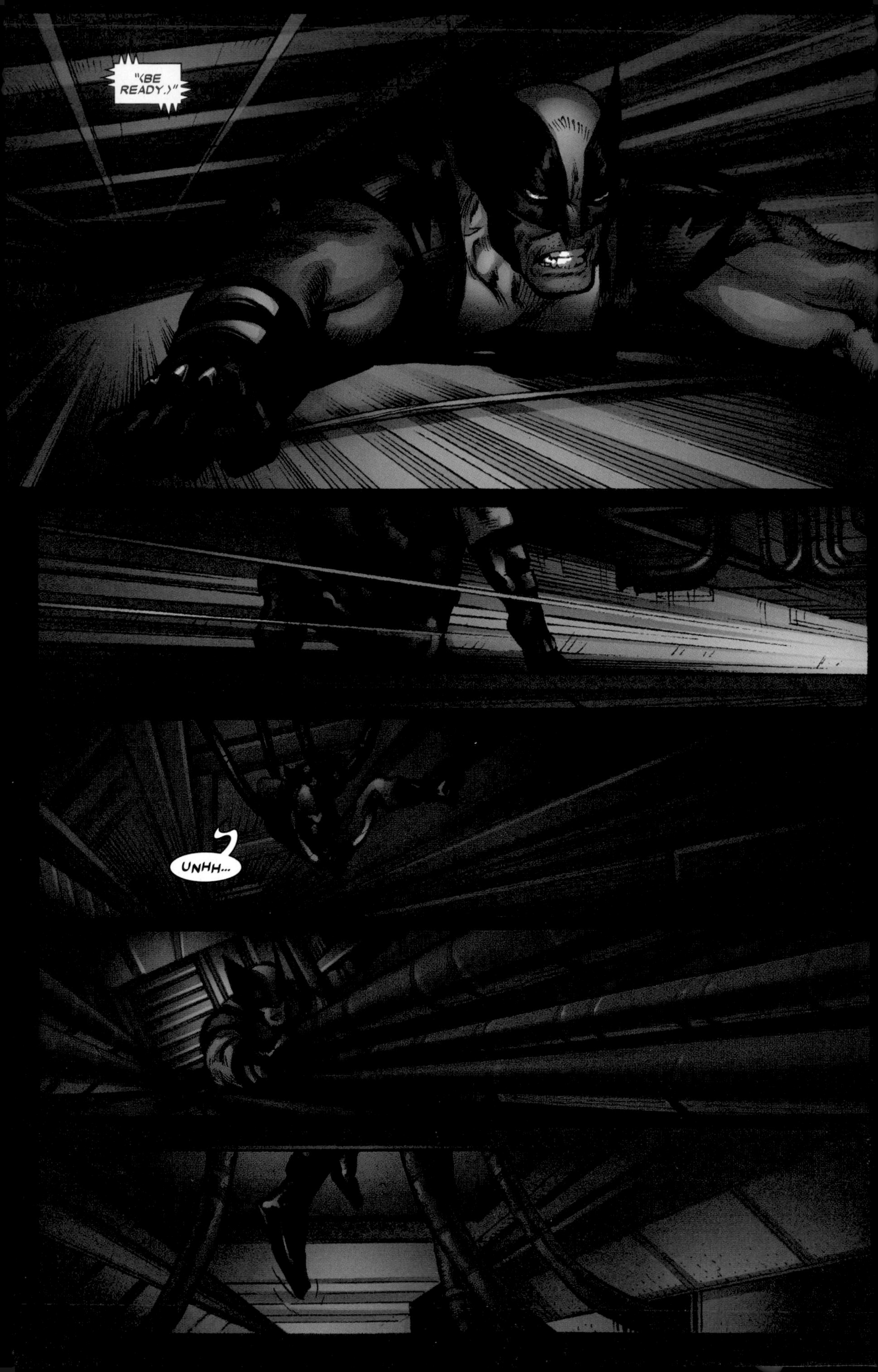
"‹BE READY.›"
UNHH...

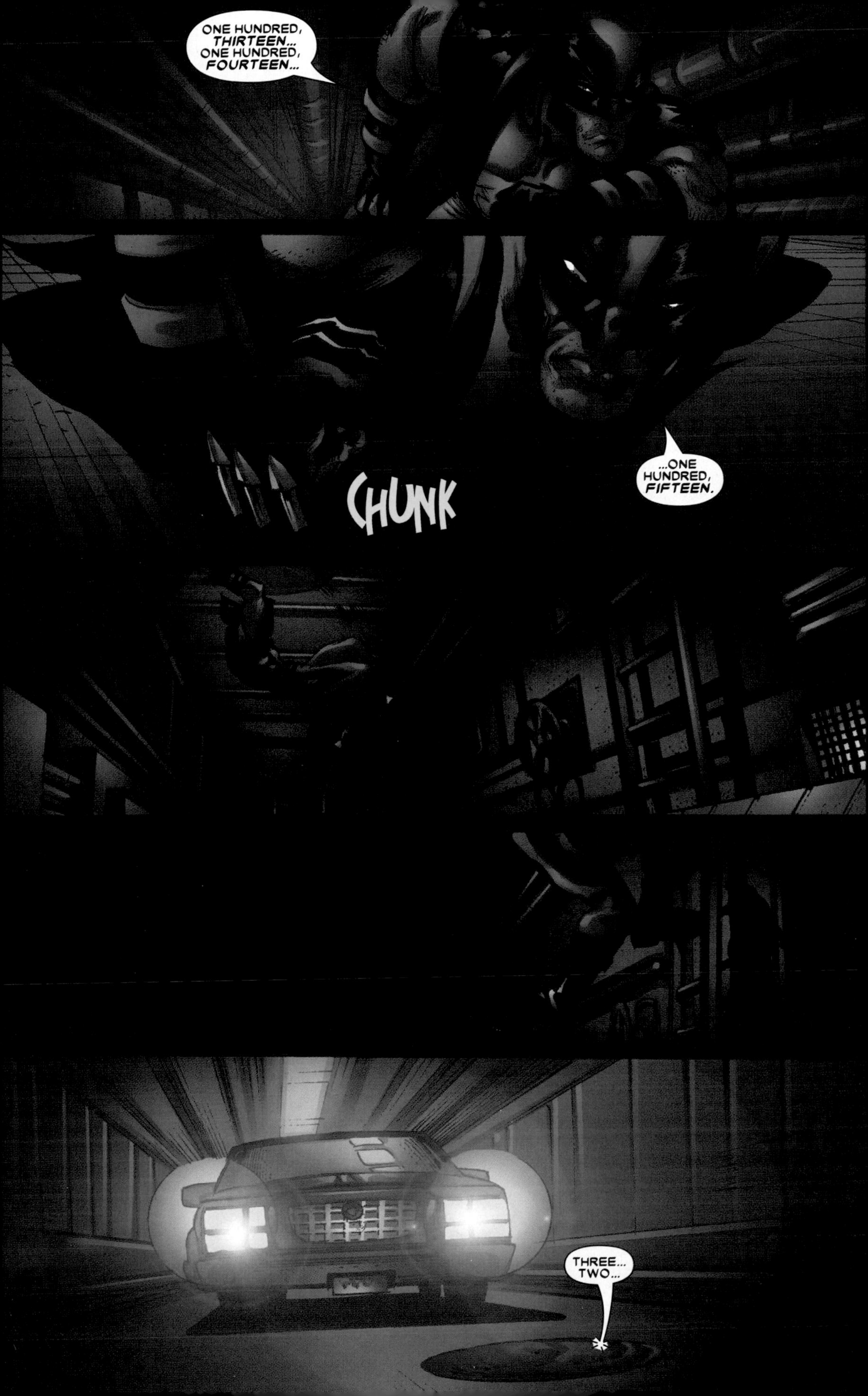
ONE HUNDRED, *THIRTEEN*... ONE HUNDRED, *FOURTEEN*...
CHUNK
...ONE HUNDRED, *FIFTEEN.*
THREE... TWO...

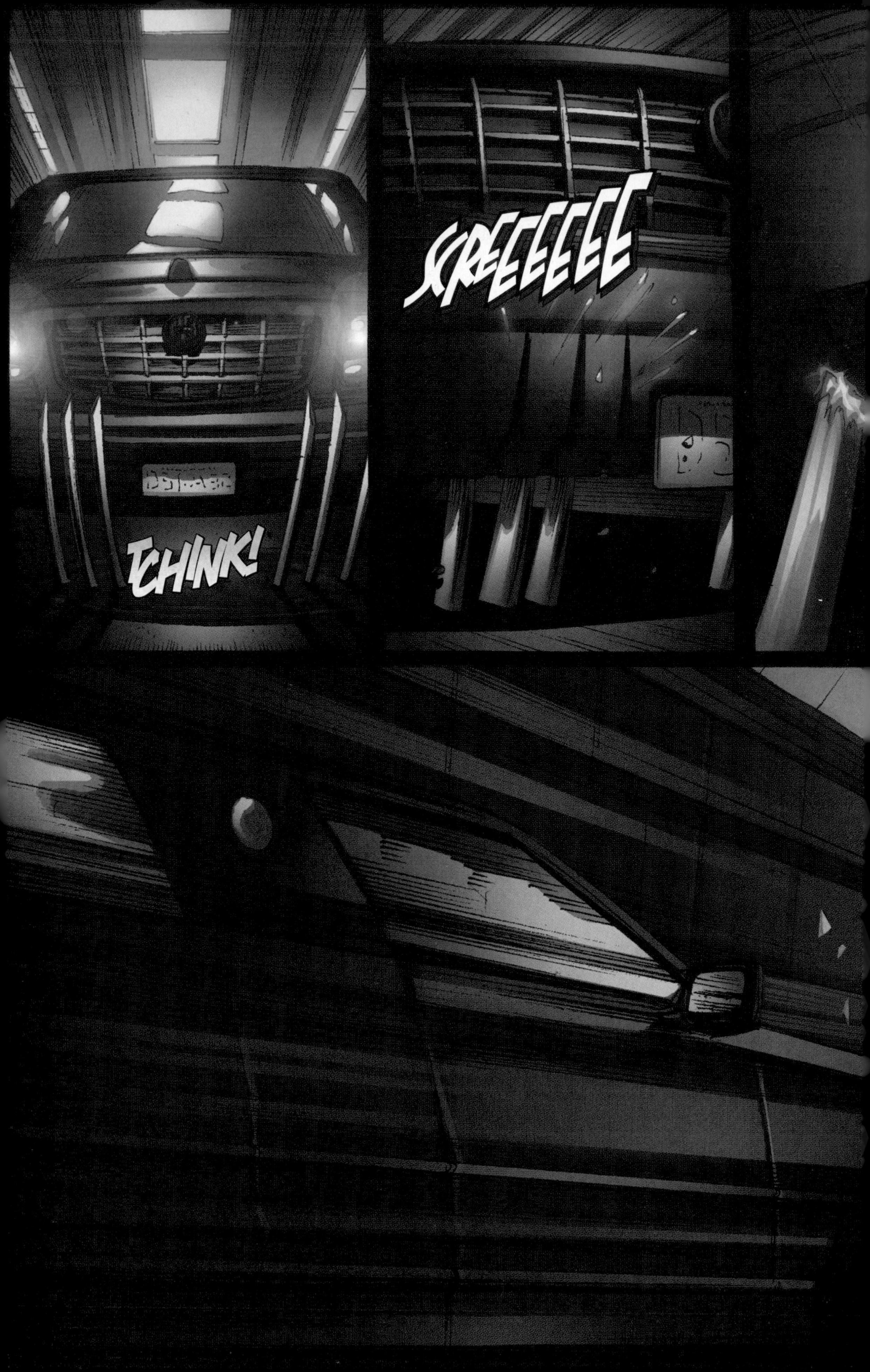
TCHINK!
SCREEEEEEE

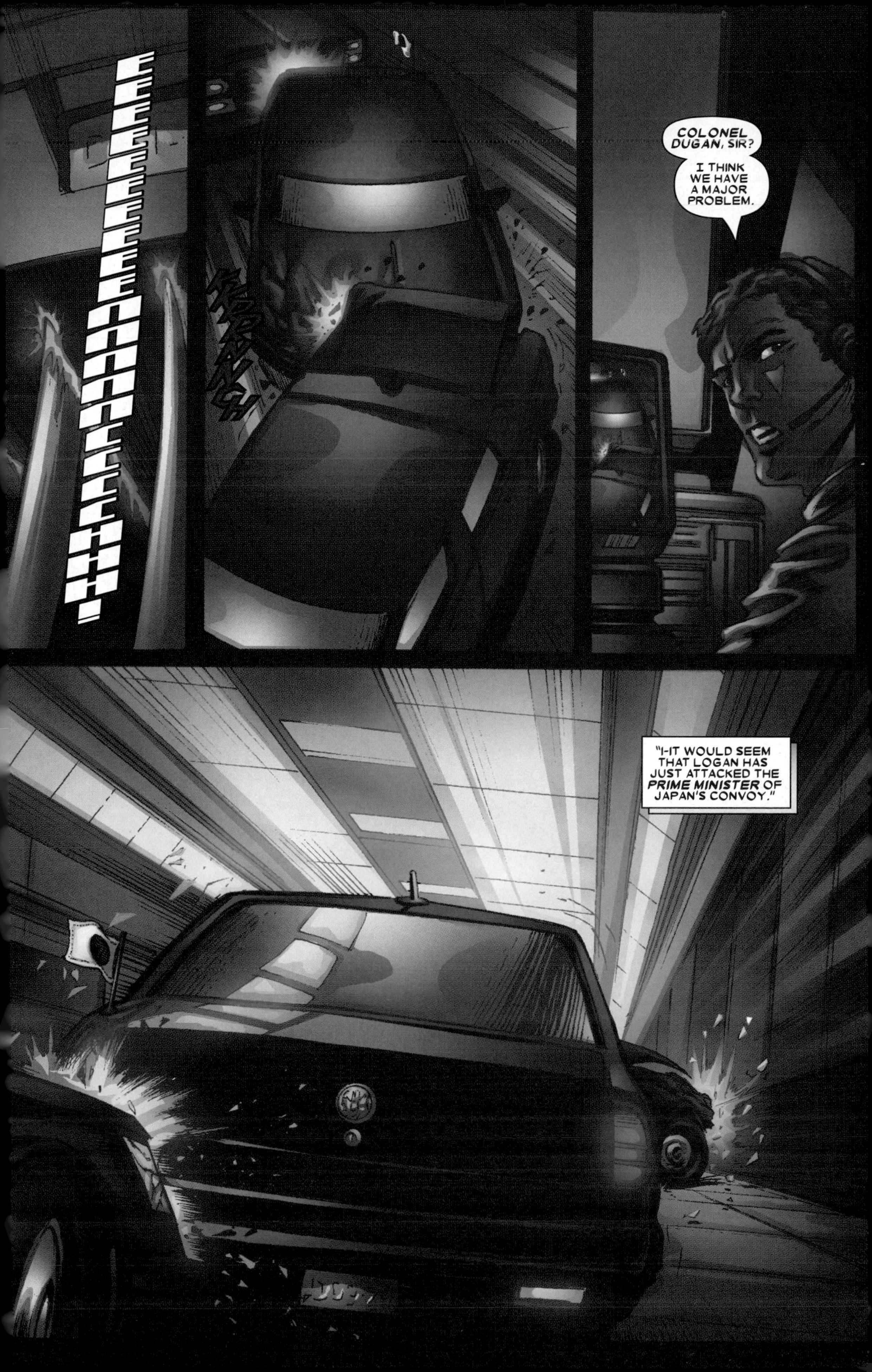
KRRANCH
COLONEL DUGAN, SIR?
I THINK WE HAVE A MAJOR PROBLEM.
"I-IT WOULD SEEM THAT LOGAN HAS JUST ATTACKED THE PRIME MINISTER OF JAPAN'S CONVOY."

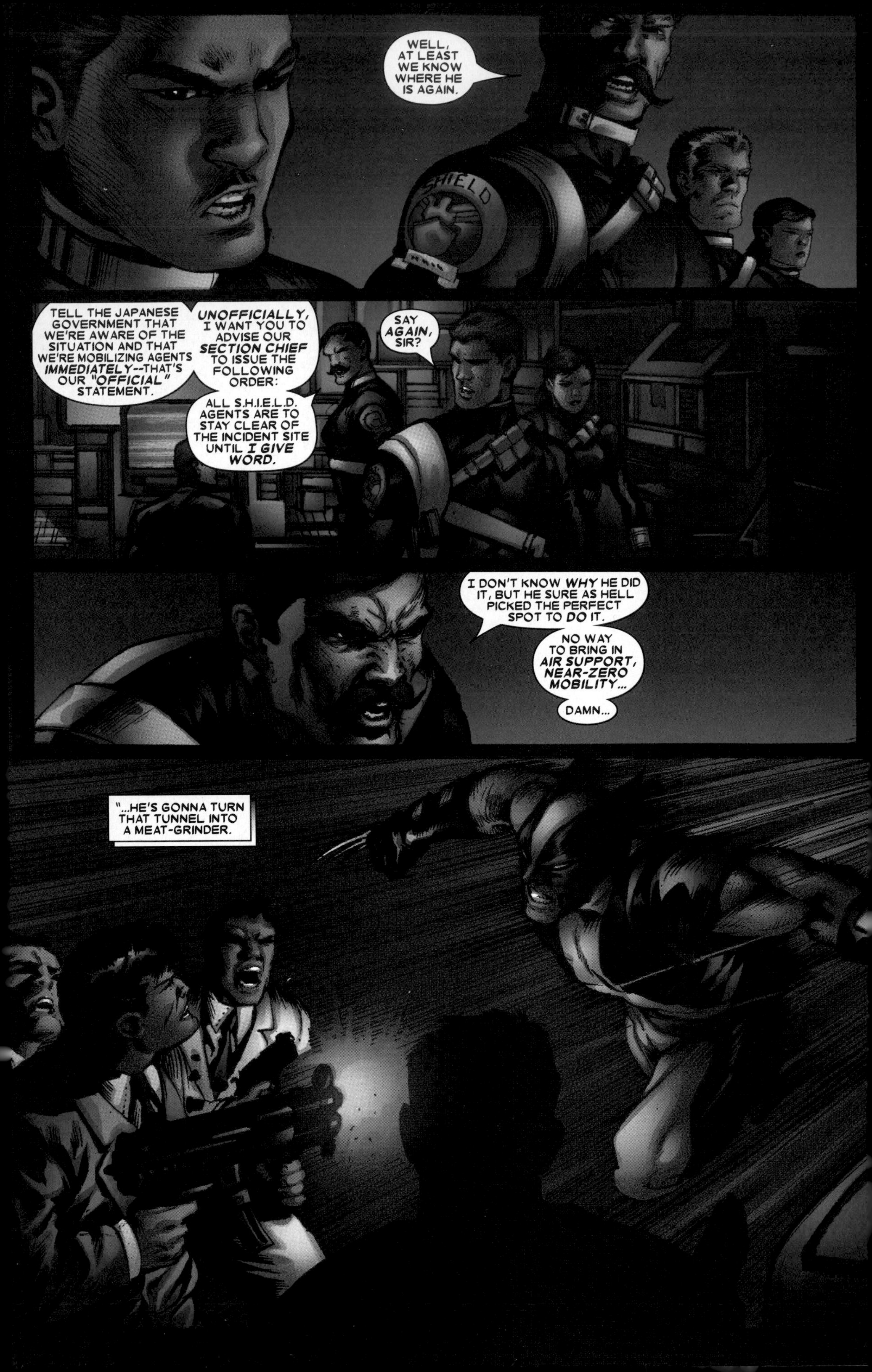
WELL, AT LEAST WE KNOW WHERE HE IS AGAIN.
TELL THE JAPANESE GOVERNMENT THAT WE'RE AWARE OF THE SITUATION AND THAT WE'RE MOBILIZING AGENTS *IMMEDIATELY*--THAT'S OUR *"OFFICIAL"* STATEMENT.
UNOFFICIALLY, I WANT YOU TO ADVISE OUR *SECTION CHIEF* TO ISSUE THE FOLLOWING ORDER:
ALL S.H.I.E.L.D. AGENTS ARE TO STAY CLEAR OF THE INCIDENT SITE UNTIL *I GIVE WORD.*
SAY *AGAIN*, SIR?
I DON'T KNOW *WHY* HE DID IT, BUT HE SURE AS HELL PICKED THE PERFECT SPOT TO *DO* IT.
NO WAY TO BRING IN *AIR SUPPORT, NEAR-ZERO MOBILITY...*
DAMN...
"...HE'S GONNA TURN THAT TUNNEL INTO A MEAT-GRINDER.

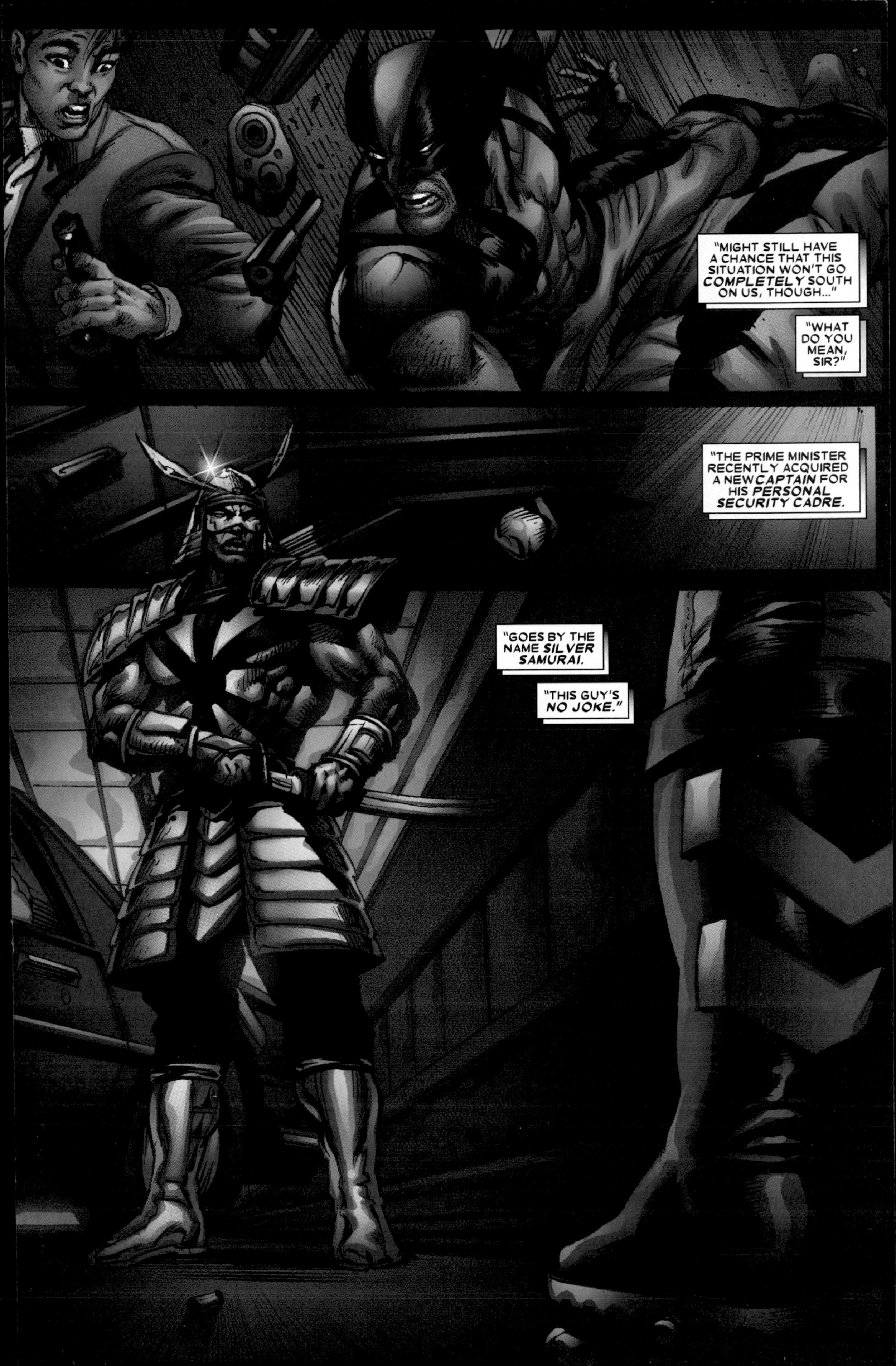
"MIGHT STILL HAVE A CHANCE THAT THIS SITUATION WON'T GO COMPLETELY SOUTH ON US, THOUGH..."
"WHAT DO YOU MEAN, SIR?"
"THE PRIME MINISTER RECENTLY ACQUIRED A NEW CAPTAIN FOR HIS PERSONAL SECURITY CADRE.
"GOES BY THE NAME SILVER SAMURAI.
"THIS GUY'S NO JOKE."

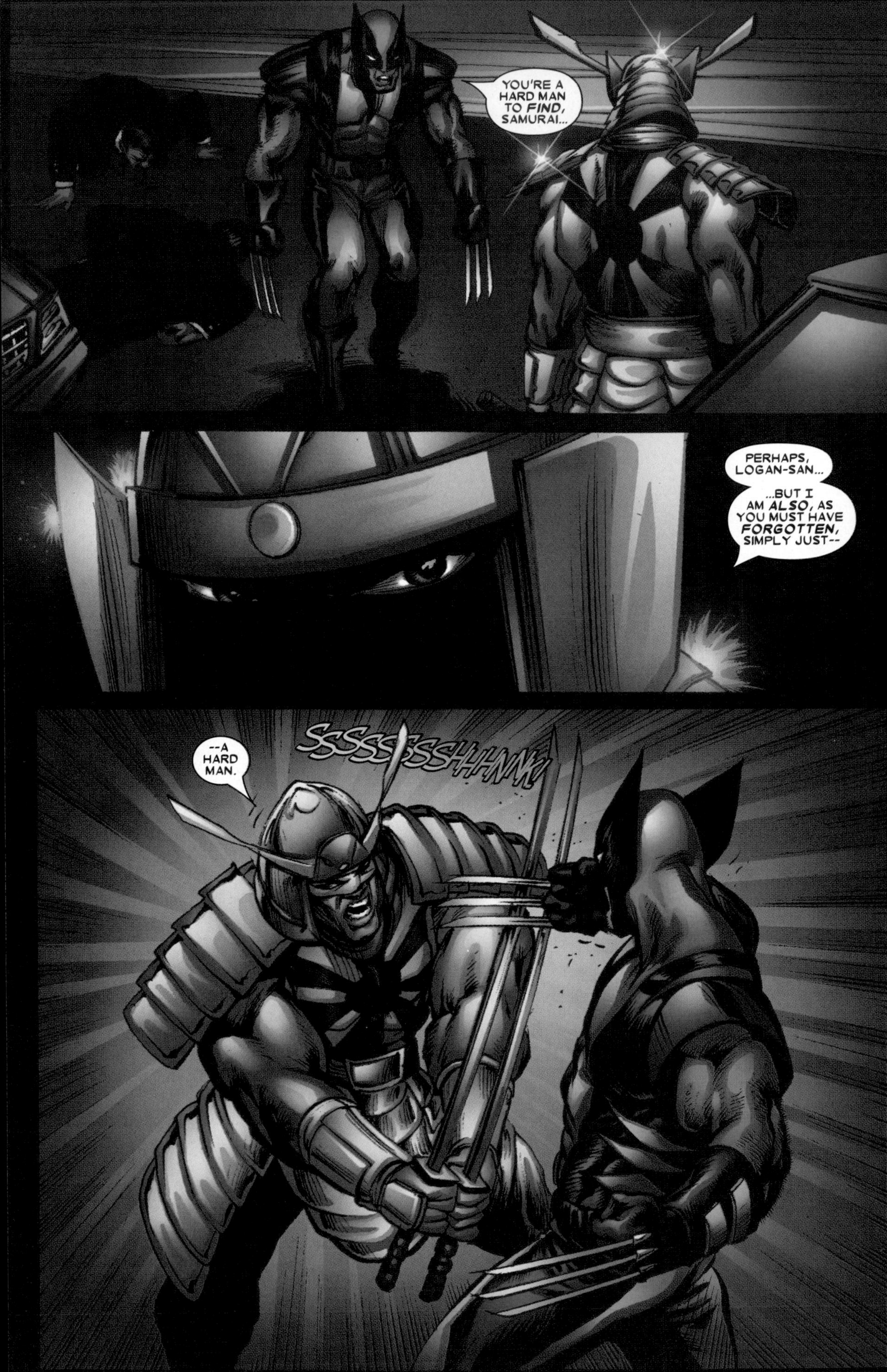
YOU'RE A HARD MAN TO *FIND*, SAMURAI...
PERHAPS, LOGAN-SAN...
...BUT I AM *ALSO*, AS YOU MUST HAVE *FORGOTTEN*, SIMPLY JUST--
--A HARD MAN.
SSSSSSSSHHNNK!

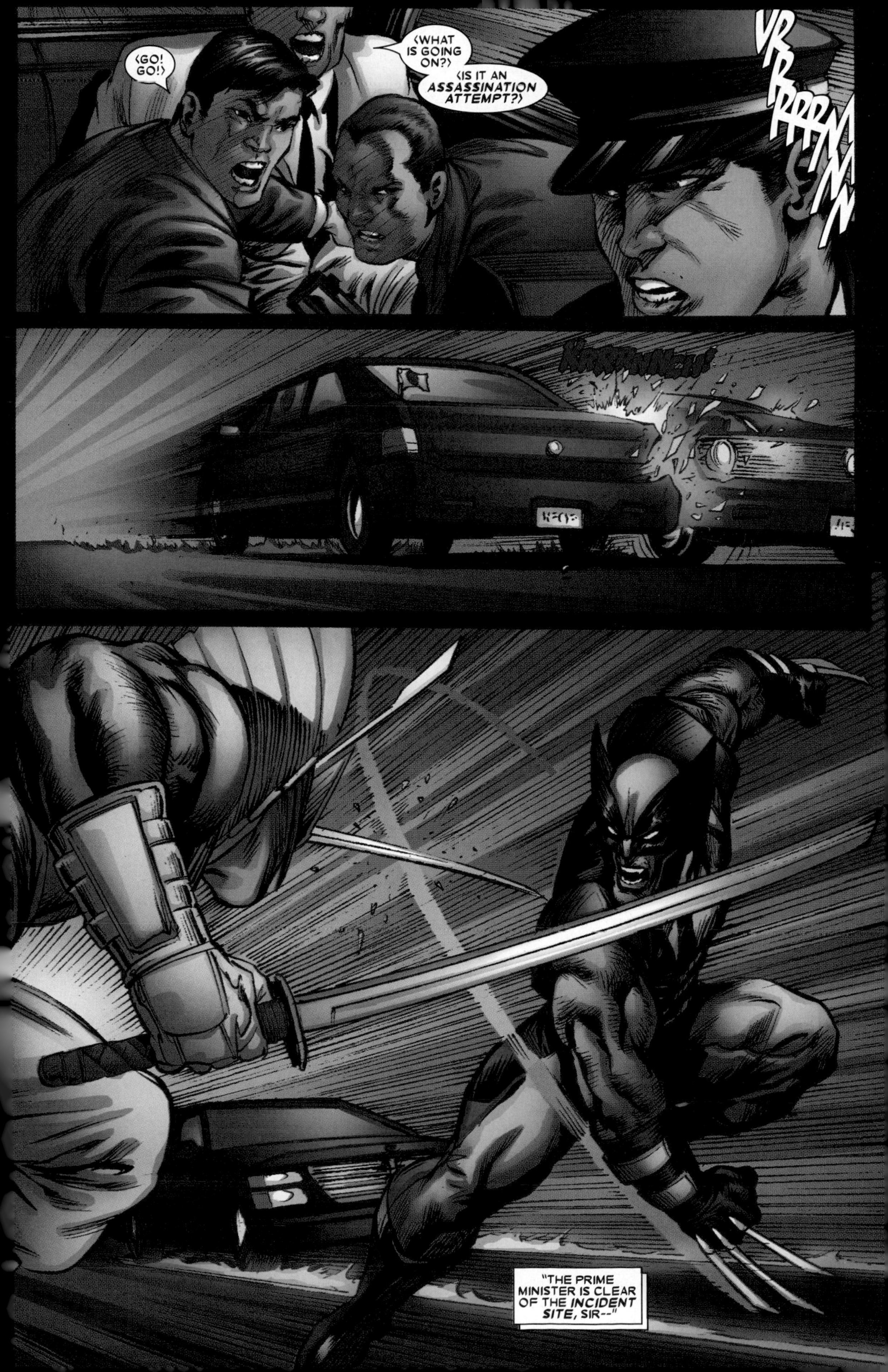
‹GO! GO!›
‹WHAT IS GOING ON?›
‹IS IT AN ASSASSINATION ATTEMPT?›
"THE PRIME MINISTER IS CLEAR OF THE INCIDENT SITE, SIR--"

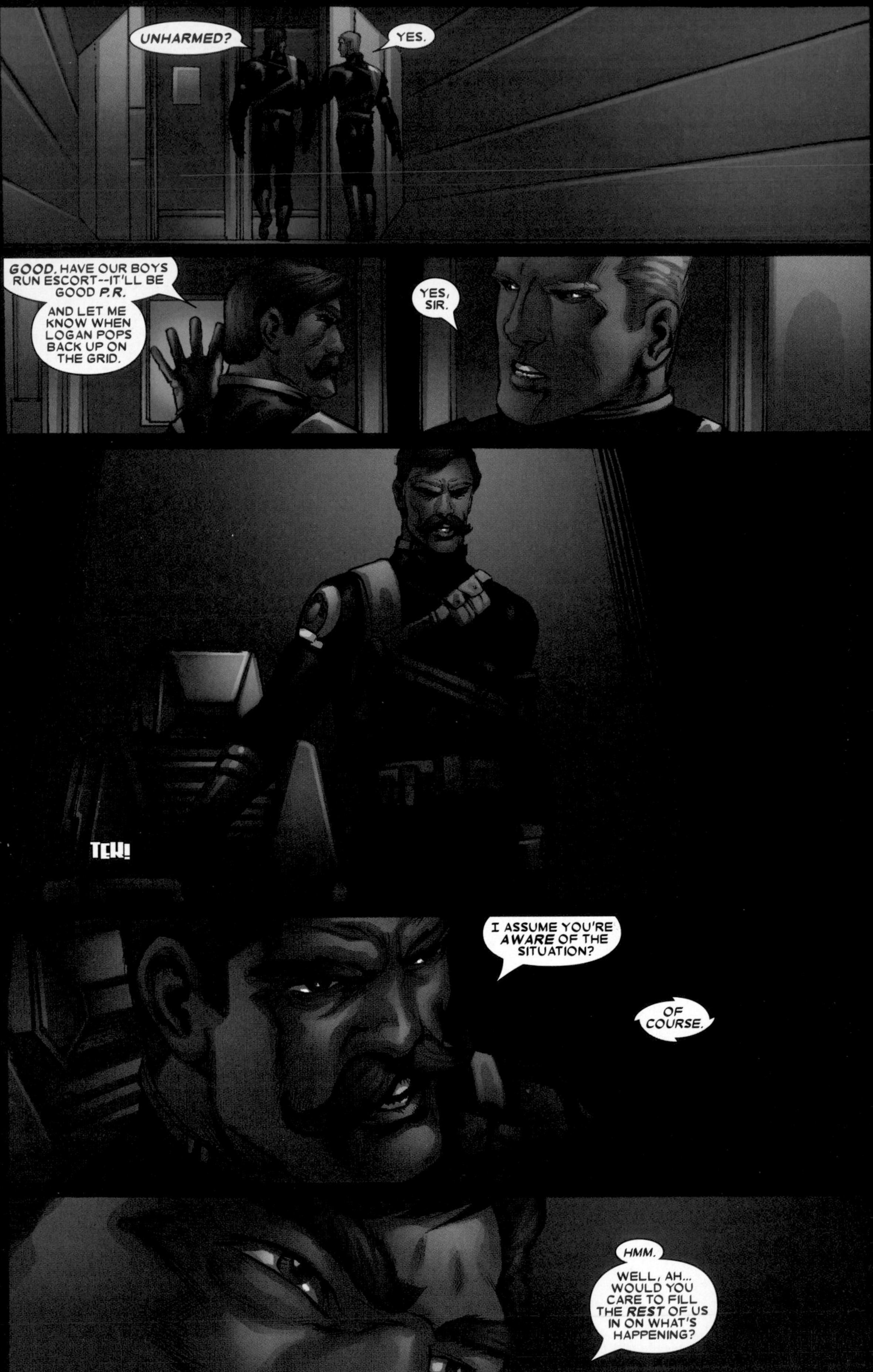
UNHARMED?
YES.
GOOD. HAVE OUR BOYS RUN ESCORT--IT'LL BE GOOD P.R.
AND LET ME KNOW WHEN LOGAN POPS BACK UP ON THE GRID.
YES, SIR.
TCK!
I ASSUME YOU'RE AWARE OF THE SITUATION?
OF COURSE.
HMM.
WELL, AH... WOULD YOU CARE TO FILL THE REST OF US IN ON WHAT'S HAPPENING?

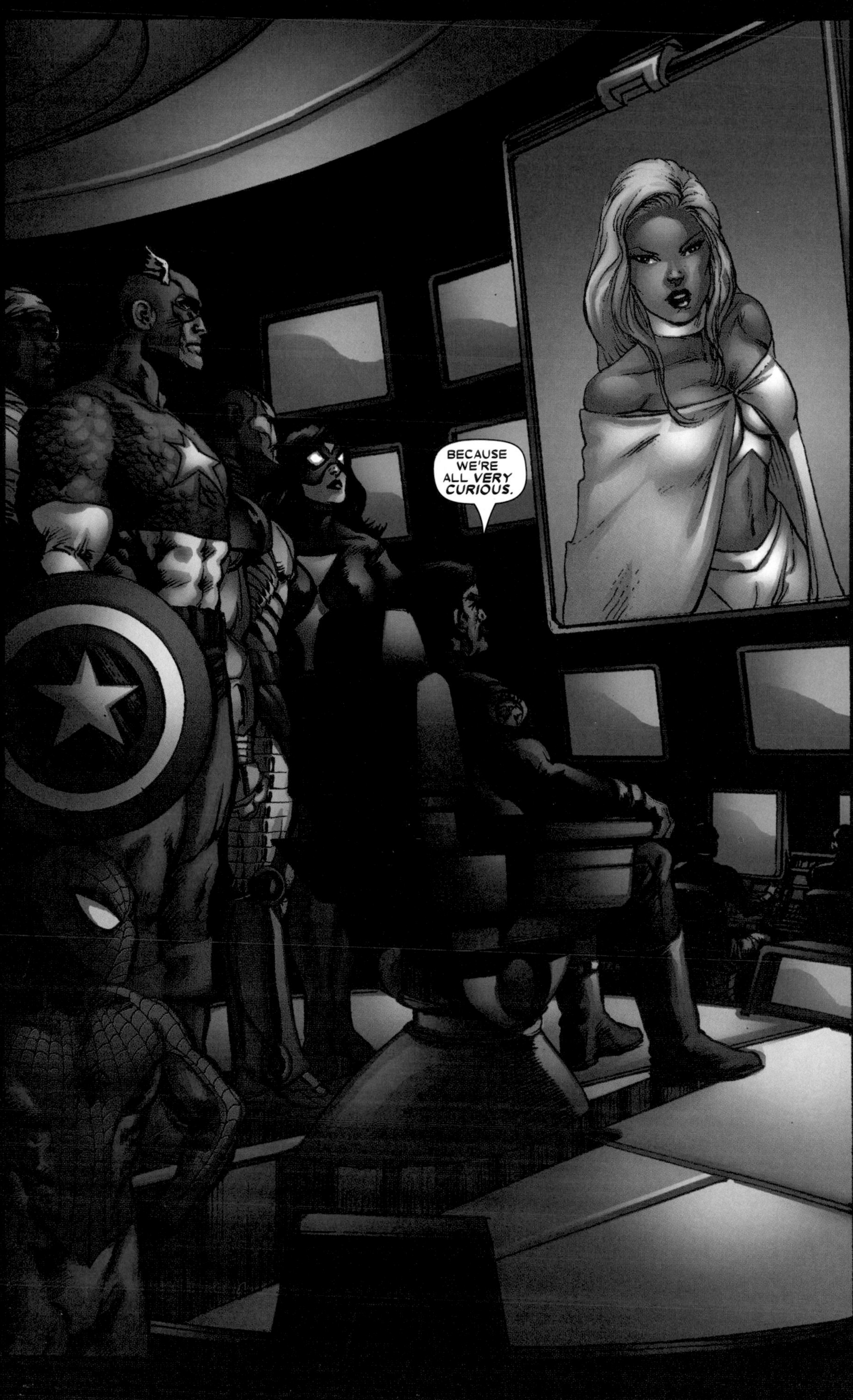
BECAUSE WE'RE ALL VERY CURIOUS.

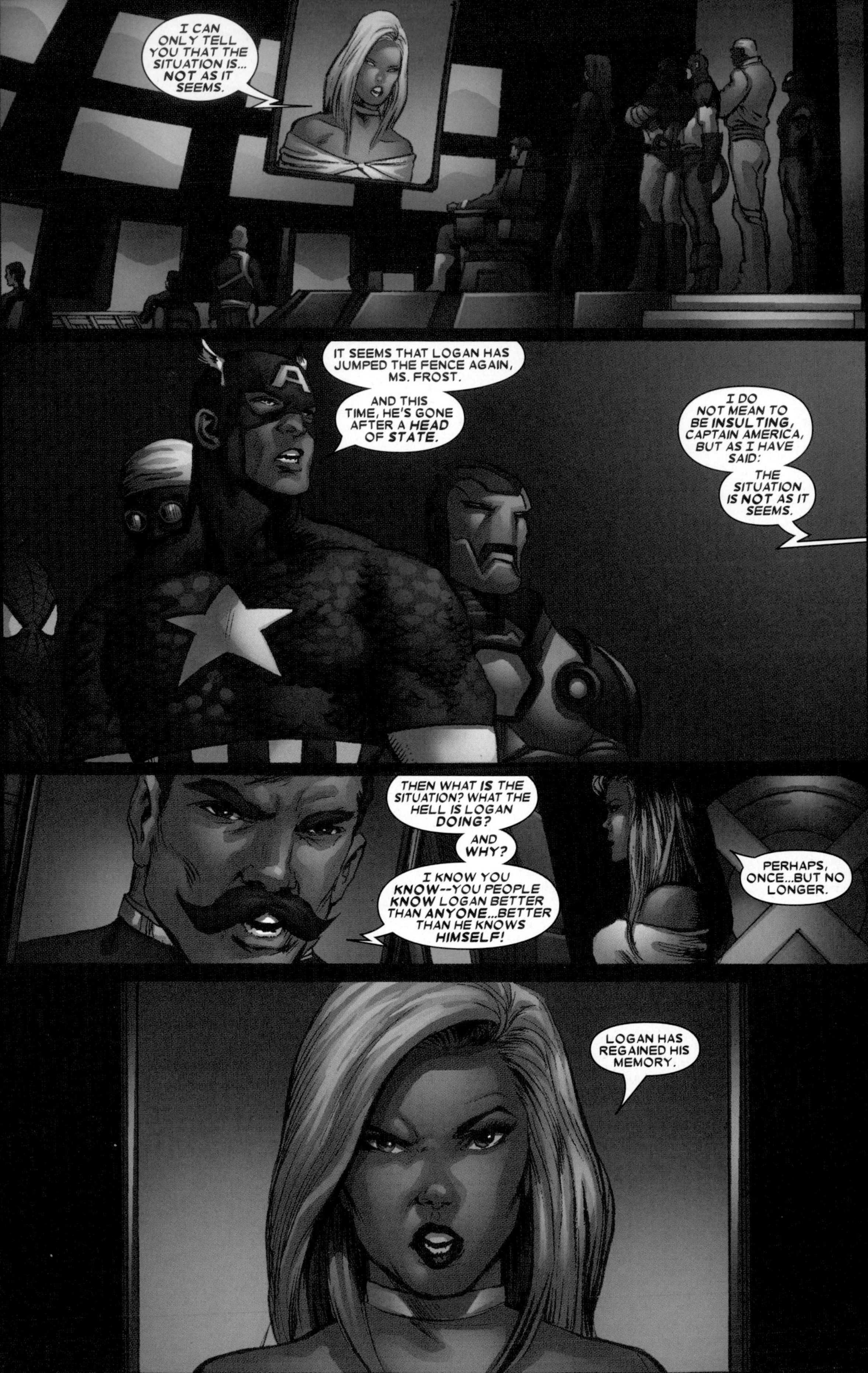
I CAN ONLY TELL YOU THAT THE SITUATION IS... NOT AS IT SEEMS.
IT SEEMS THAT LOGAN HAS JUMPED THE FENCE AGAIN, MS. FROST.
AND THIS TIME, HE'S GONE AFTER A HEAD OF STATE.
I DO NOT MEAN TO BE INSULTING, CAPTAIN AMERICA, BUT AS I HAVE SAID:
THE SITUATION IS NOT AS IT SEEMS.
THEN WHAT IS THE SITUATION? WHAT THE HELL IS LOGAN DOING?
AND WHY?
I KNOW YOU KNOW--YOU PEOPLE KNOW LOGAN BETTER THAN ANYONE...BETTER THAN HE KNOWS HIMSELF!
PERHAPS, ONCE...BUT NO LONGER.
LOGAN HAS REGAINED HIS MEMORY.

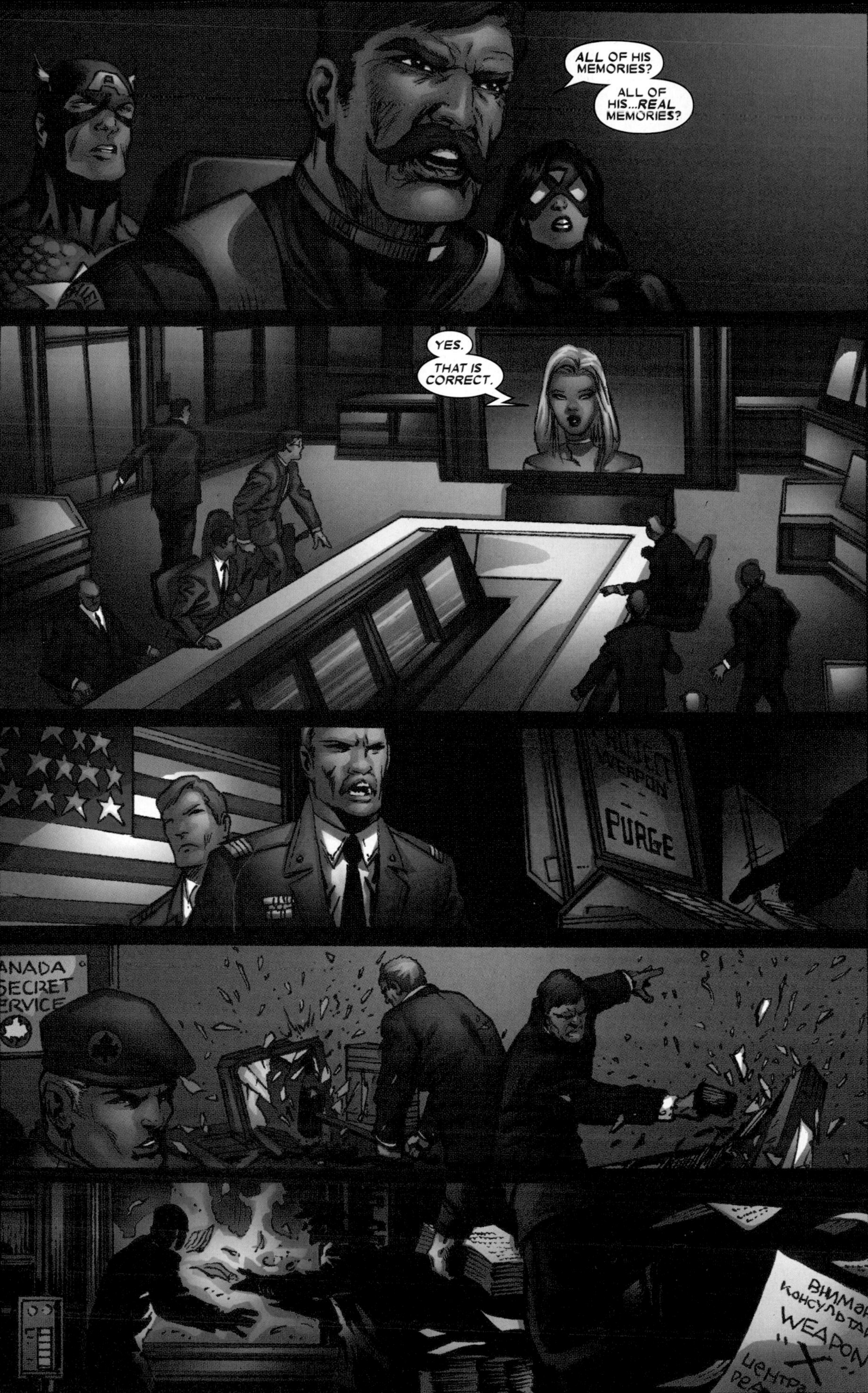
ALL OF HIS MEMORIES?
ALL OF HIS...REAL MEMORIES?
YES. THAT IS CORRECT.
WEAPON
PURGE
ANADA
SECRET
ERVICE
WEAPON
X

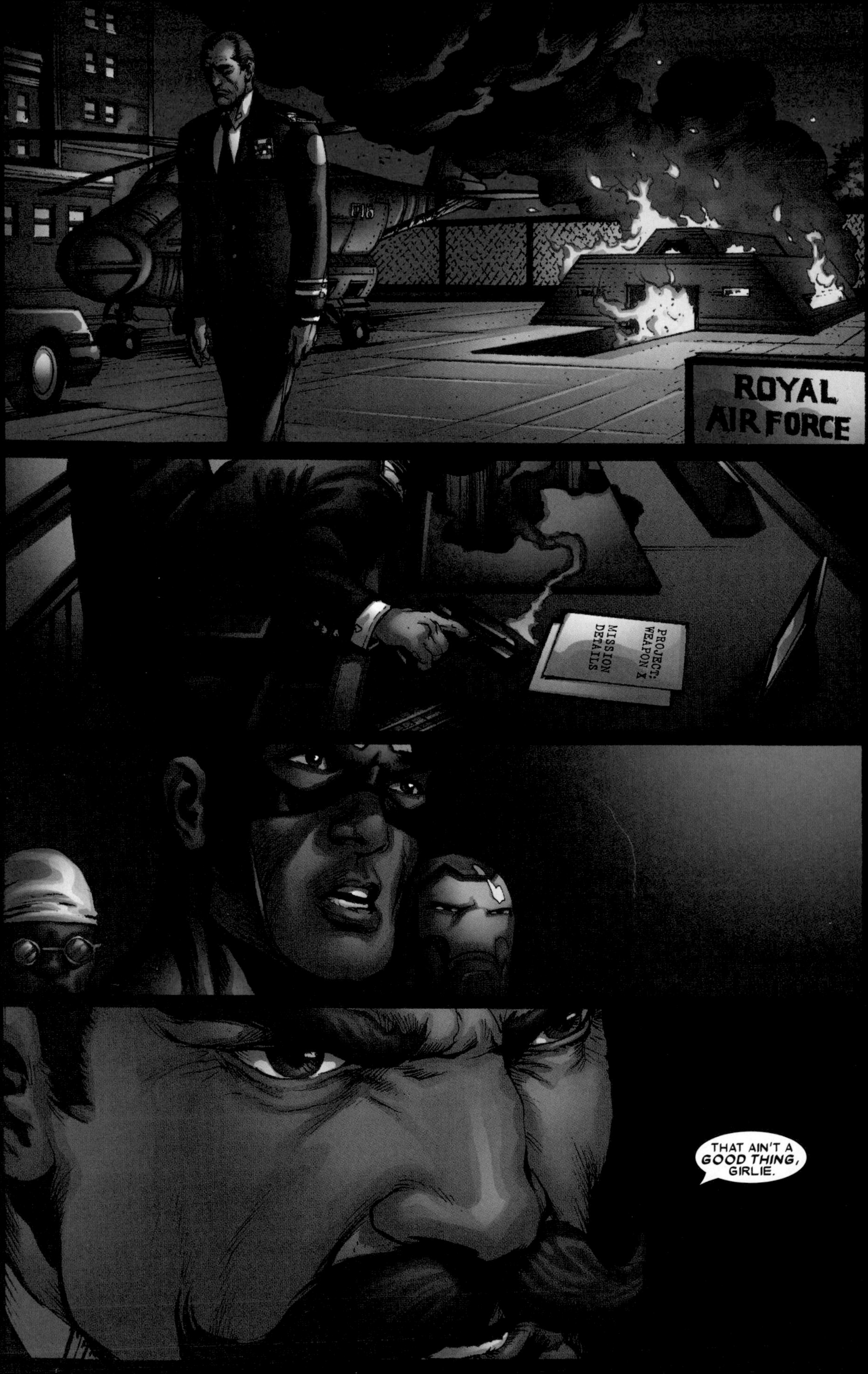
ROYAL AIR FORCE
PROJECT: WEAPON X
MISSION DETAILS
THAT AIN'T A *GOOD THING,* GIRLIE.

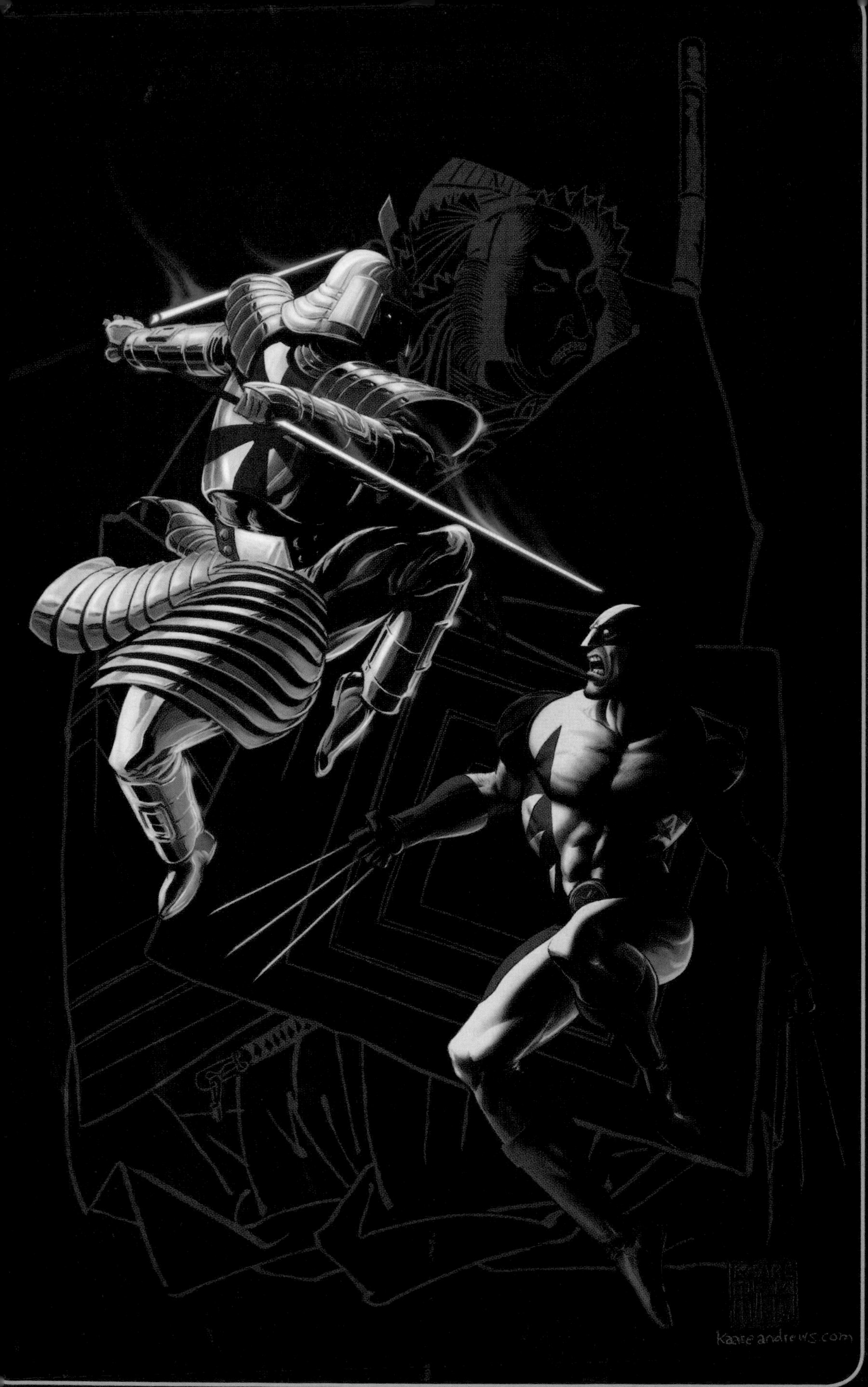
kaareandrews.com

ISSUE #37

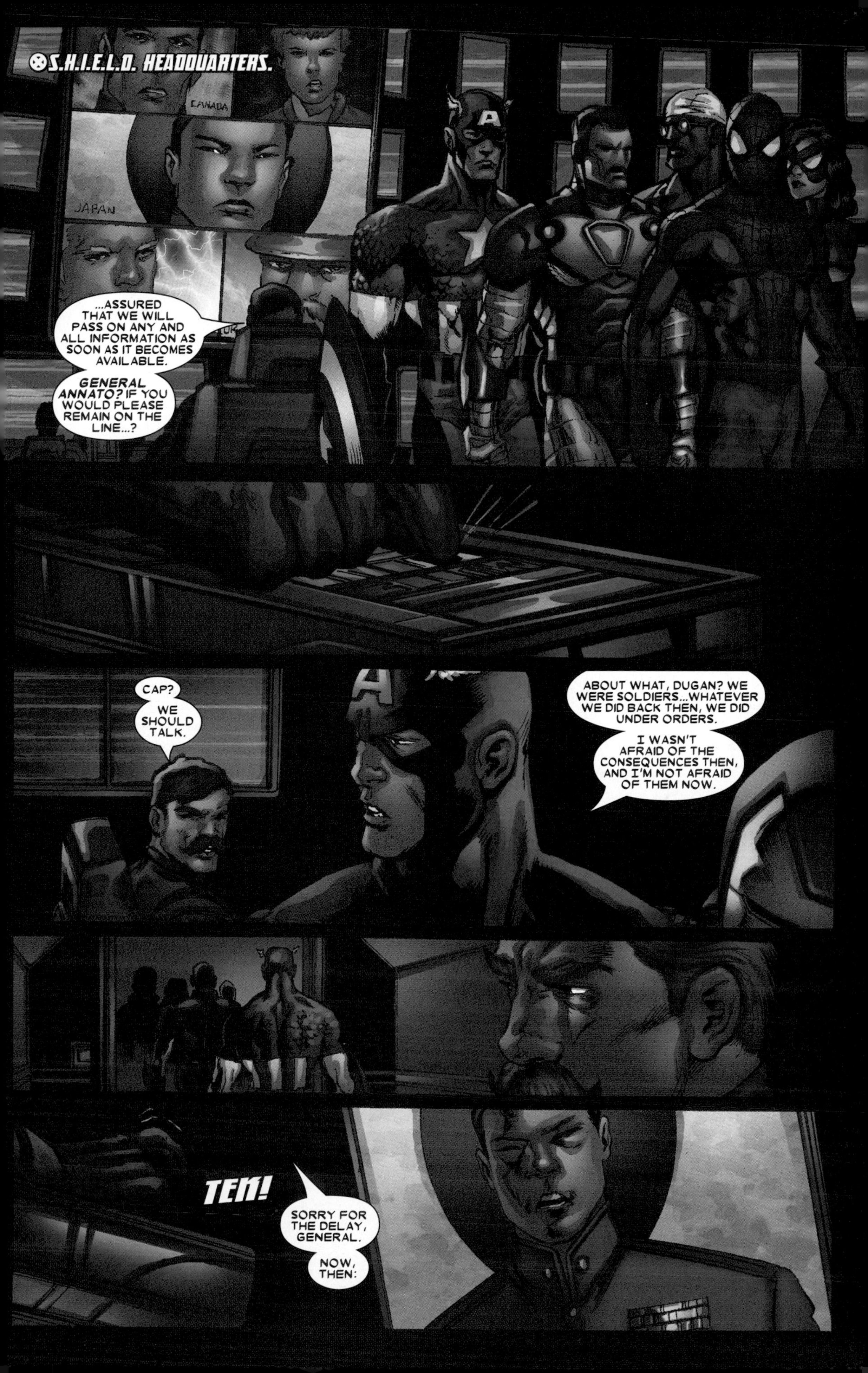
S.H.I.E.L.D. HEADQUARTERS.
CANADA
JAPAN
...ASSURED THAT WE WILL PASS ON ANY AND ALL INFORMATION AS SOON AS IT BECOMES AVAILABLE.
GENERAL ANNATO? IF YOU WOULD PLEASE REMAIN ON THE LINE...?
CAP? WE SHOULD TALK.
ABOUT WHAT, DUGAN? WE WERE SOLDIERS...WHATEVER WE DID BACK THEN, WE DID UNDER ORDERS.
I WASN'T AFRAID OF THE CONSEQUENCES THEN, AND I'M NOT AFRAID OF THEM NOW.
TEN!
SORRY FOR THE DELAY, GENERAL.
NOW, THEN:

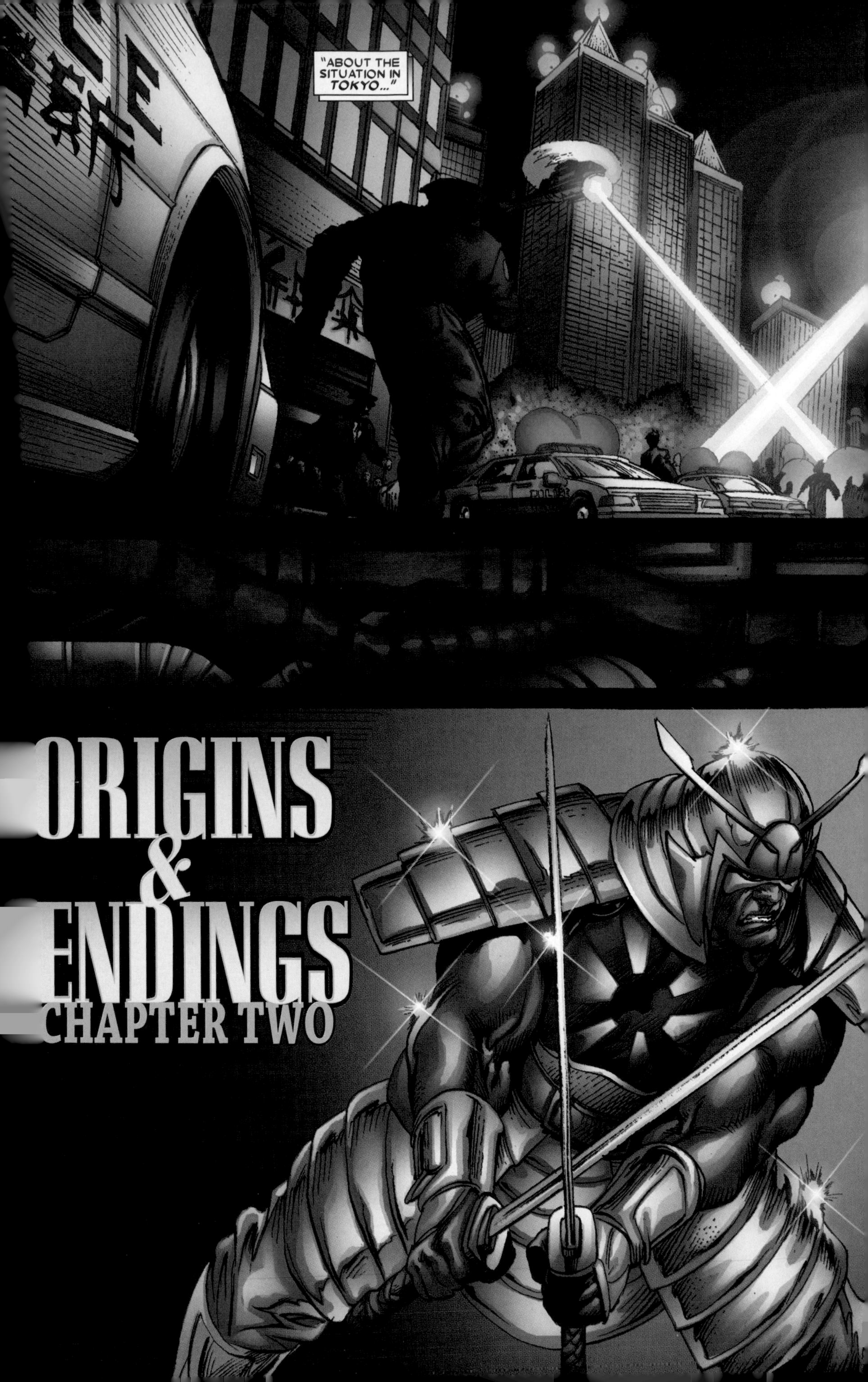
"ABOUT THE SITUATION IN *TOKYO*..."
ORIGINS
&
ENDINGS
CHAPTER TWO

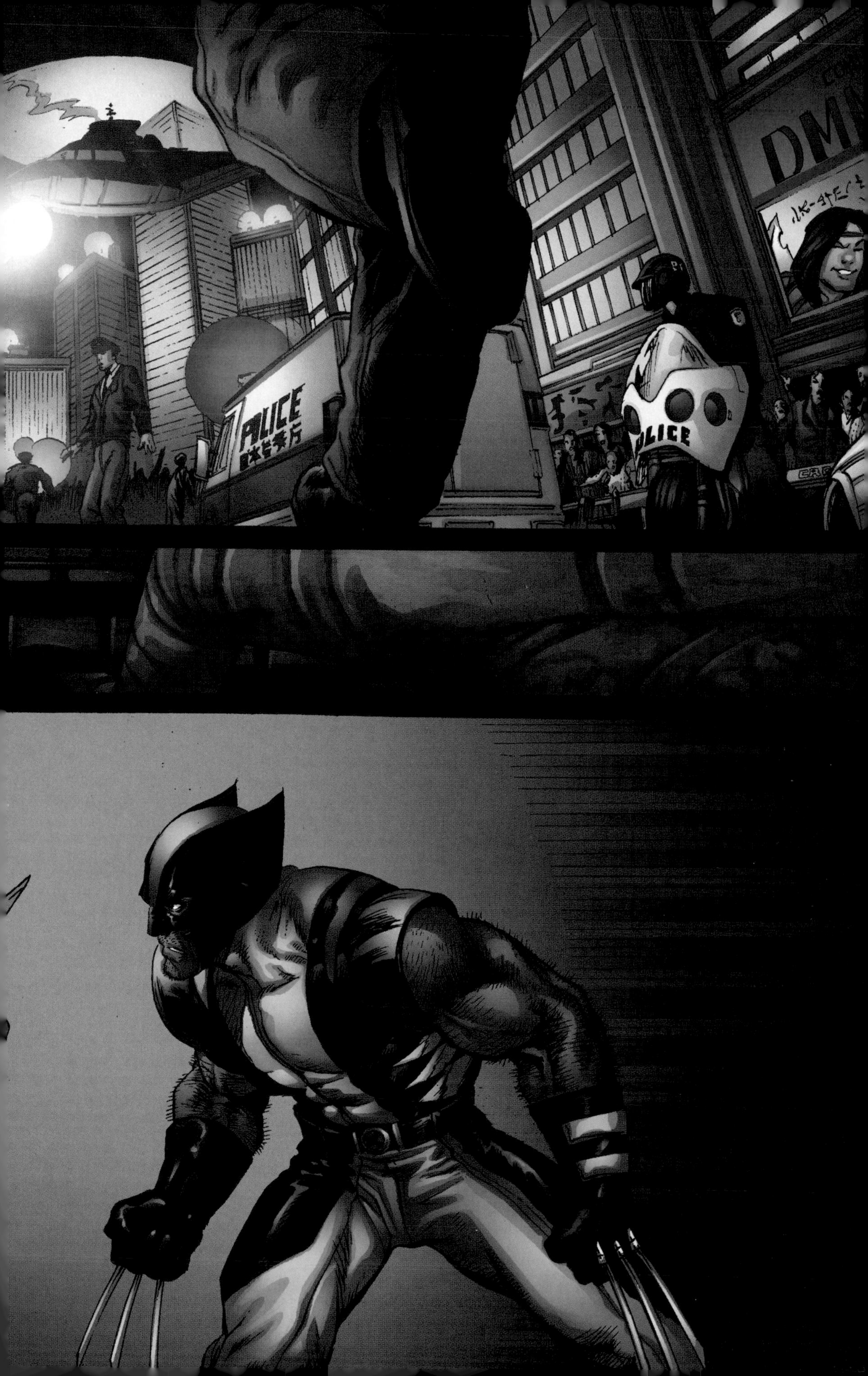
POLICE

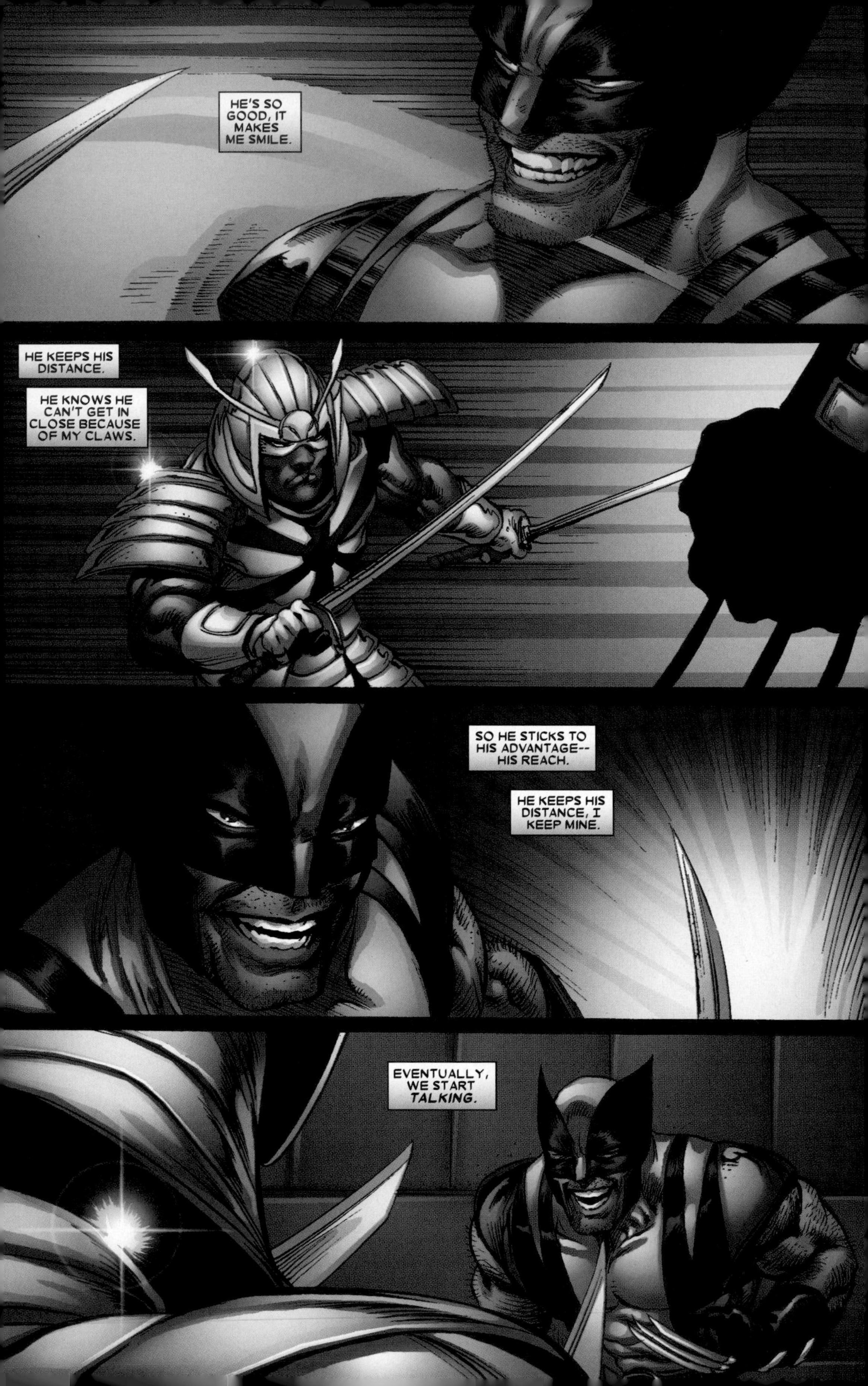
HE'S SO GOOD, IT MAKES ME SMILE.
HE KEEPS HIS DISTANCE.
HE KNOWS HE CAN'T GET IN CLOSE BECAUSE OF MY CLAWS.
SO HE STICKS TO HIS ADVANTAGE-- HIS REACH.
HE KEEPS HIS DISTANCE, I KEEP MINE.
EVENTUALLY, WE START *TALKING*.

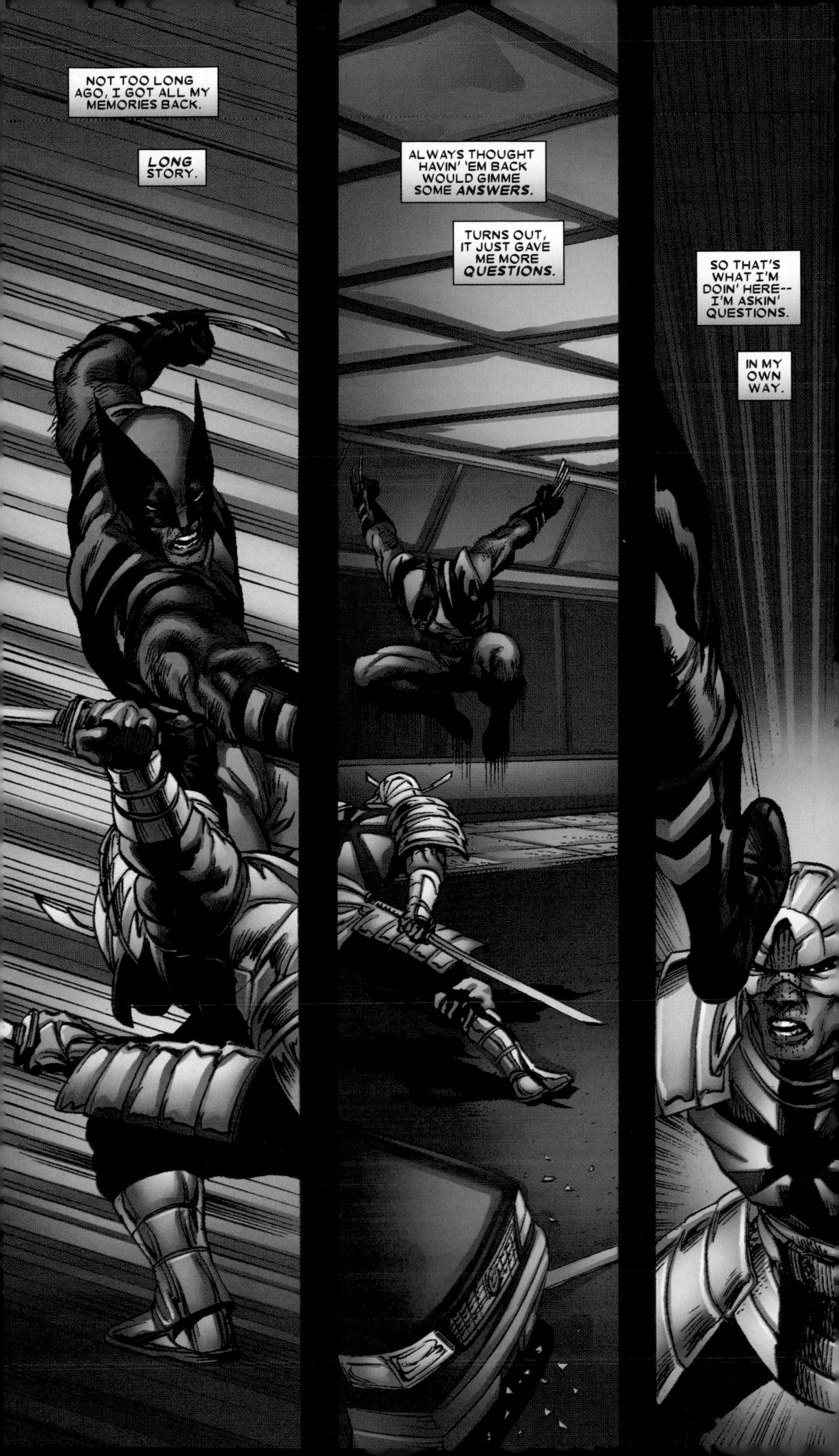
NOT TOO LONG AGO, I GOT ALL MY MEMORIES BACK.
LONG STORY.
ALWAYS THOUGHT HAVIN' 'EM BACK WOULD GIMME SOME ANSWERS.
TURNS OUT, IT JUST GAVE ME MORE QUESTIONS.
SO THAT'S WHAT I'M DOIN' HERE-- I'M ASKIN' QUESTIONS.
IN MY OWN WAY.

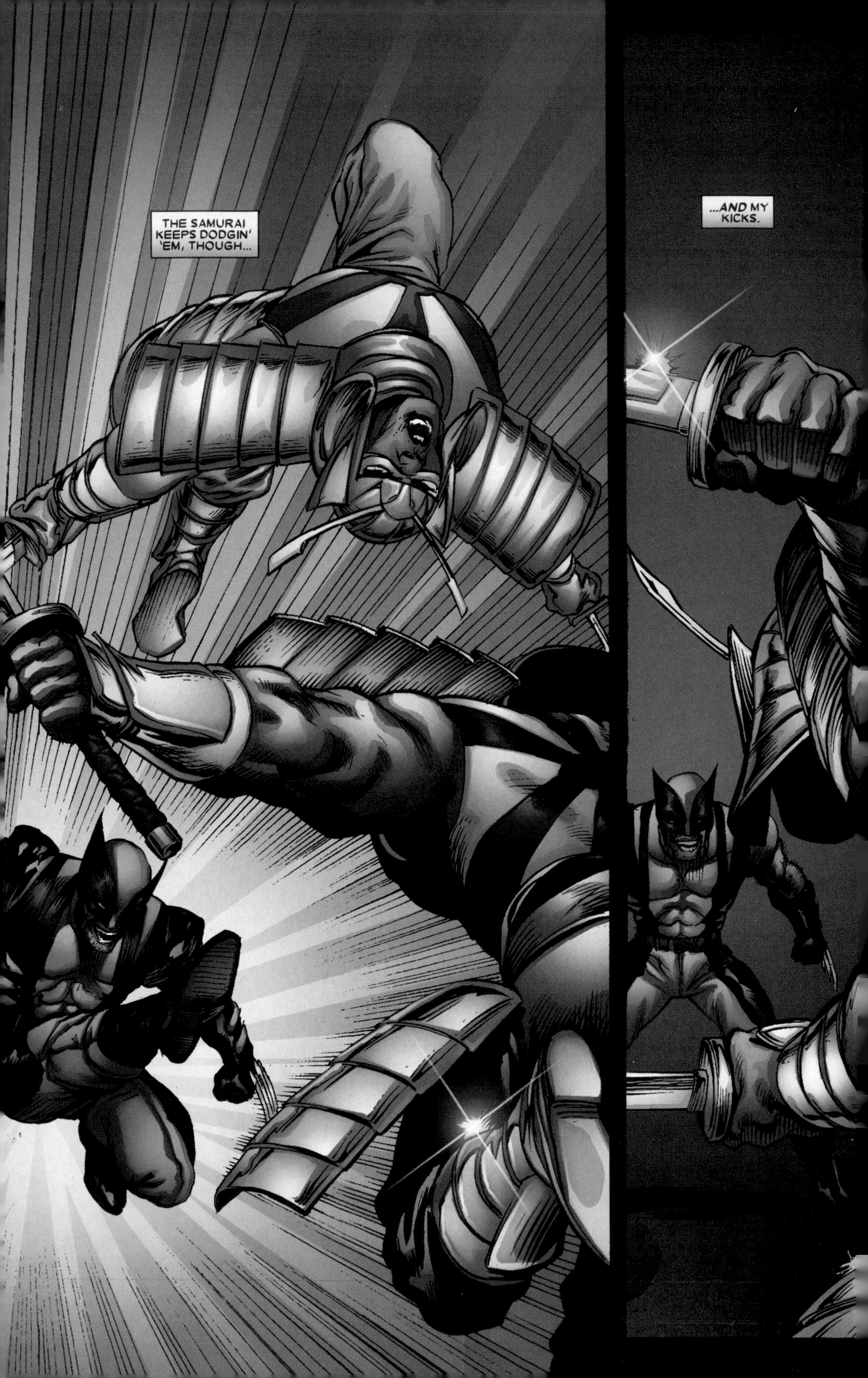
THE SAMURAI KEEPS DODGIN' 'EM, THOUGH...
...AND MY KICKS.

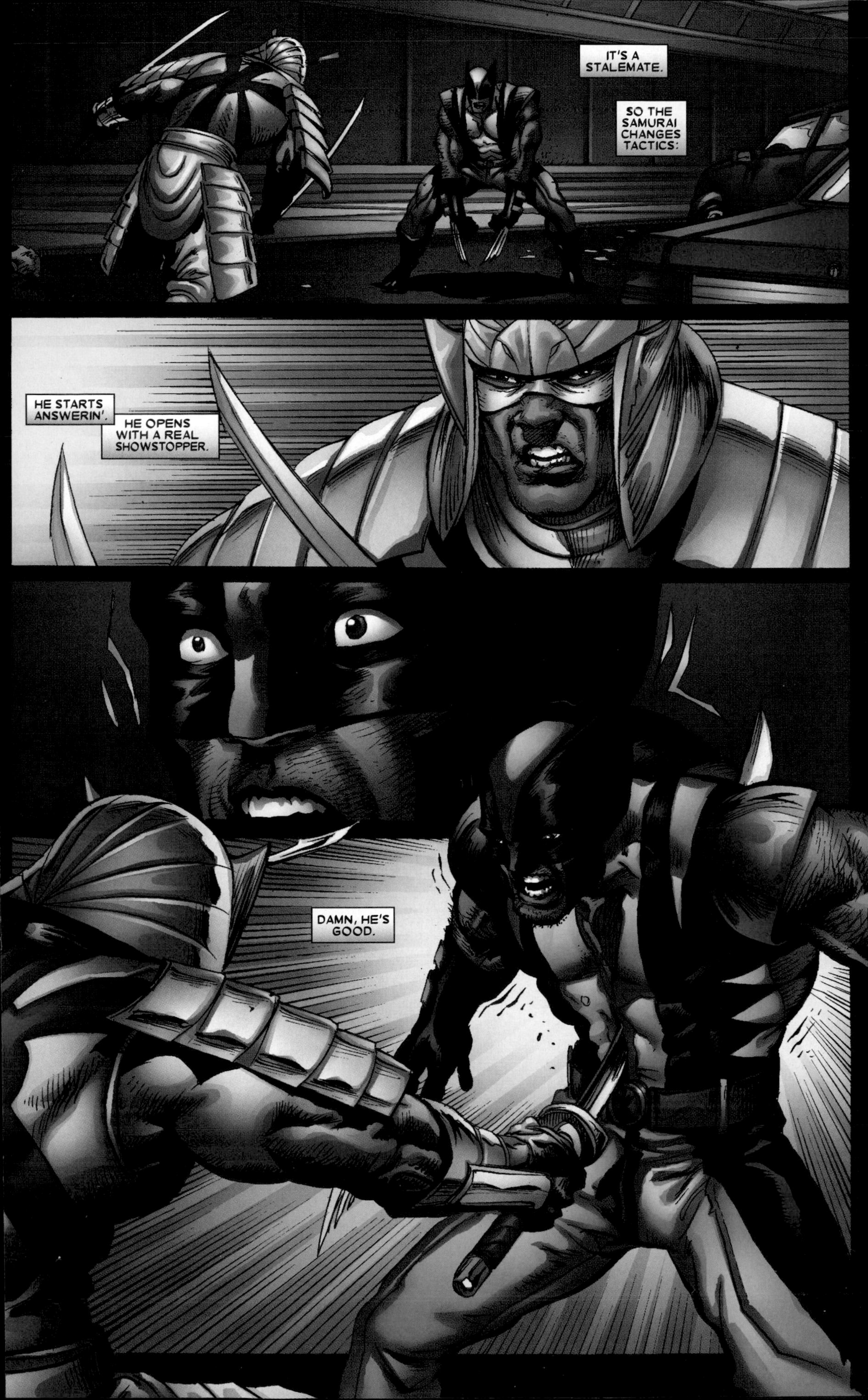
IT'S A STALEMATE.
SO THE SAMURAI CHANGES TACTICS:
HE STARTS ANSWERIN'.
HE OPENS WITH A REAL SHOWSTOPPER.
DAMN, HE'S GOOD.

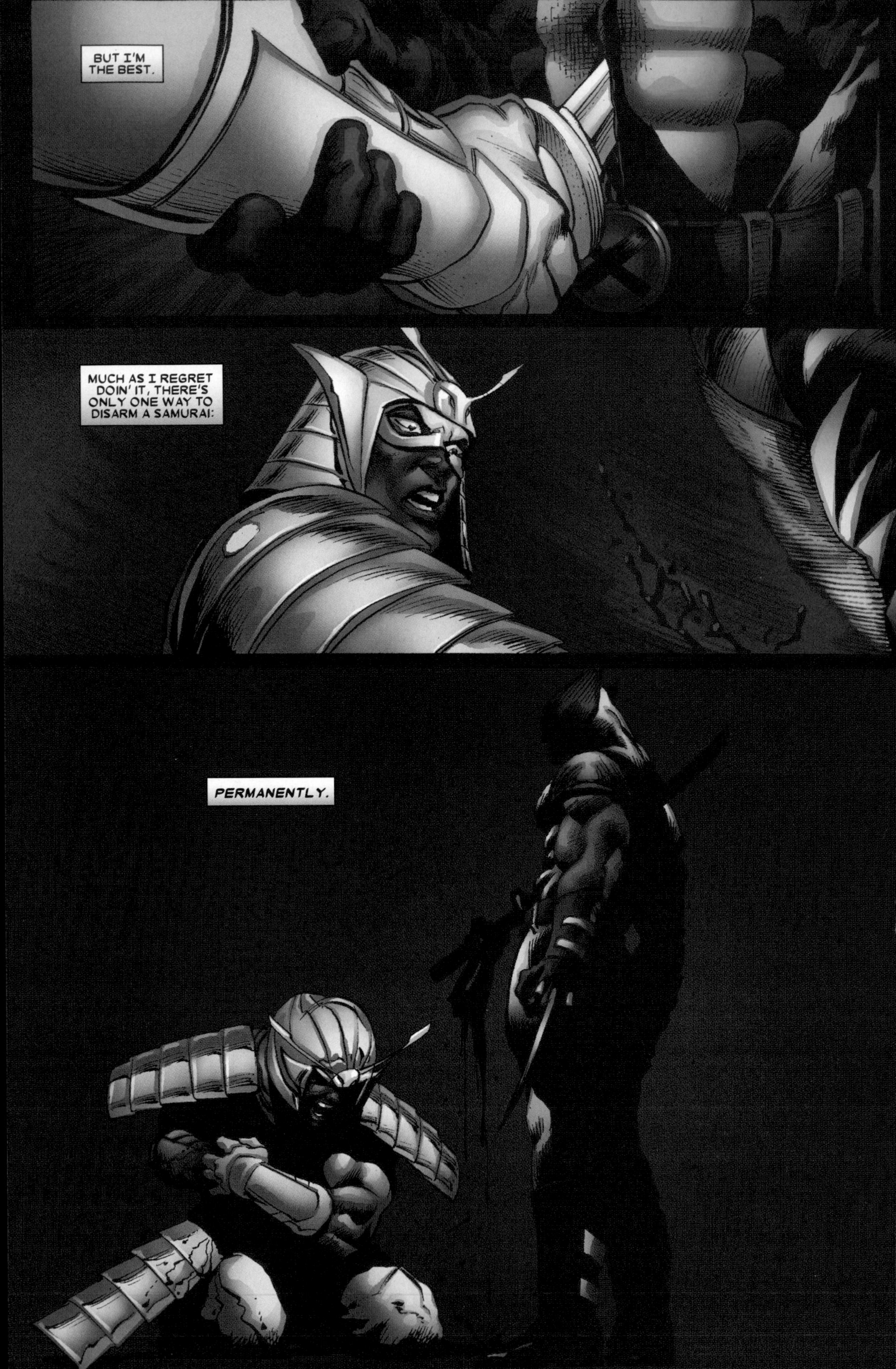
BUT I'M THE BEST.
MUCH AS I REGRET DOIN' IT, THERE'S ONLY ONE WAY TO DISARM A SAMURAI:
PERMANENTLY.

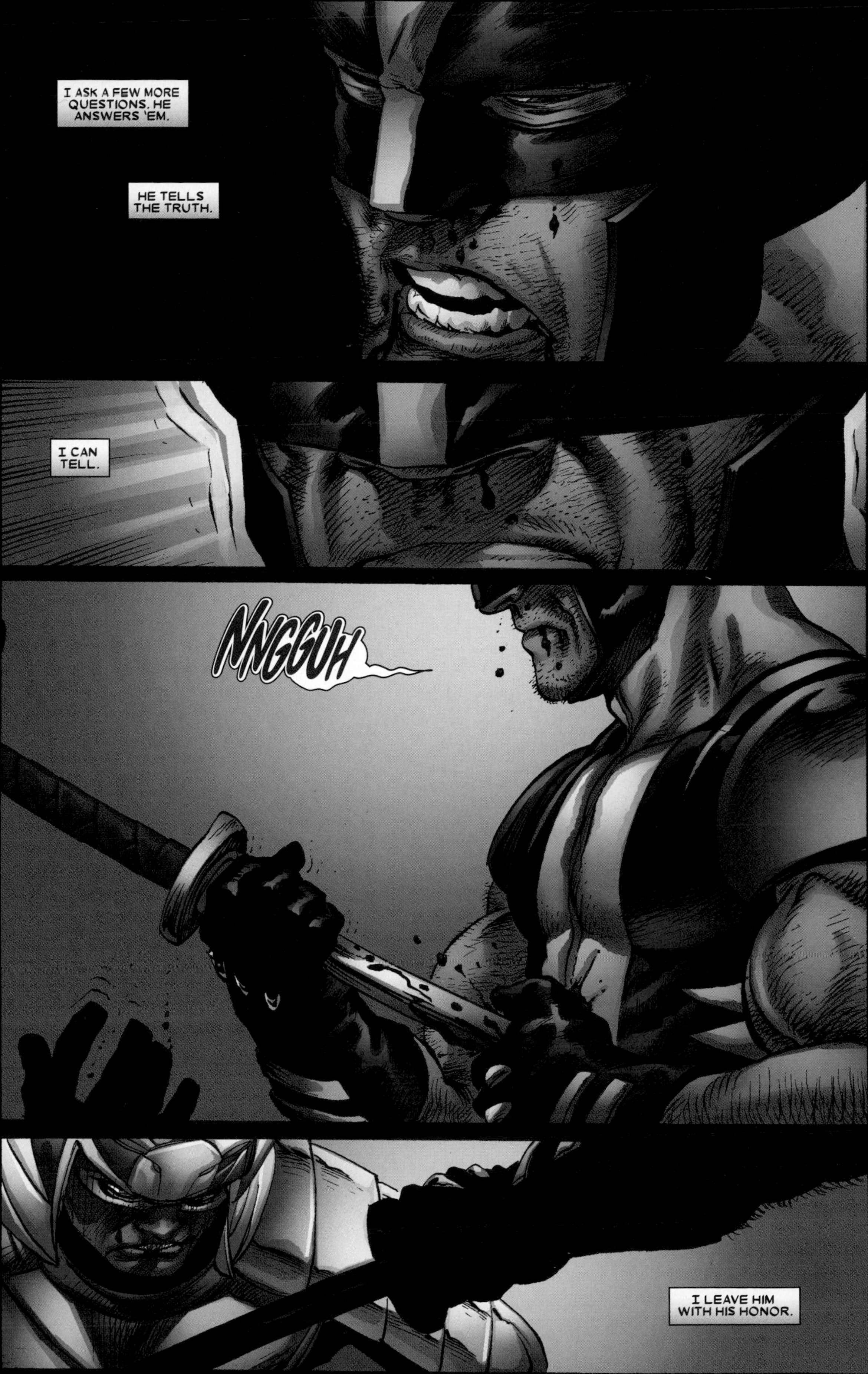
I ASK A FEW MORE QUESTIONS. HE ANSWERS 'EM.
HE TELLS THE TRUTH.
I CAN TELL.
NNGGUH
I LEAVE HIM WITH HIS HONOR.

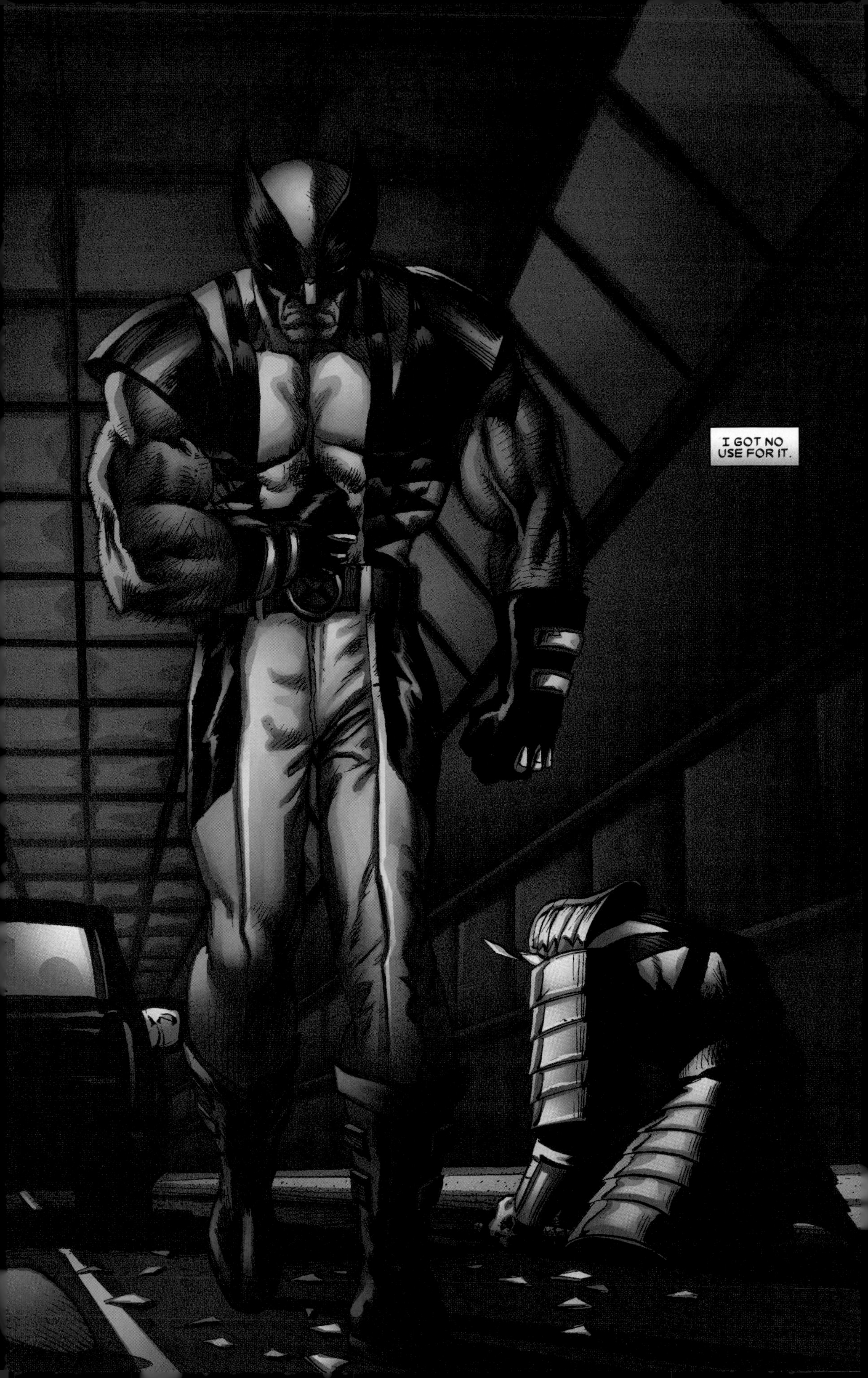
I GOT NO USE FOR IT.

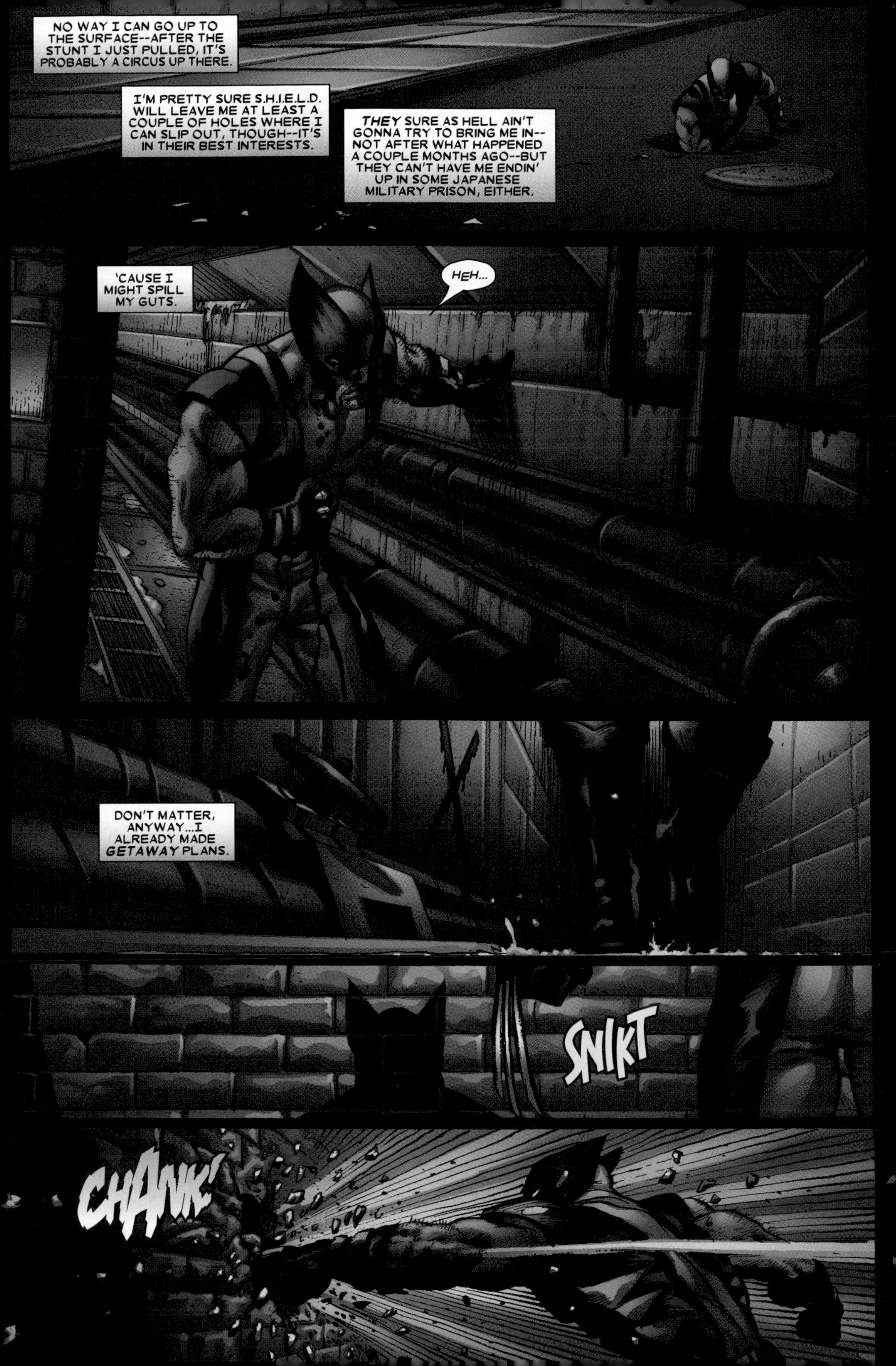
NO WAY I CAN GO UP TO THE SURFACE--AFTER THE STUNT I JUST PULLED, IT'S PROBABLY A CIRCUS UP THERE.
I'M PRETTY SURE S.H.I.E.L.D. WILL LEAVE ME AT LEAST A COUPLE OF HOLES WHERE I CAN SLIP OUT, THOUGH--IT'S IN THEIR BEST INTERESTS.
THEY SURE AS HELL AIN'T GONNA TRY TO BRING ME IN--NOT AFTER WHAT HAPPENED A COUPLE MONTHS AGO--BUT THEY CAN'T HAVE ME ENDIN' UP IN SOME JAPANESE MILITARY PRISON, EITHER.
'CAUSE I MIGHT SPILL MY GUTS.
HEH...
DON'T MATTER, ANYWAY...I ALREADY MADE *GETAWAY* PLANS.
SNIKT
CHANK!

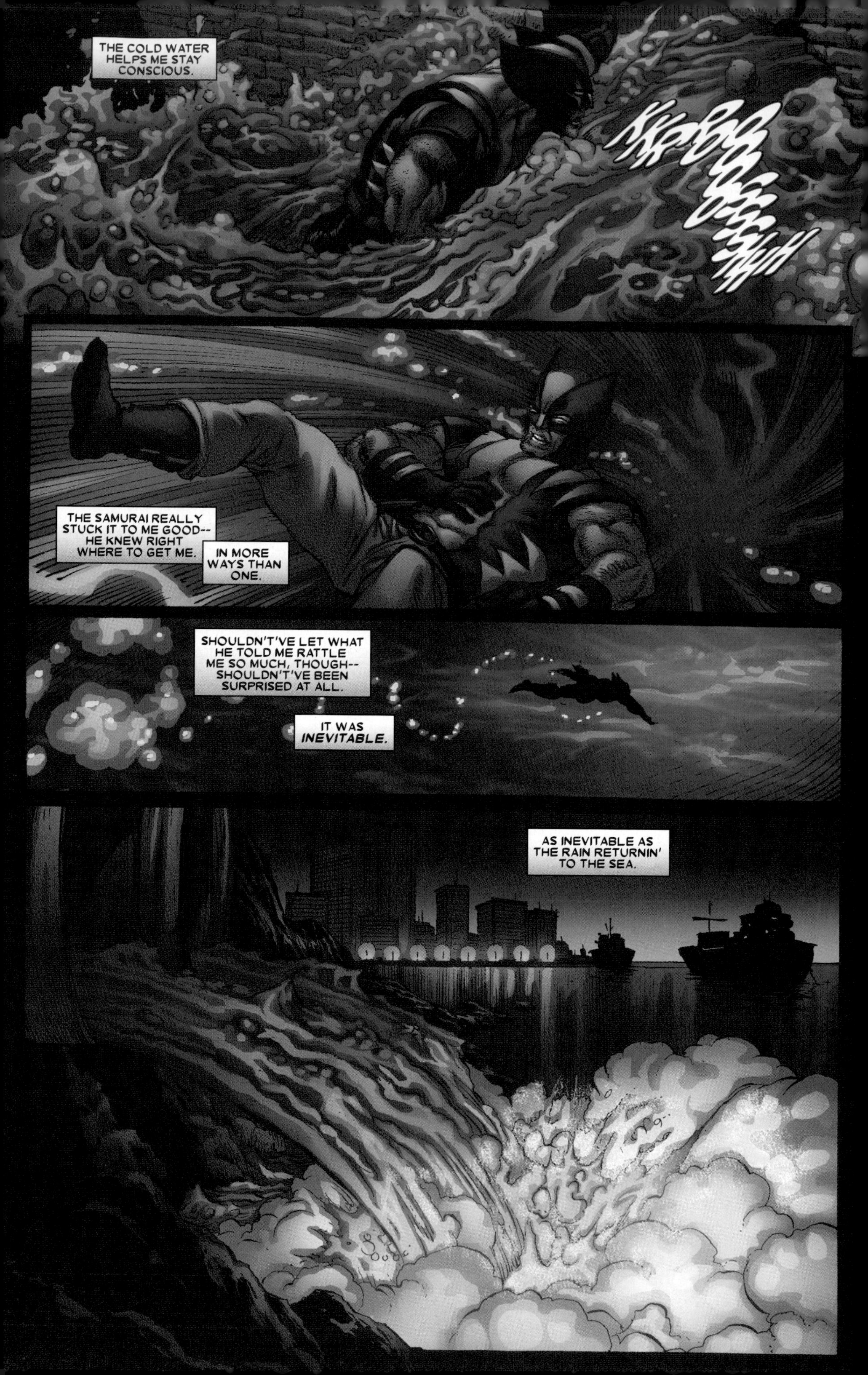
THE COLD WATER HELPS ME STAY CONSCIOUS.
KKRRBBOOSSSHHH
THE SAMURAI REALLY STUCK IT TO ME GOOD-- HE KNEW RIGHT WHERE TO GET ME.
IN MORE WAYS THAN ONE.
SHOULDN'T'VE LET WHAT HE TOLD ME RATTLE ME SO MUCH, THOUGH-- SHOULDN'T'VE BEEN SURPRISED AT ALL.
IT WAS *INEVITABLE.*
AS INEVITABLE AS THE RAIN RETURNIN' TO THE SEA.

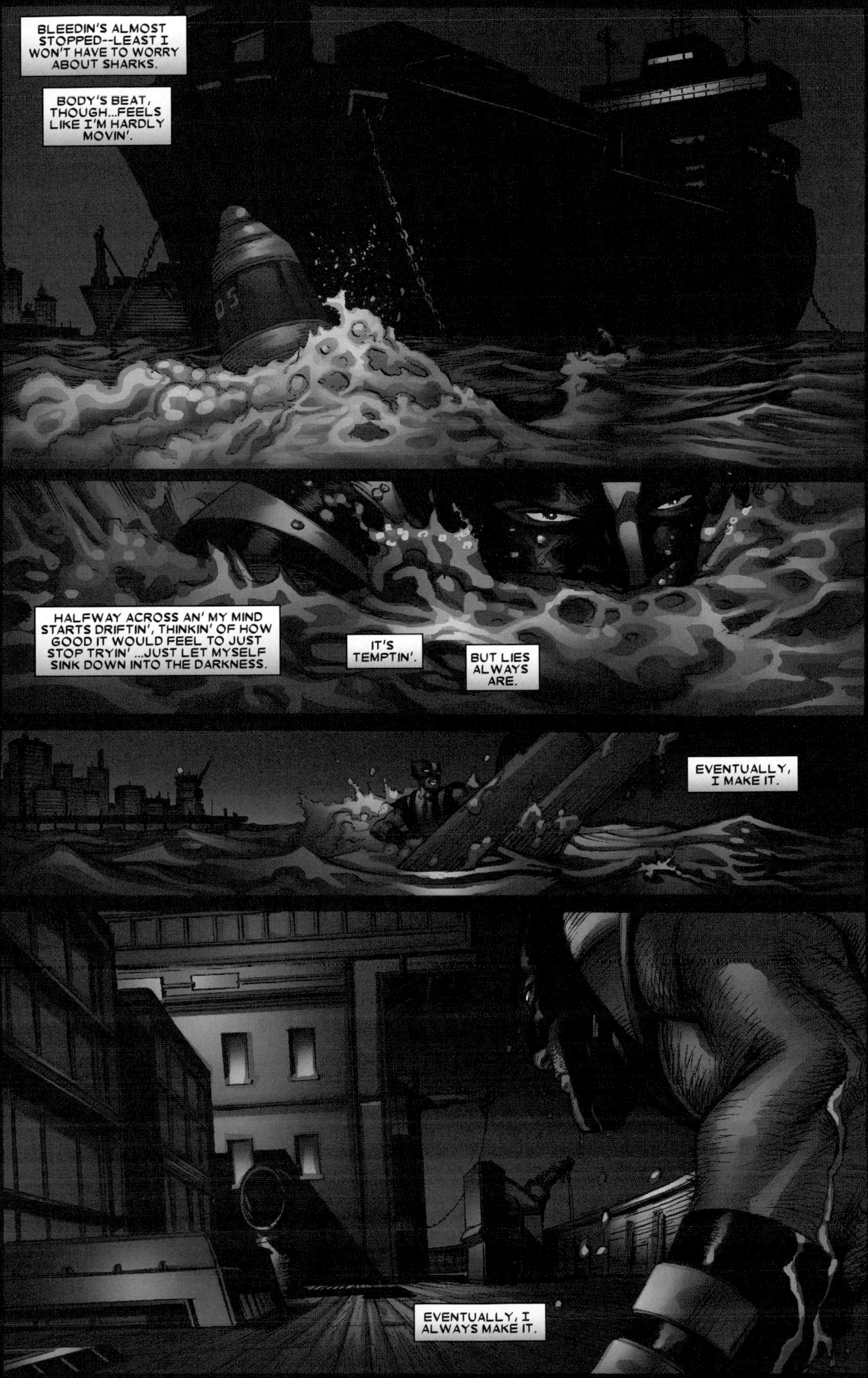
BLEEDIN'S ALMOST STOPPED--LEAST I WON'T HAVE TO WORRY ABOUT SHARKS.
BODY'S BEAT, THOUGH...FEELS LIKE I'M HARDLY MOVIN'.
HALFWAY ACROSS AN' MY MIND STARTS DRIFTIN', THINKIN' OF HOW GOOD IT WOULD FEEL TO JUST STOP TRYIN' ...JUST LET MYSELF SINK DOWN INTO THE DARKNESS.
IT'S TEMPTIN'.
BUT LIES ALWAYS ARE.
EVENTUALLY, I MAKE IT.
EVENTUALLY, I ALWAYS MAKE IT.

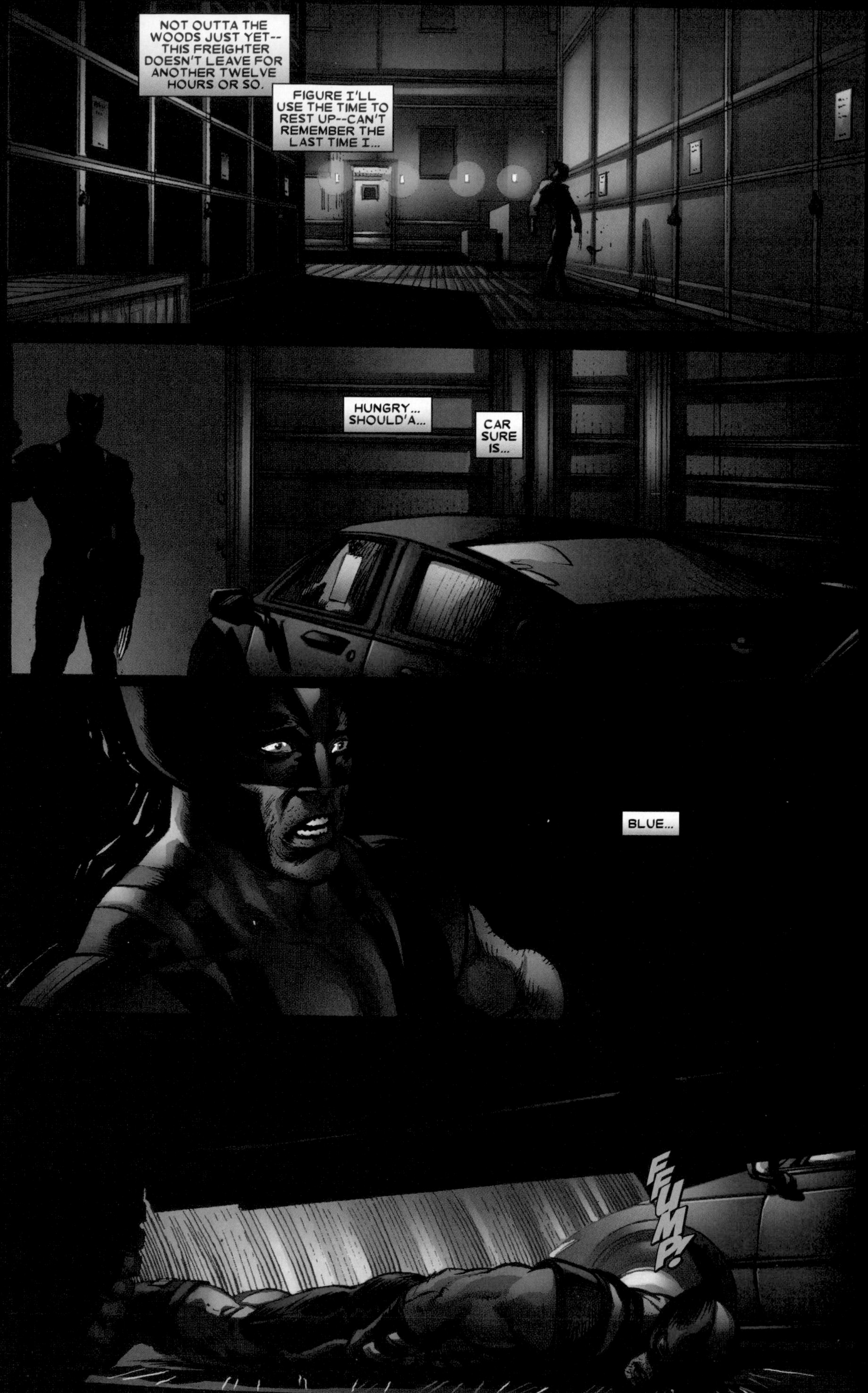
NOT OUTTA THE WOODS JUST YET-- THIS FREIGHTER DOESN'T LEAVE FOR ANOTHER TWELVE HOURS OR SO.
FIGURE I'LL USE THE TIME TO REST UP--CAN'T REMEMBER THE LAST TIME I...
HUNGRY... SHOULD'A...
CAR SURE IS...
BLUE...
FFUMP!

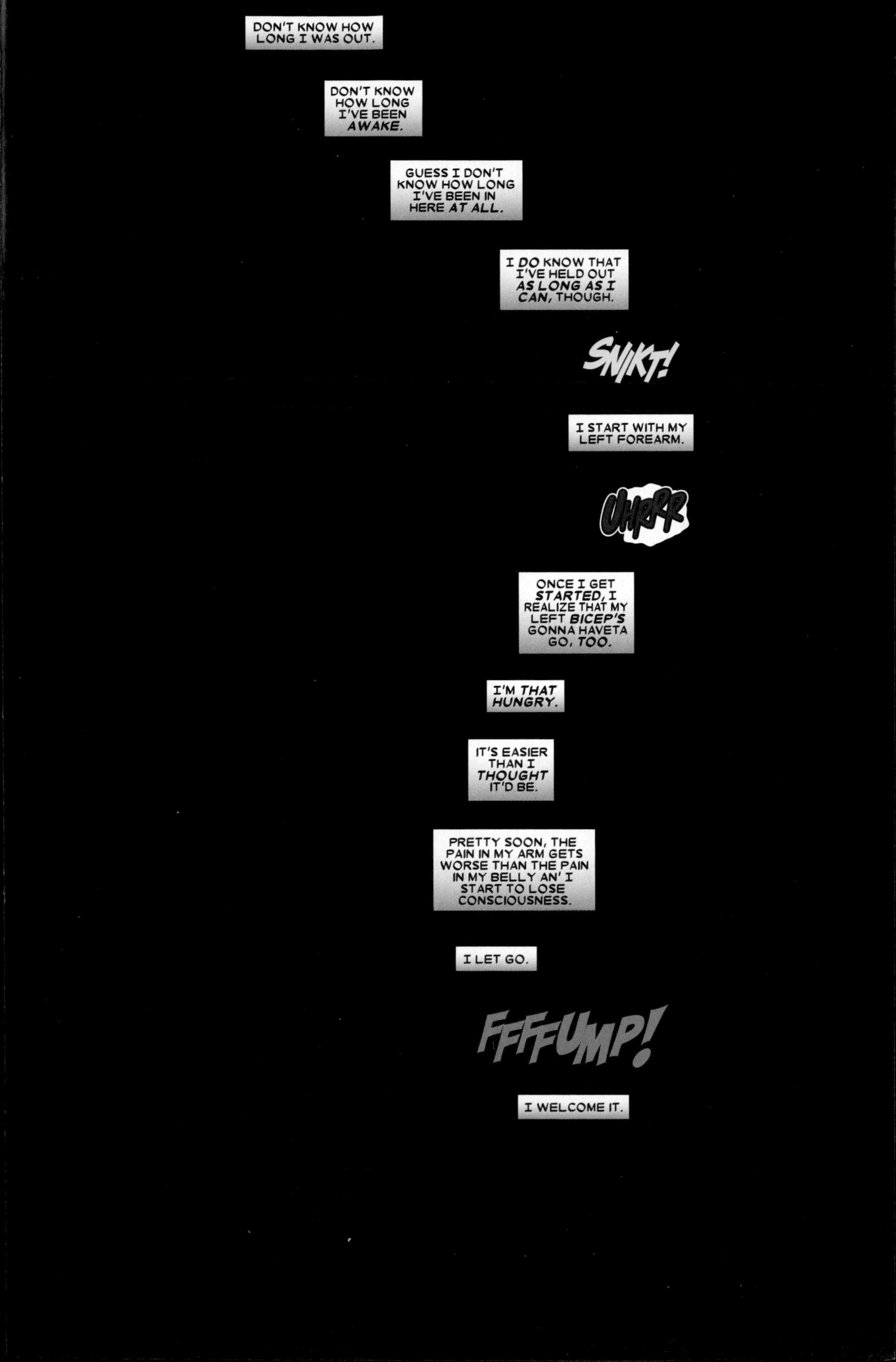
DON'T KNOW HOW LONG I WAS OUT.
DON'T KNOW HOW LONG I'VE BEEN AWAKE.
GUESS I DON'T KNOW HOW LONG I'VE BEEN IN HERE AT ALL.
I DO KNOW THAT I'VE HELD OUT AS LONG AS I CAN, THOUGH.
SNIKT!
I START WITH MY LEFT FOREARM.
UHRRR
ONCE I GET STARTED, I REALIZE THAT MY LEFT BICEP'S GONNA HAVETA GO, TOO.
I'M THAT HUNGRY.
IT'S EASIER THAN I THOUGHT IT'D BE.
PRETTY SOON, THE PAIN IN MY ARM GETS WORSE THAN THE PAIN IN MY BELLY AN' I START TO LOSE CONSCIOUSNESS.
I LET GO.
FFFFUMP!
I WELCOME IT.

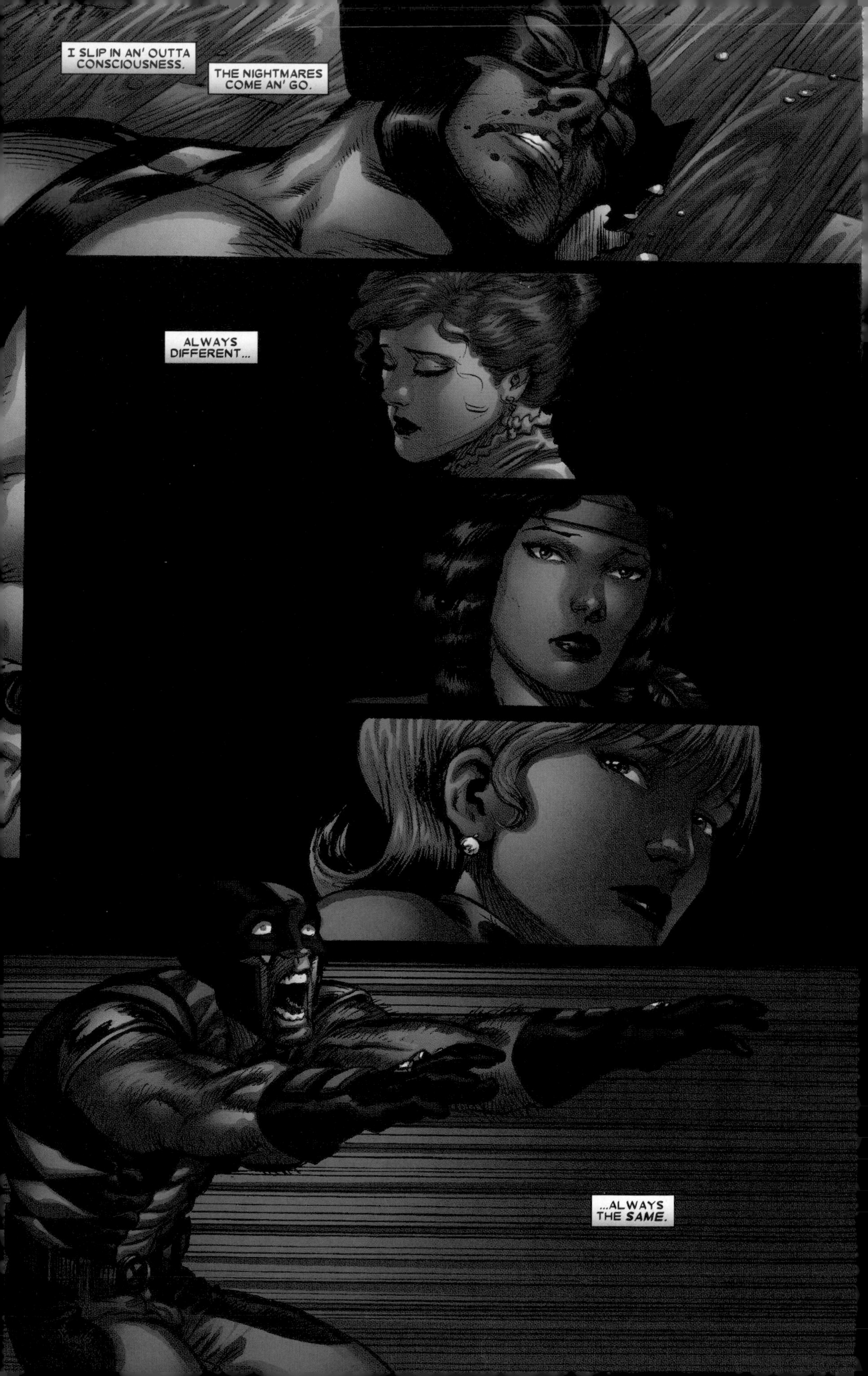
I SLIP IN AN' OUTTA CONSCIOUSNESS.
THE NIGHTMARES COME AN' GO.
ALWAYS DIFFERENT...
...ALWAYS THE SAME.

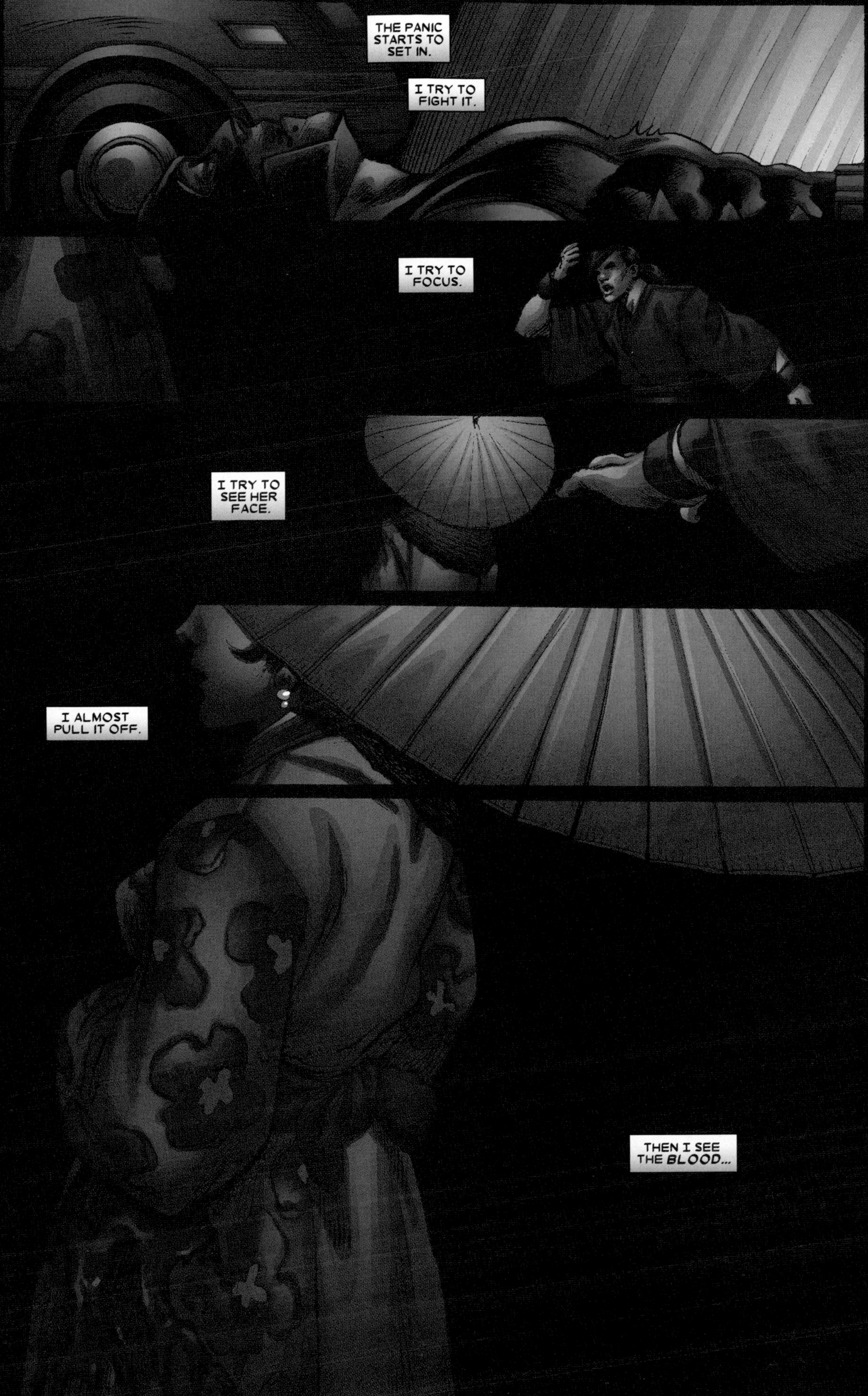
THE PANIC STARTS TO SET IN.
I TRY TO FIGHT IT.
I TRY TO FOCUS.
I TRY TO SEE HER FACE.
I ALMOST PULL IT OFF.
THEN I SEE THE BLOOD...

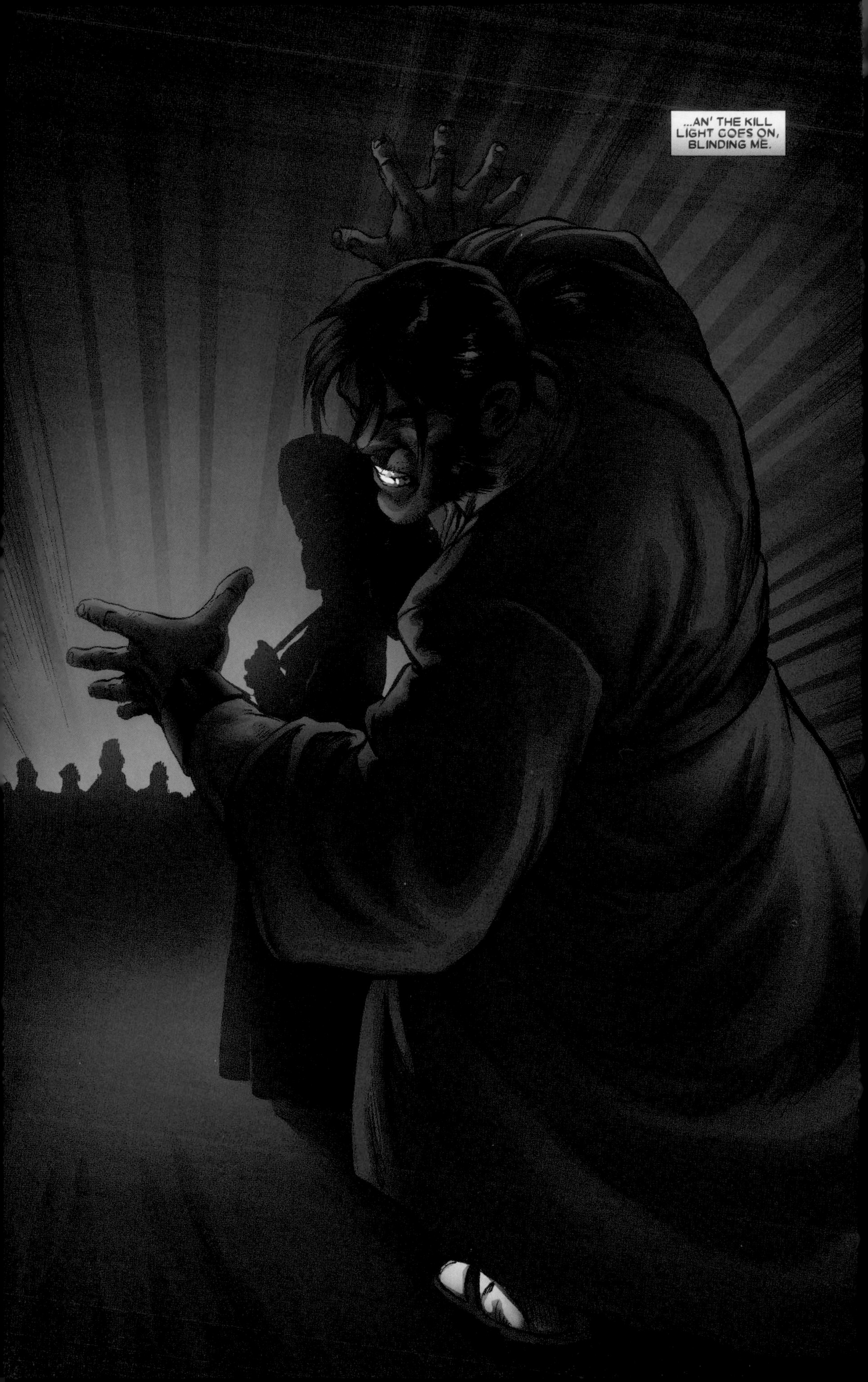
...AN' THE KILL LIGHT GOES ON, BLINDING ME.

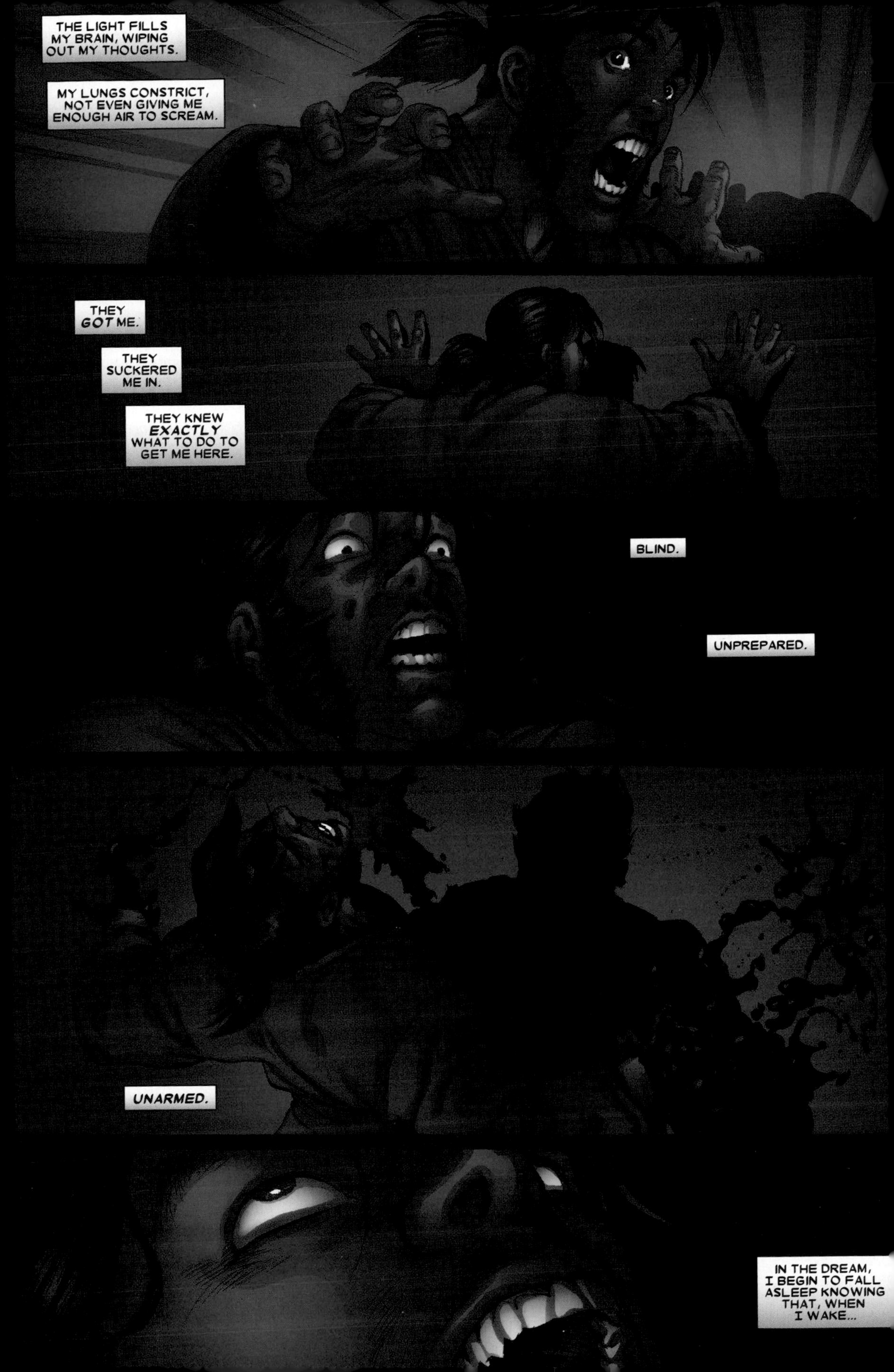
THE LIGHT FILLS MY BRAIN, WIPING OUT MY THOUGHTS.
MY LUNGS CONSTRICT, NOT EVEN GIVING ME ENOUGH AIR TO SCREAM.
THEY *GOT* ME.
THEY SUCKERED ME IN.
THEY KNEW *EXACTLY* WHAT TO DO TO GET ME HERE.
BLIND.
UNPREPARED.
UNARMED.
IN THE DREAM, I BEGIN TO FALL ASLEEP KNOWING THAT, WHEN I WAKE...

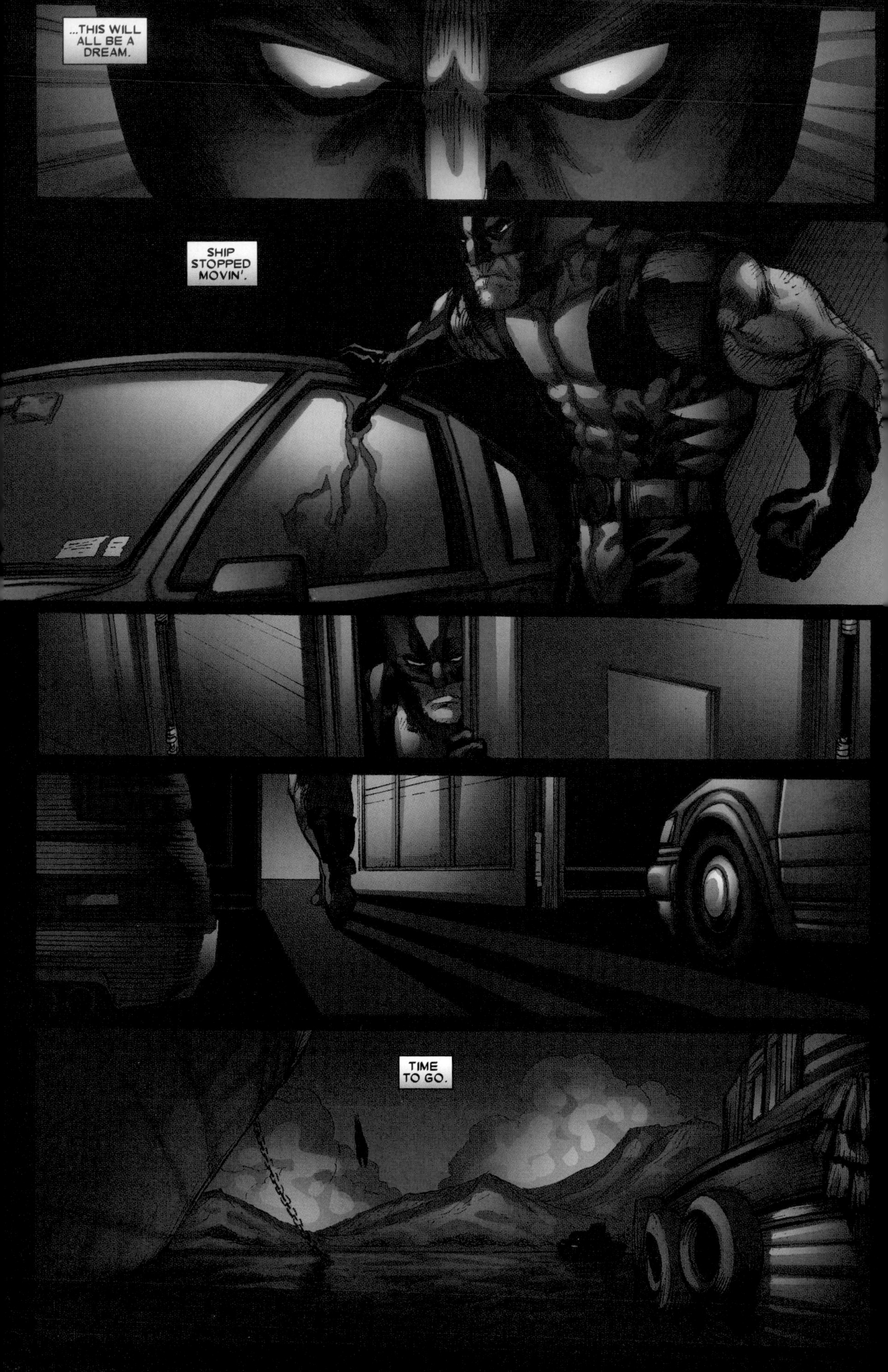
...THIS WILL ALL BE A DREAM.
SHIP STOPPED MOVIN'.
TIME TO GO.

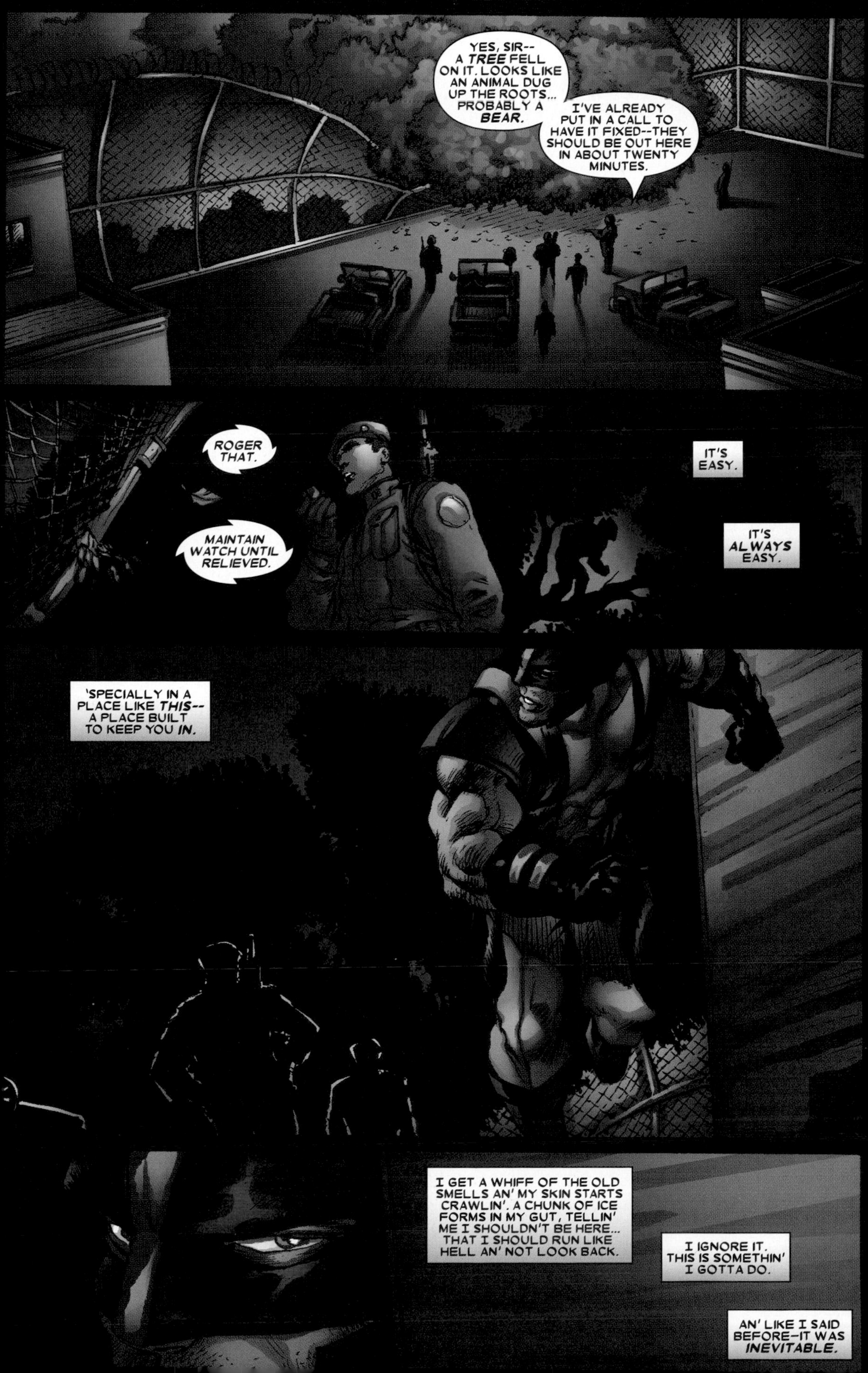

YES, SIR-- A TREE FELL ON IT. LOOKS LIKE AN ANIMAL DUG UP THE ROOTS... PROBABLY A BEAR.
I'VE ALREADY PUT IN A CALL TO HAVE IT FIXED--THEY SHOULD BE OUT HERE IN ABOUT TWENTY MINUTES.
ROGER THAT.
MAINTAIN WATCH UNTIL RELIEVED.
IT'S EASY.
IT'S ALWAYS EASY.
'SPECIALLY IN A PLACE LIKE THIS-- A PLACE BUILT TO KEEP YOU IN.
I GET A WHIFF OF THE OLD SMELLS AN' MY SKIN STARTS CRAWLIN'. A CHUNK OF ICE FORMS IN MY GUT, TELLIN' ME I SHOULDN'T BE HERE... THAT I SHOULD RUN LIKE HELL AN' NOT LOOK BACK.
I IGNORE IT. THIS IS SOMETHIN' I GOTTA DO.
AN' LIKE I SAID BEFORE--IT WAS INEVITABLE.

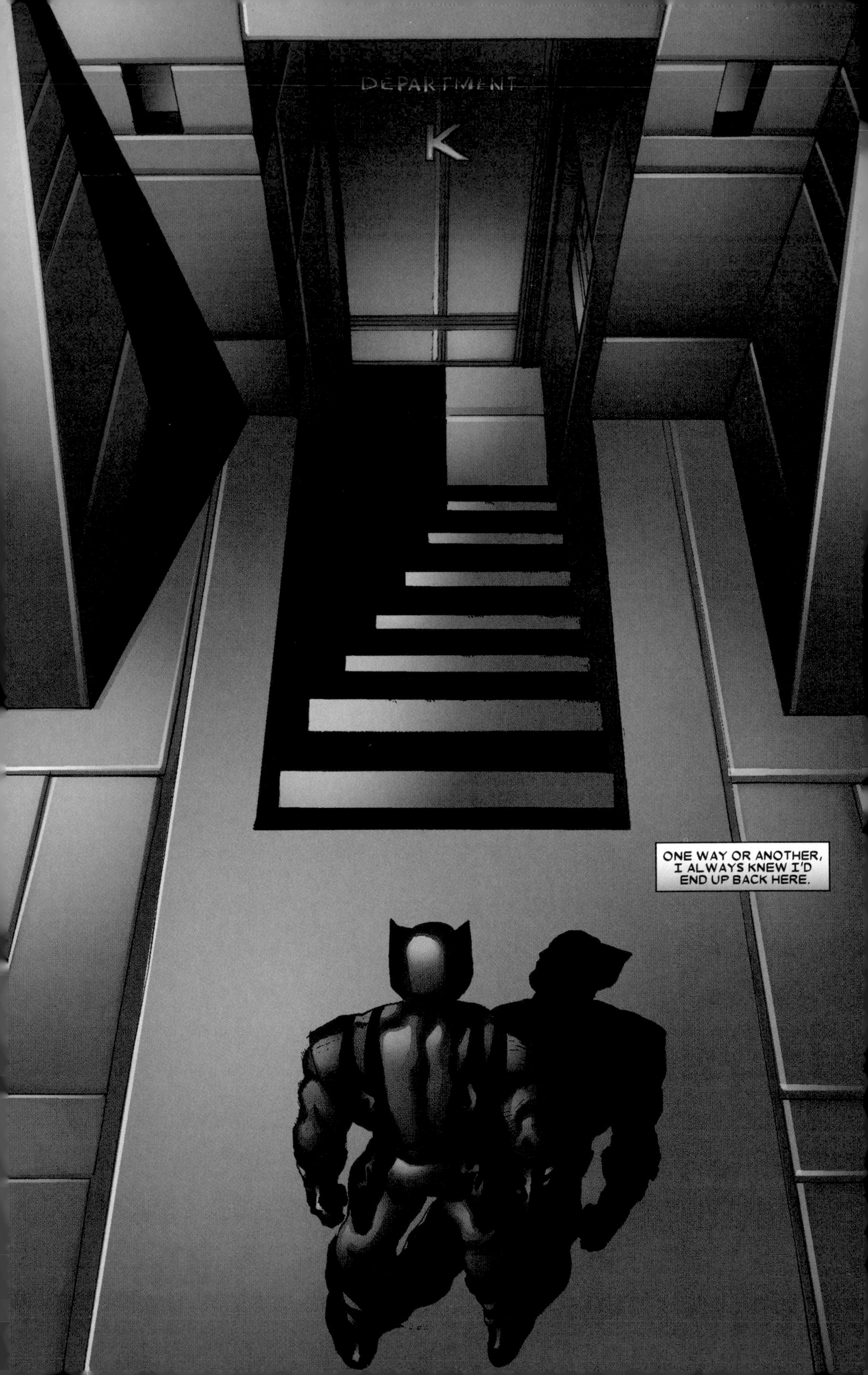
DEPARTMENT
K
ONE WAY OR ANOTHER, I ALWAYS KNEW I'D END UP BACK HERE.

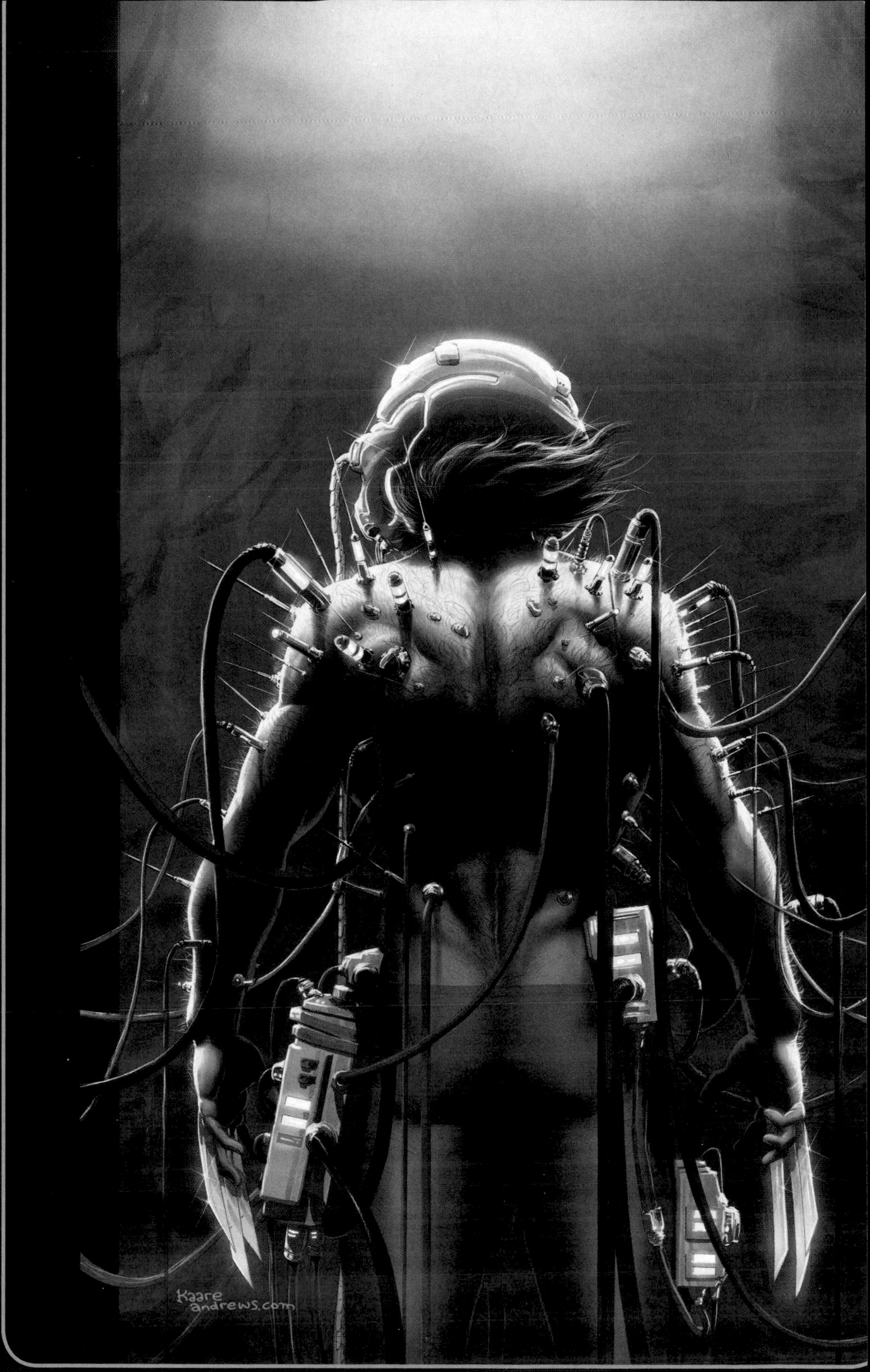
Kaare
andrews.com

ISSUE #38

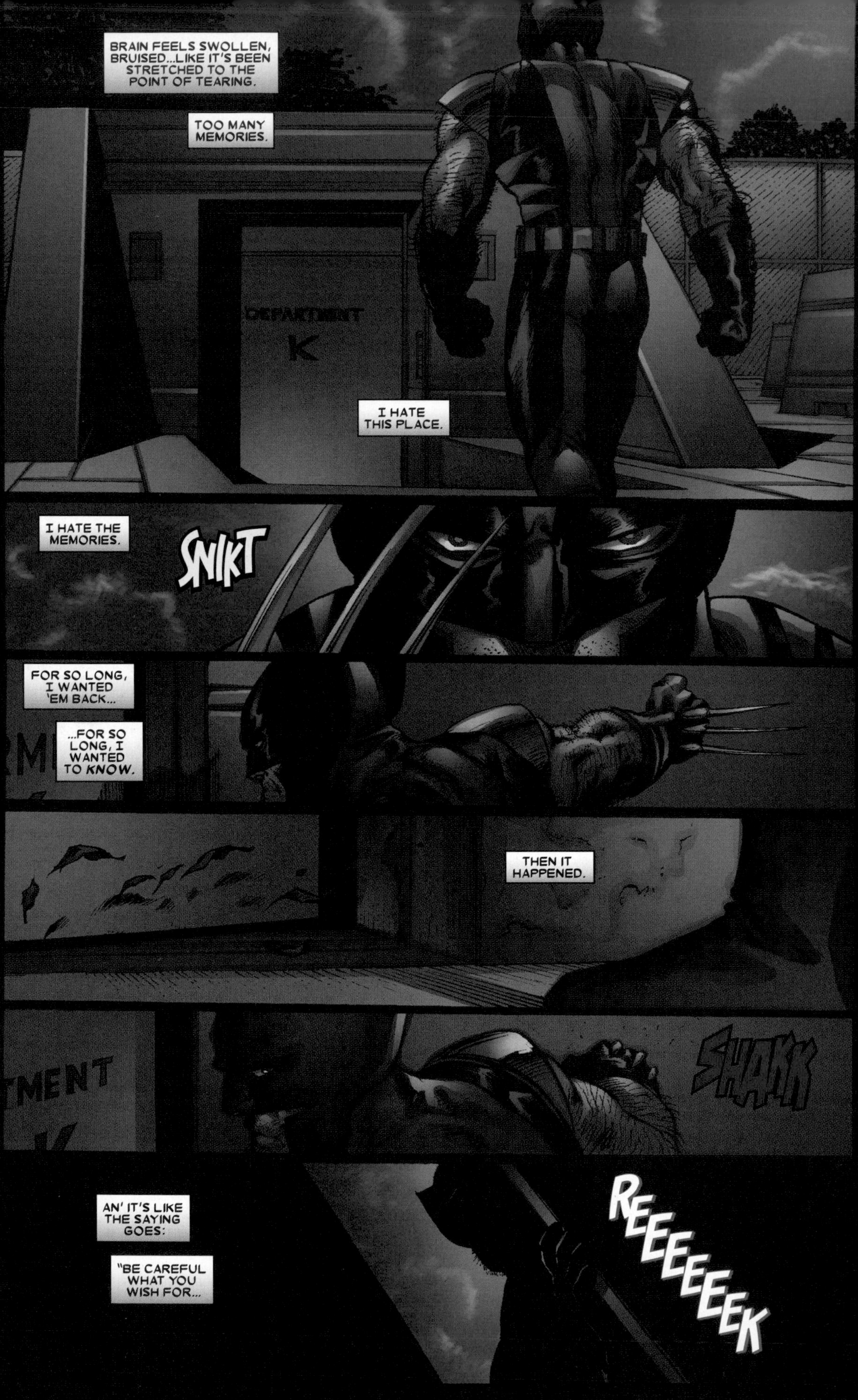
BRAIN FEELS SWOLLEN, BRUISED...LIKE IT'S BEEN STRETCHED TO THE POINT OF TEARING.
TOO MANY MEMORIES.
DEPARTMENT K
I HATE THIS PLACE.
I HATE THE MEMORIES.
SNIKT
FOR SO LONG, I WANTED 'EM BACK...
...FOR SO LONG, I WANTED TO *KNOW*.
THEN IT HAPPENED.
MENT
SHAKK
AN' IT'S LIKE THE SAYING GOES:
"BE CAREFUL WHAT YOU WISH FOR...
REEEEEEEK

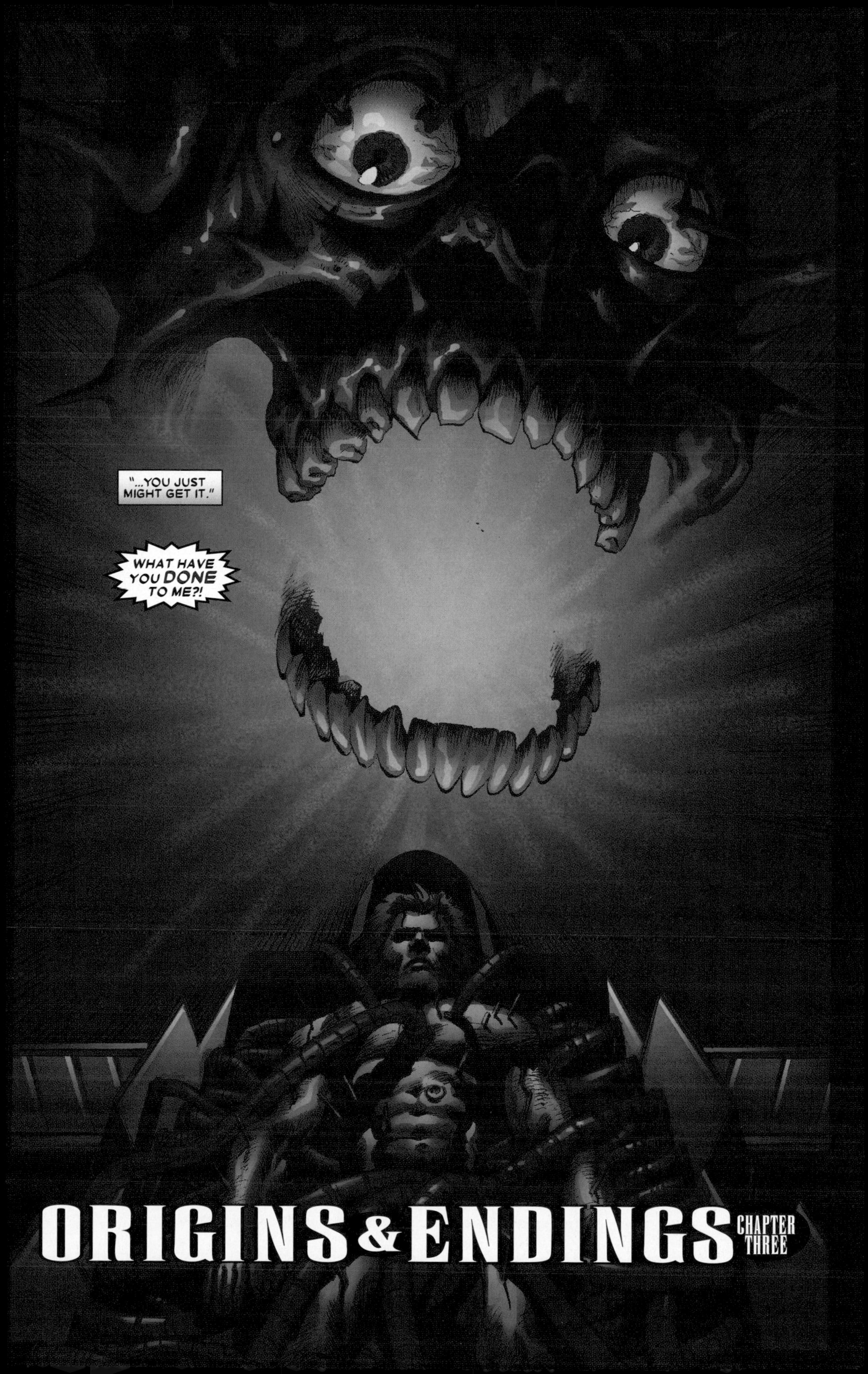
"...YOU JUST MIGHT GET IT."
WHAT HAVE YOU DONE TO ME?!
ORIGINS & ENDINGS CHAPTER THREE

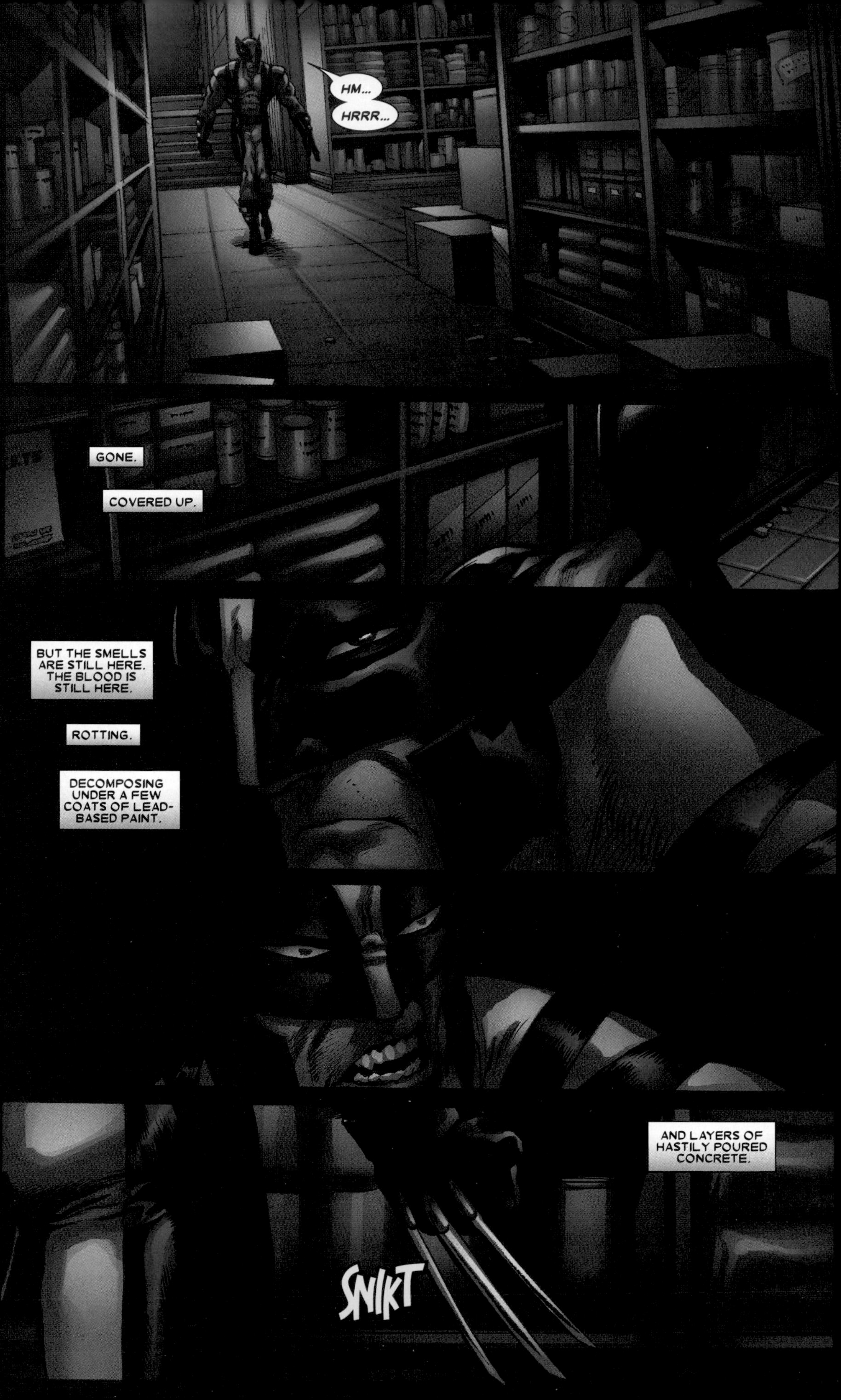
HM...
HRRR...
GONE.
COVERED UP.
BUT THE SMELLS ARE STILL HERE. THE BLOOD IS STILL HERE.
ROTTING.
DECOMPOSING UNDER A FEW COATS OF LEAD-BASED PAINT.
AND LAYERS OF HASTILY POURED CONCRETE.
SNIKT

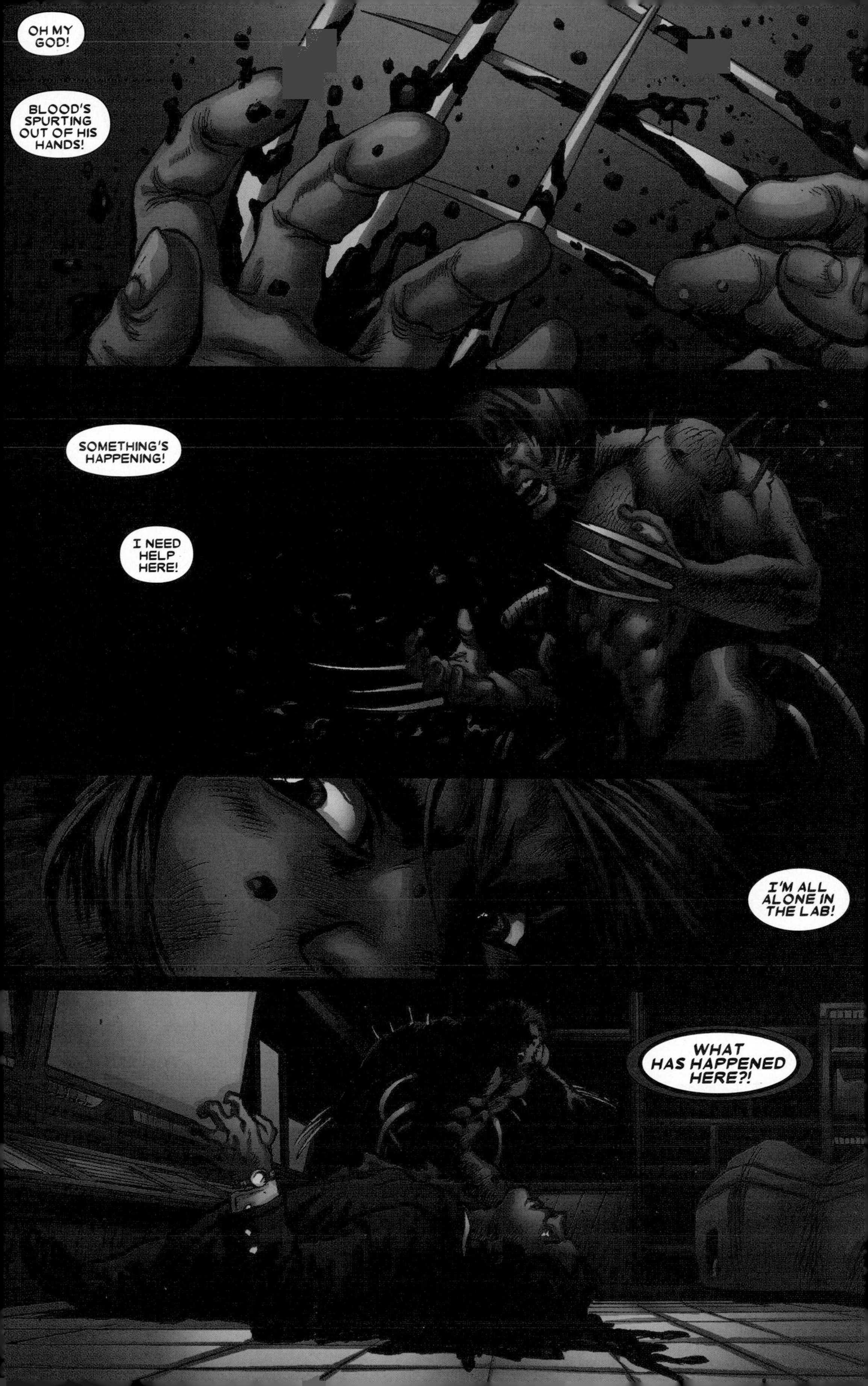
OH MY GOD!
BLOOD'S SPURTING OUT OF HIS HANDS!
SOMETHING'S HAPPENING!
I NEED HELP HERE!
I'M ALL ALONE IN THE LAB!
WHAT HAS HAPPENED HERE?!

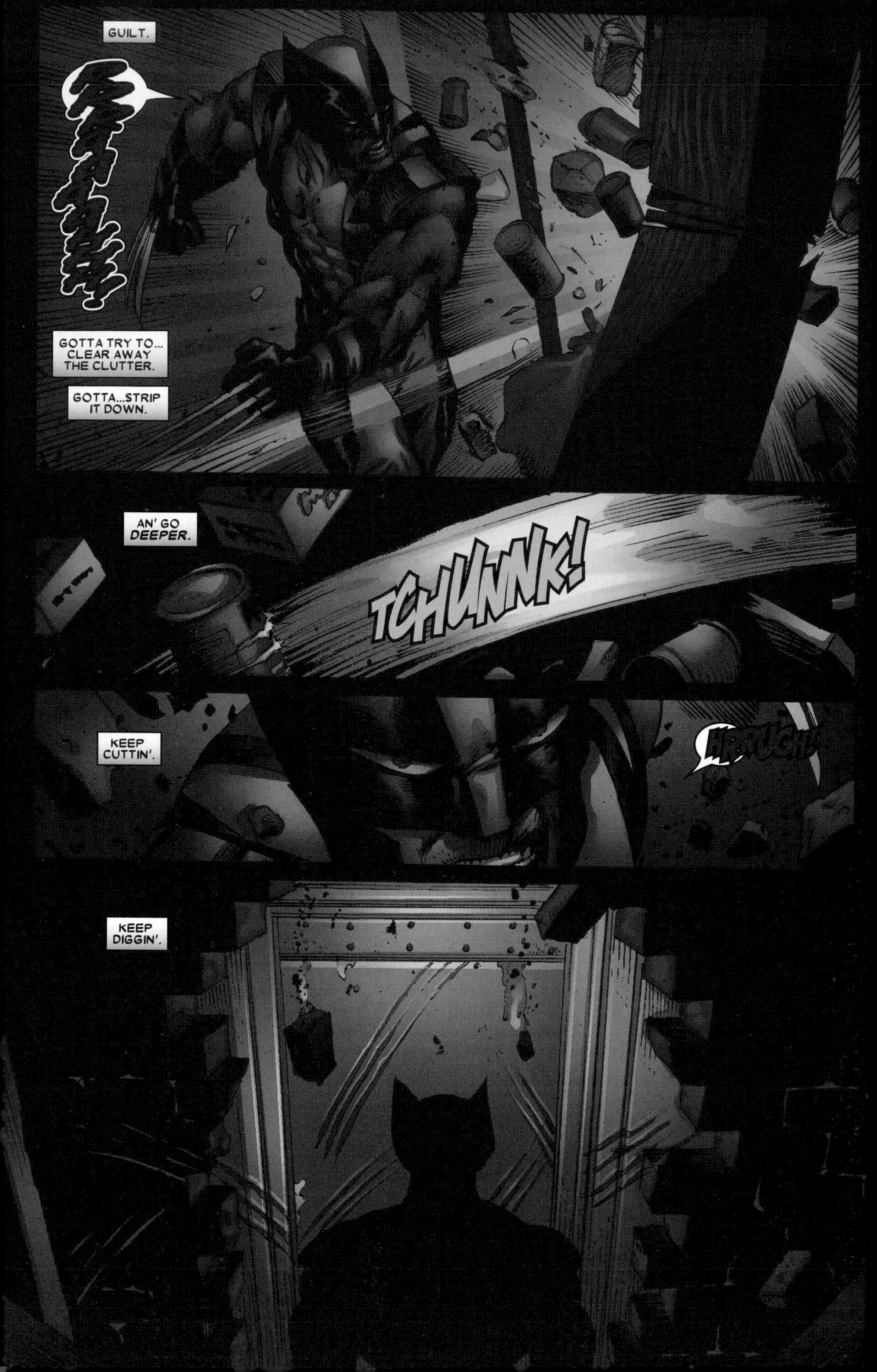
GUILT.
GOTTA TRY TO... CLEAR AWAY THE CLUTTER.
GOTTA...STRIP IT DOWN.
AN' GO DEEPER.
TCHUNNK!
KEEP CUTTIN'.
KEEP DIGGIN'.

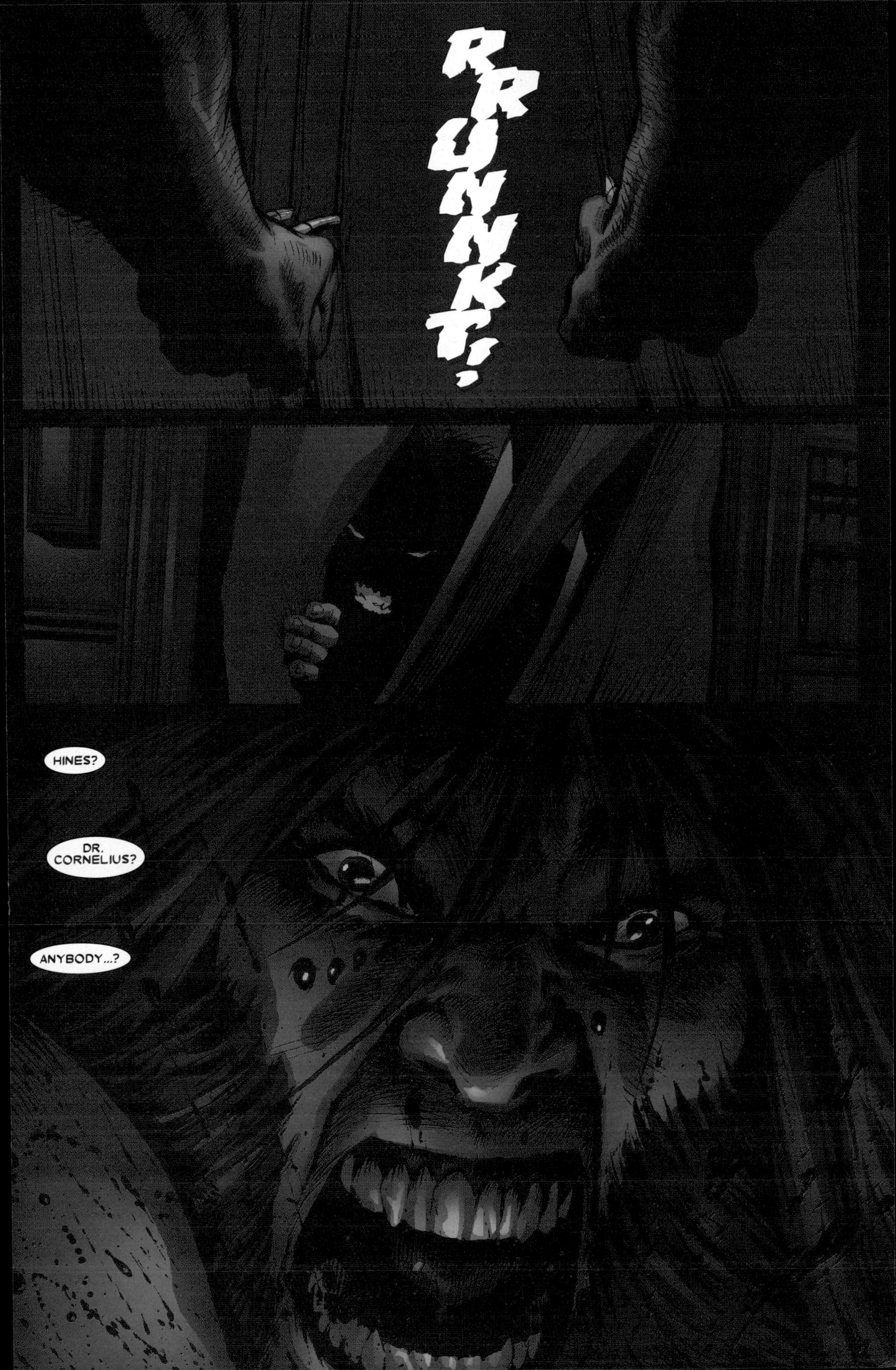
RRUNKT!
HINES?
DR. CORNELIUS?
ANYBODY...?

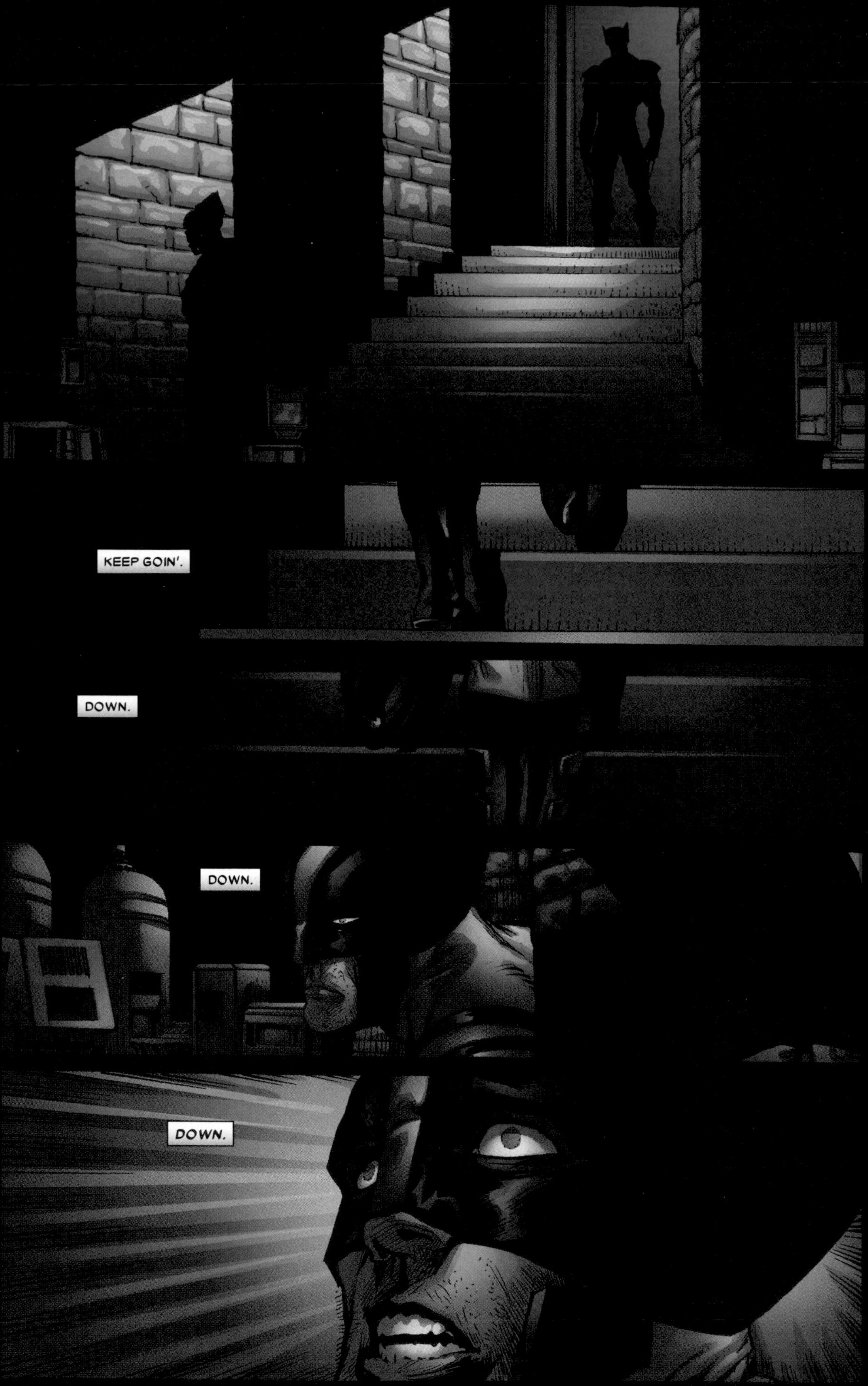
KEEP GOIN'.
DOWN.
DOWN.
DOWN.

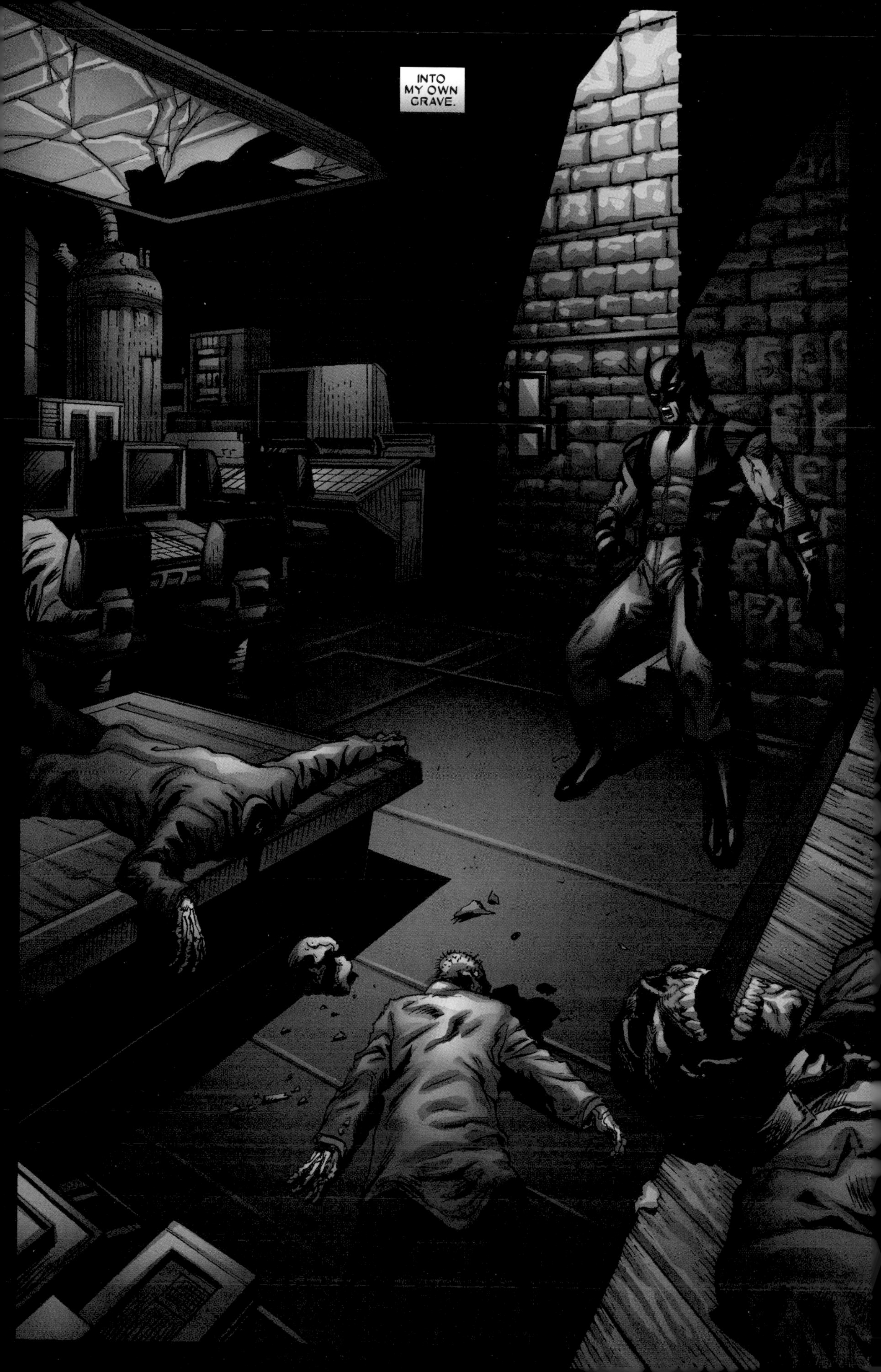
INTO MY OWN GRAVE.

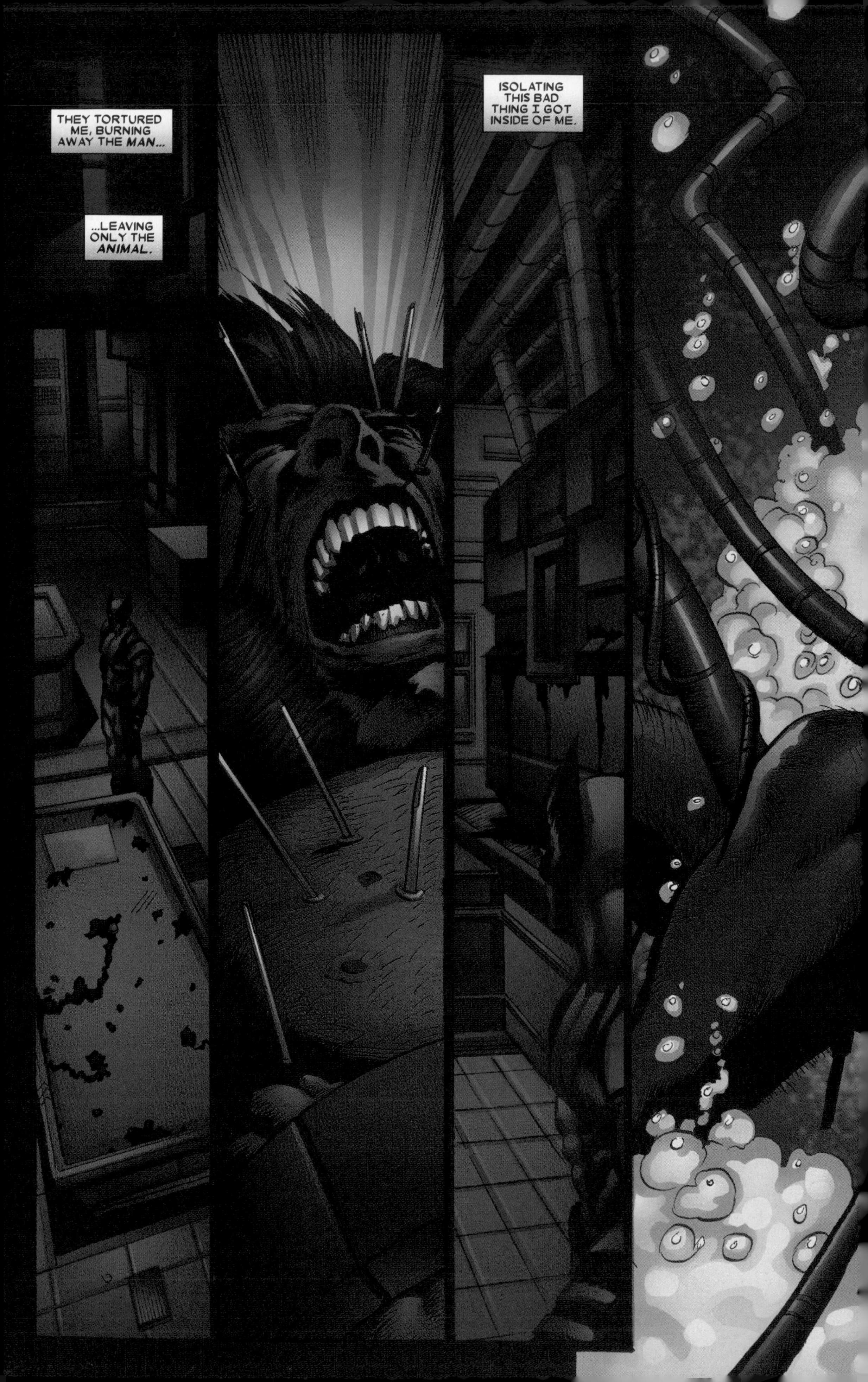
THEY TORTURED ME, BURNING AWAY THE *MAN*...
...LEAVING ONLY THE *ANIMAL*.
ISOLATING THIS BAD THING I GOT INSIDE OF ME.

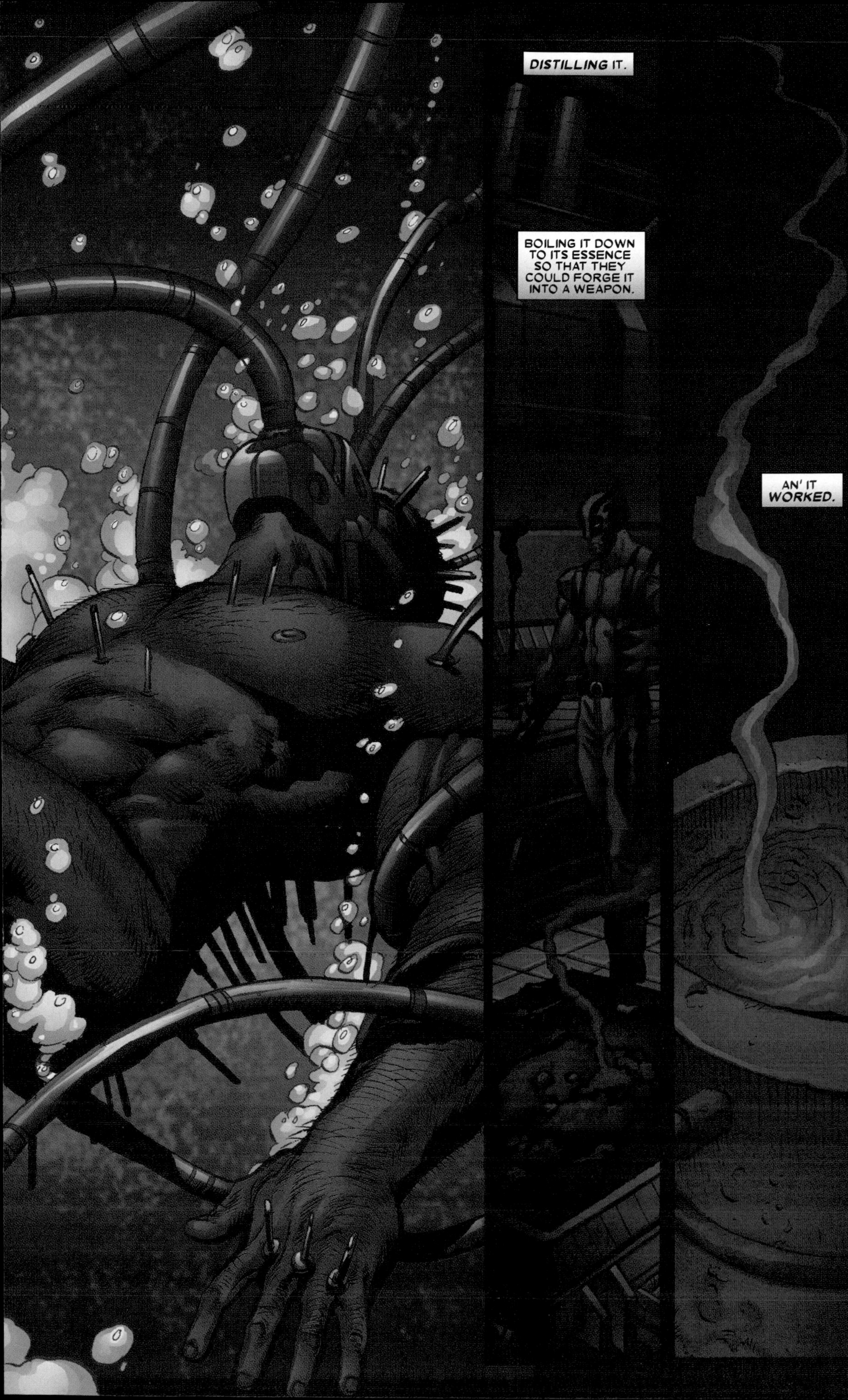
DISTILLING IT.
BOILING IT DOWN TO ITS ESSENCE SO THAT THEY COULD FORGE IT INTO A WEAPON.
AN' IT *WORKED.*

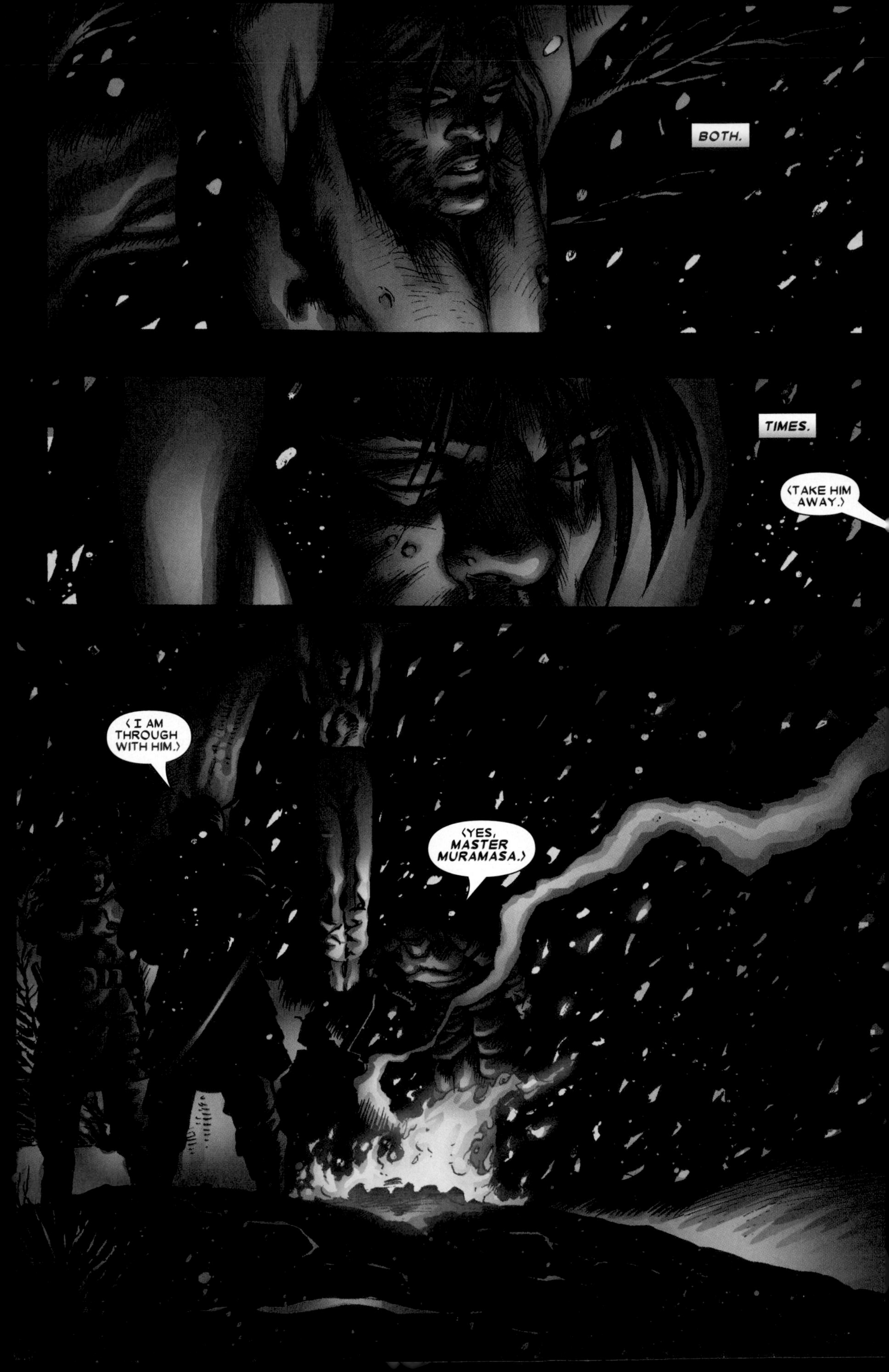
BOTH.
TIMES.
‹TAKE HIM AWAY.›
‹I AM THROUGH WITH HIM.›
‹YES, MASTER MURAMASA.›

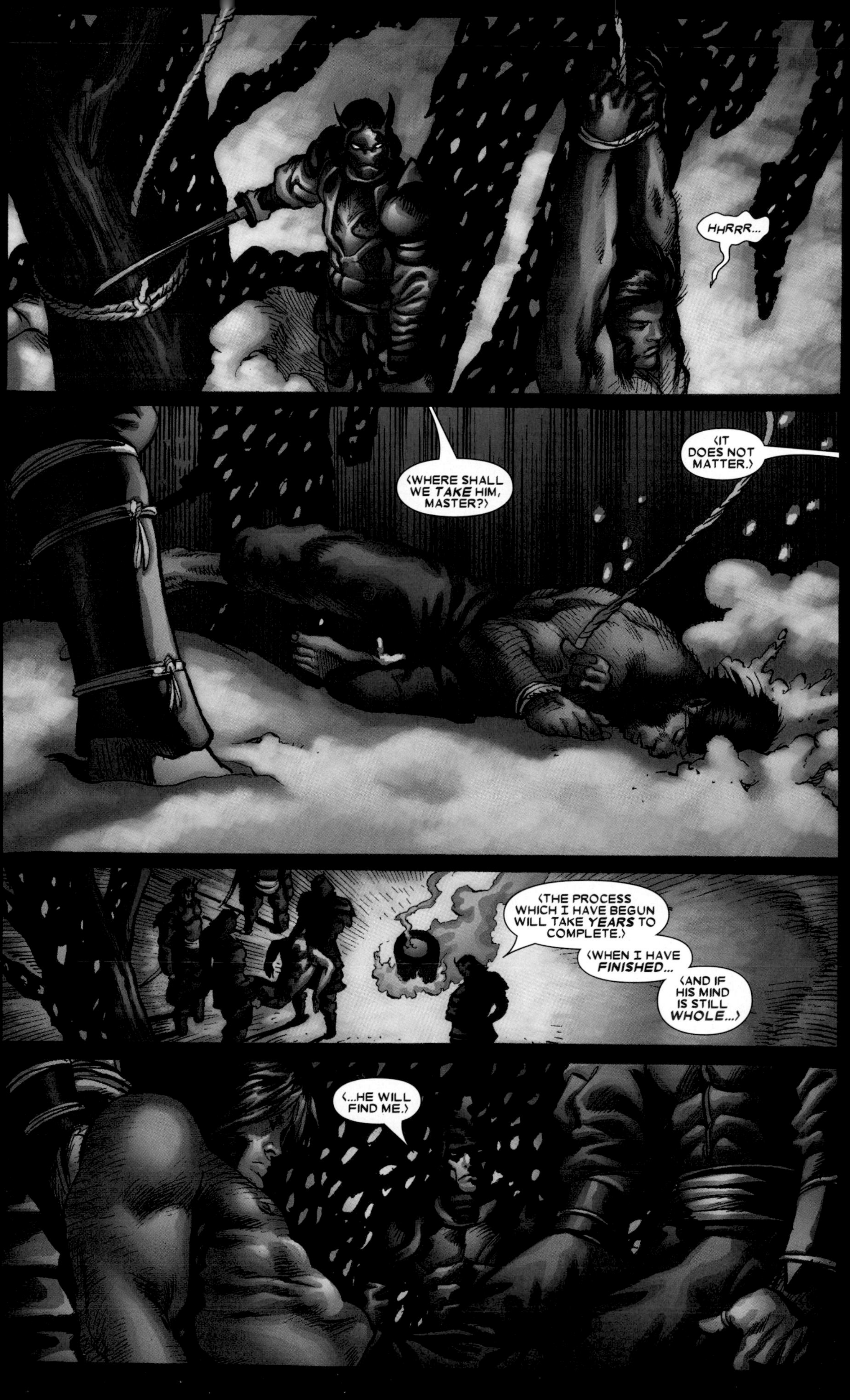
HHRRR...
‹WHERE SHALL WE TAKE HIM, MASTER?›
‹IT DOES NOT MATTER.›
‹THE PROCESS WHICH I HAVE BEGUN WILL TAKE YEARS TO COMPLETE.›
‹WHEN I HAVE FINISHED...
‹AND IF HIS MIND IS STILL WHOLE...›
‹...HE WILL FIND ME.›

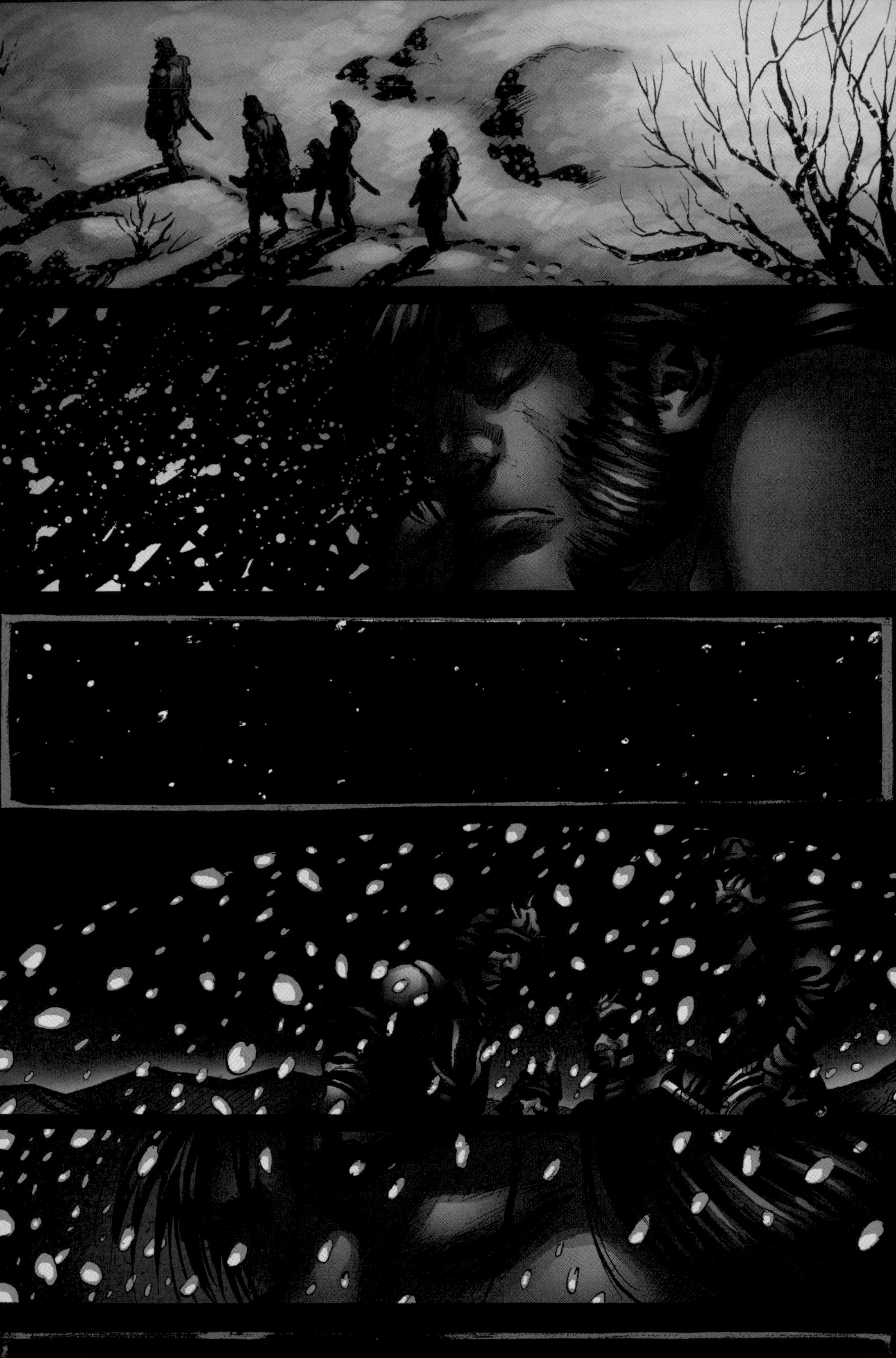

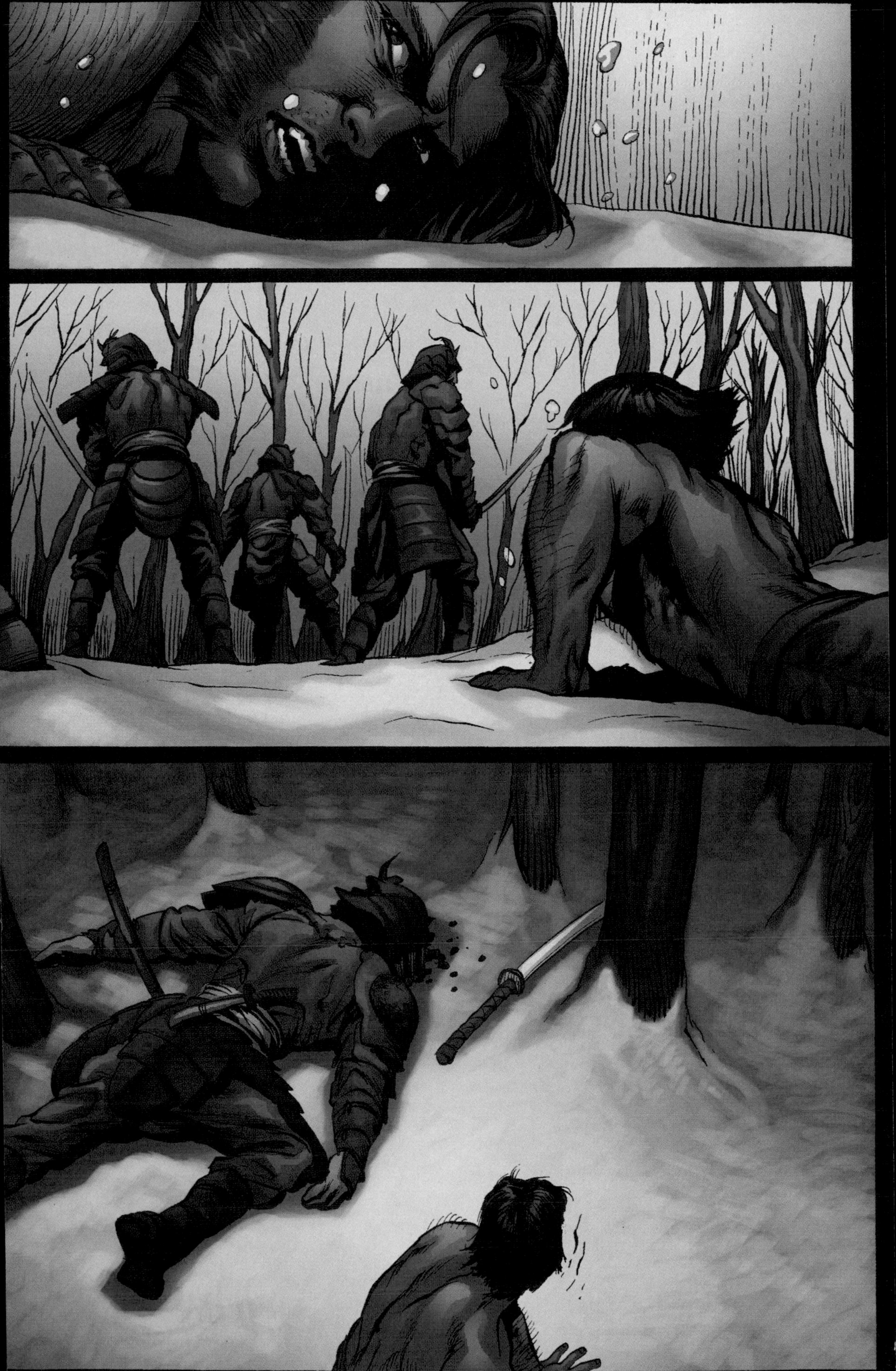

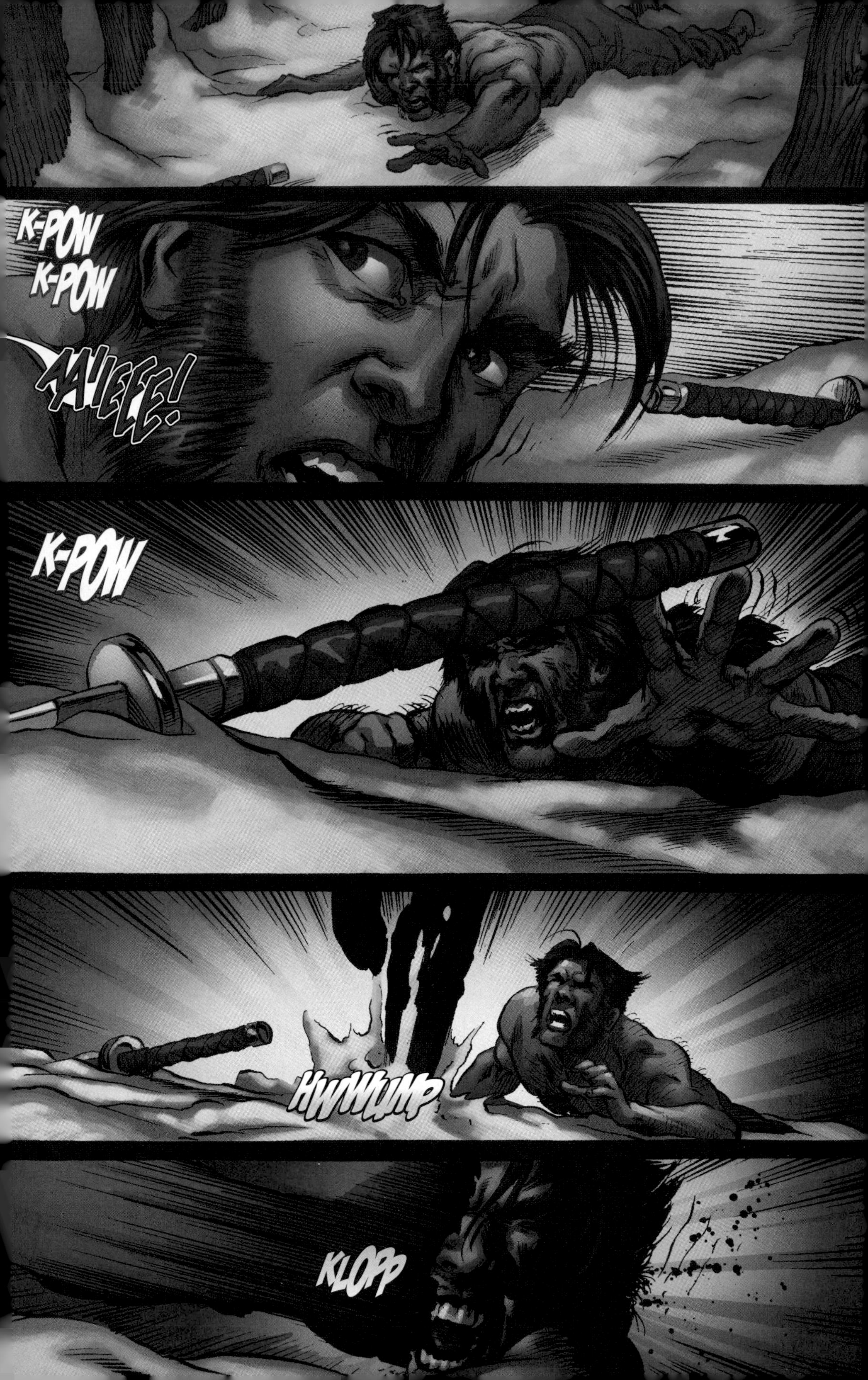
K-POW
K-POW
AAIIEEEE!
K-POW
HWWUMP
KLOPP

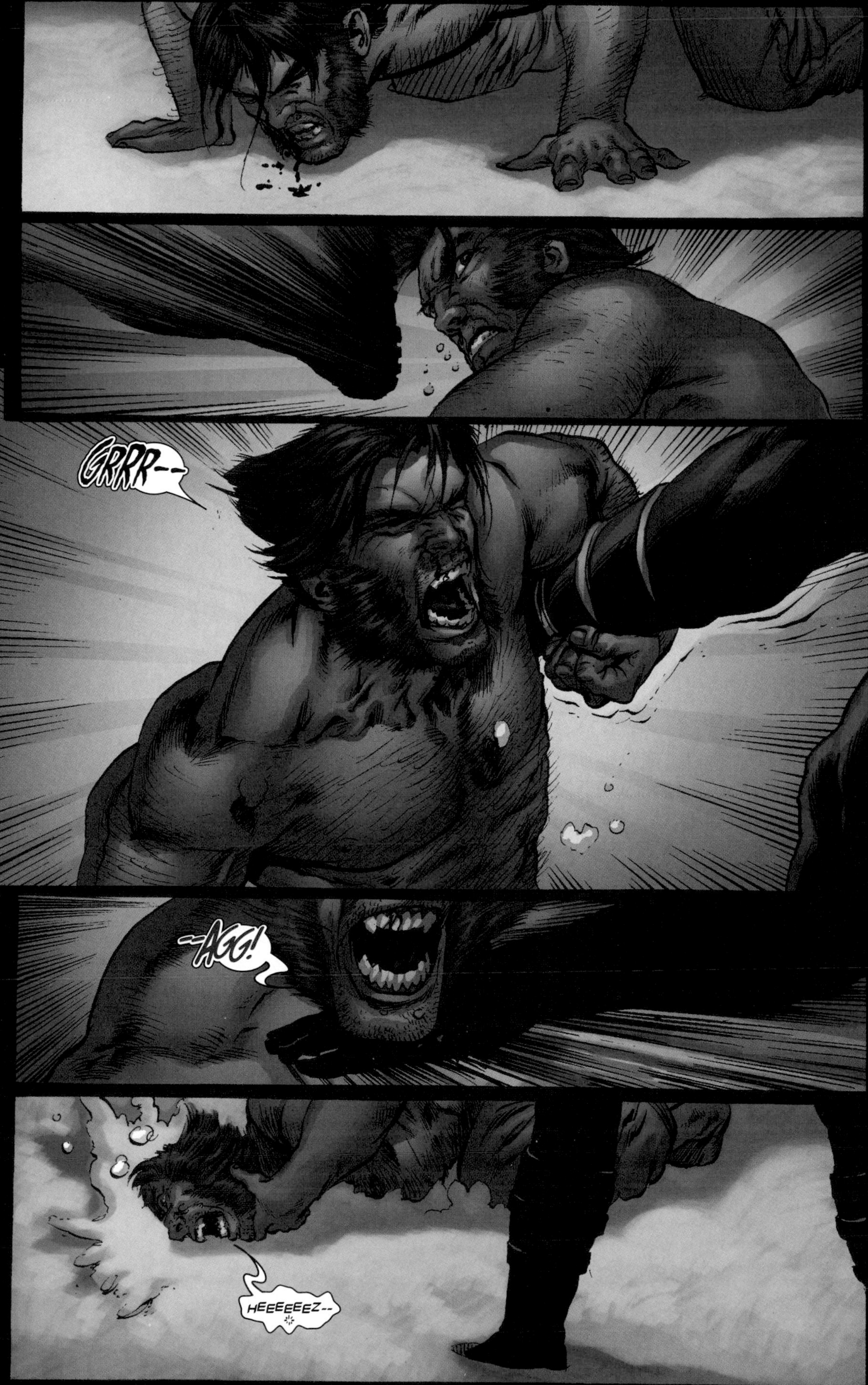
GRRR--
--AGG!
HEEEEEEZ--

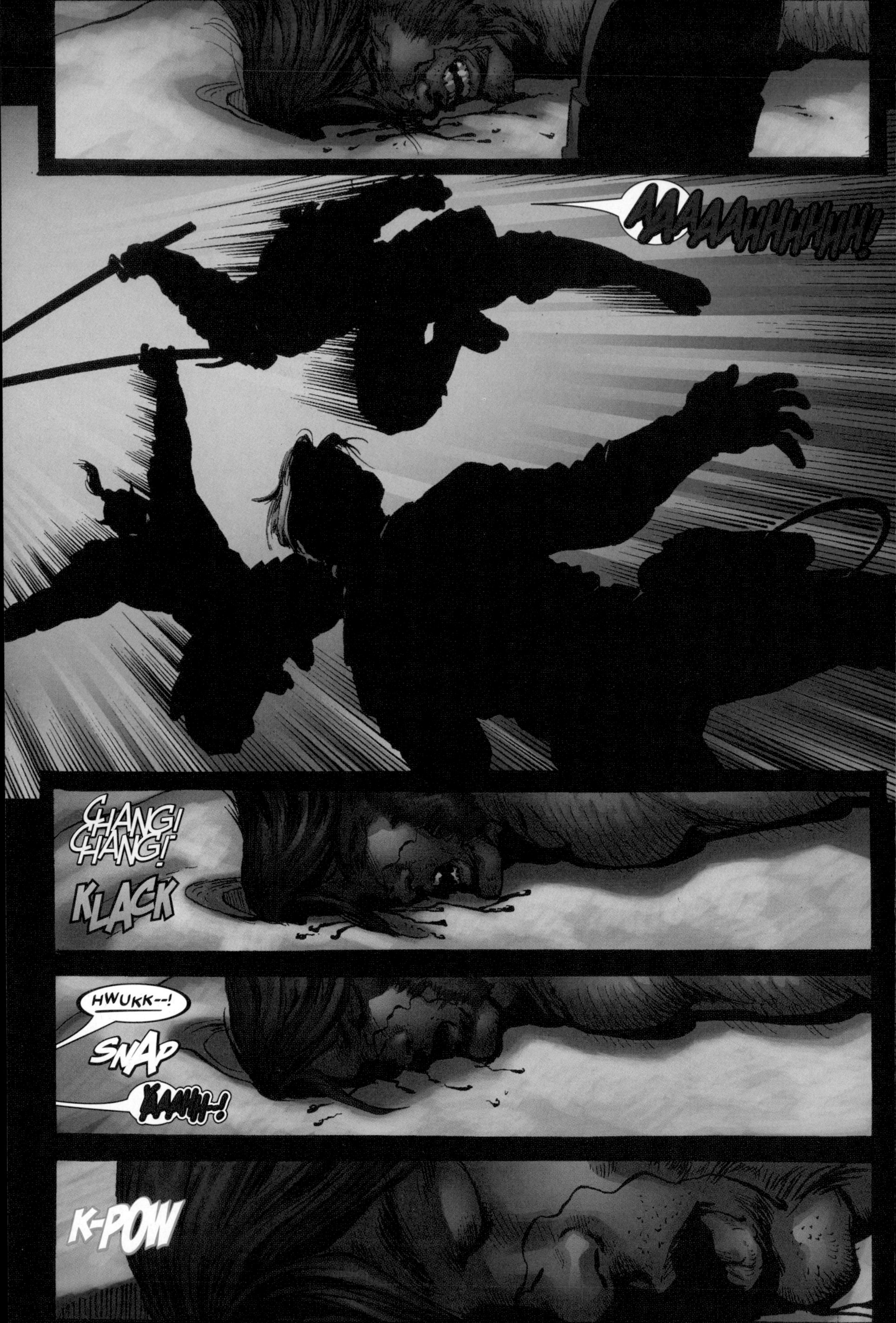
AAAAAHHHHHH!
CHANG!
CHANG!
KLACK
HWUKK--!
SNAP
KAAHH--!
K-POW

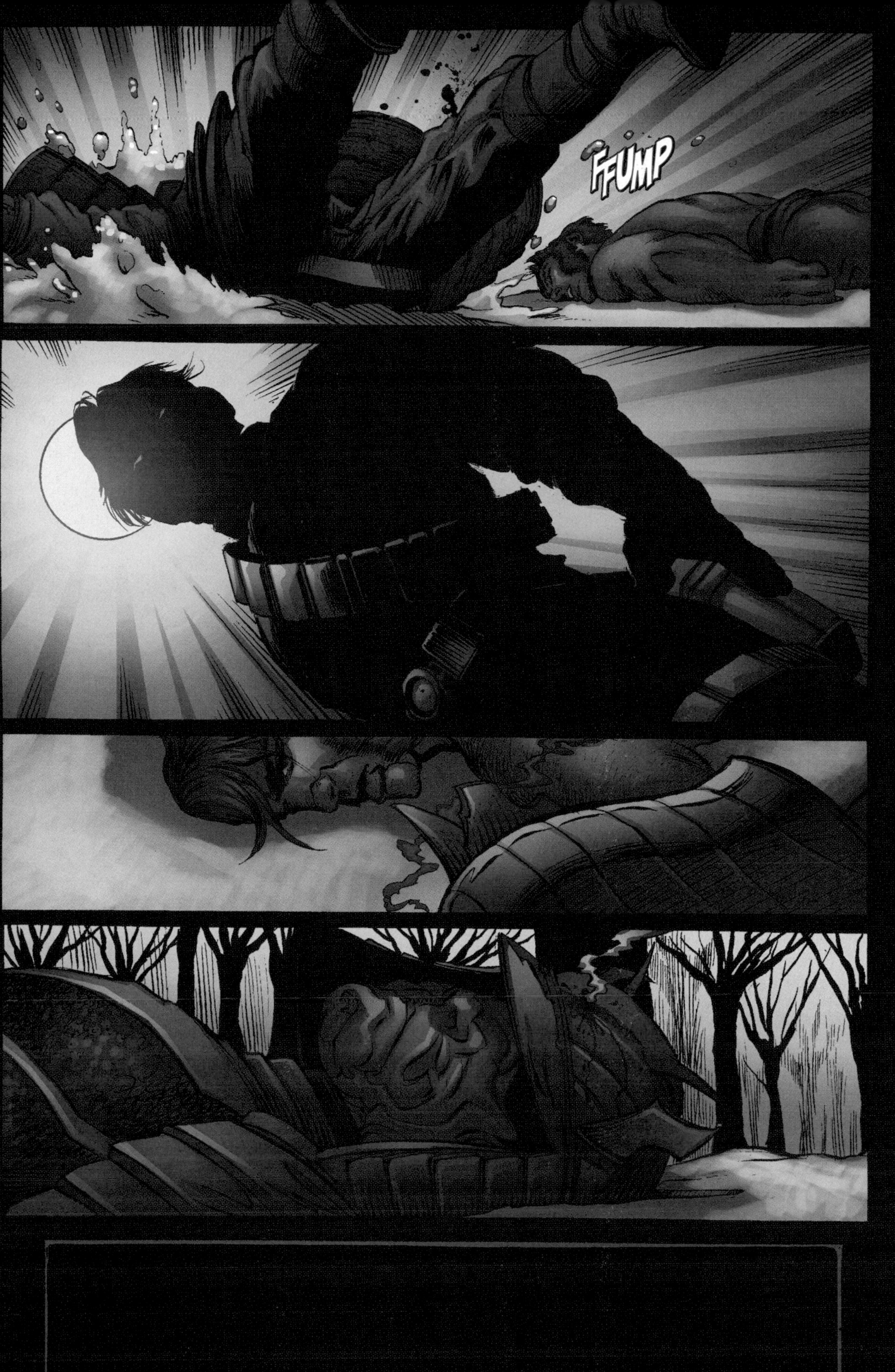
FFUMP

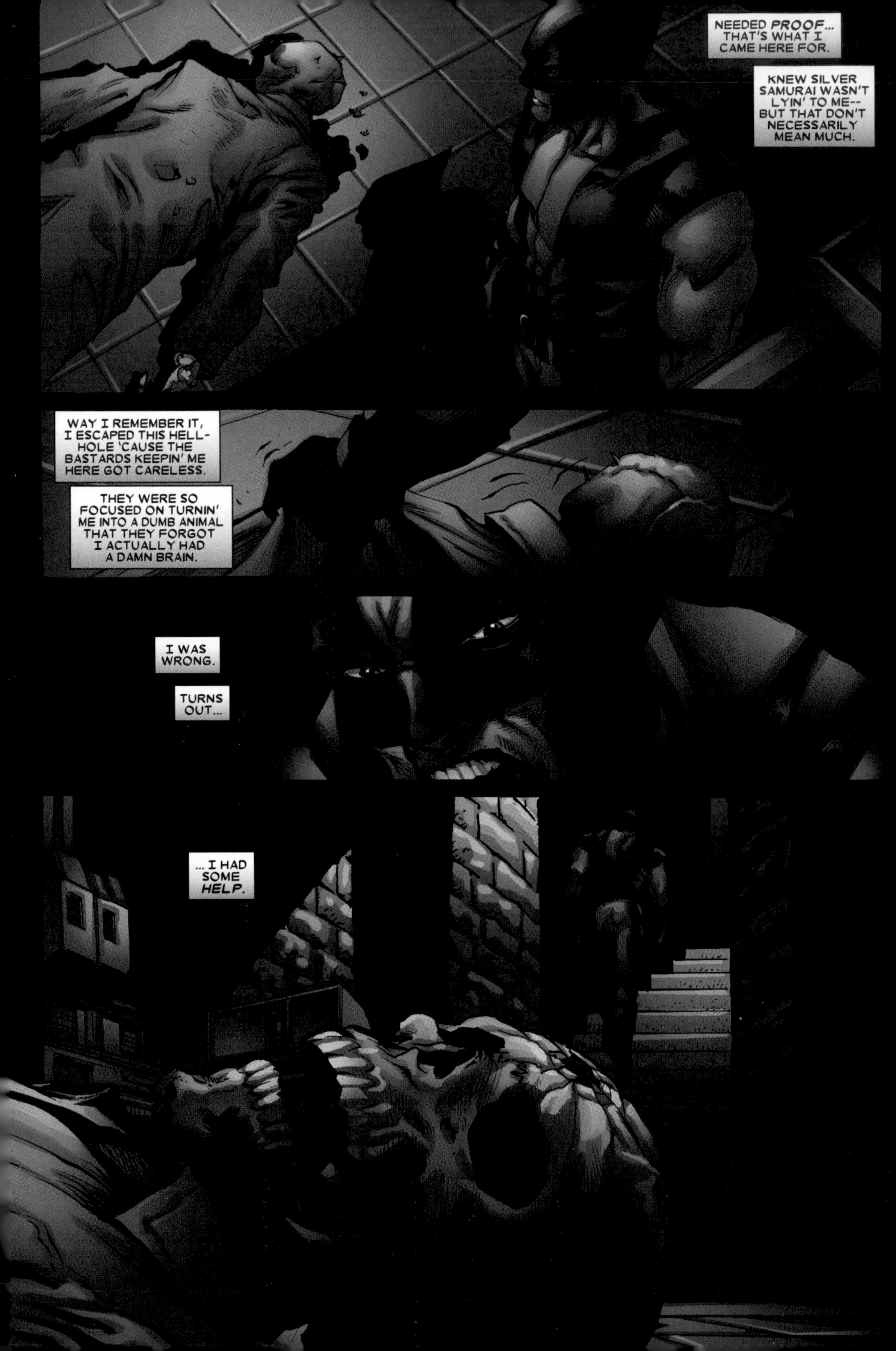
NEEDED *PROOF*... THAT'S WHAT I CAME HERE FOR.
KNEW SILVER SAMURAI WASN'T LYIN' TO ME-- BUT THAT DON'T NECESSARILY MEAN MUCH.
WAY I REMEMBER IT, I ESCAPED THIS HELL-HOLE 'CAUSE THE BASTARDS KEEPIN' ME HERE GOT CARELESS.
THEY WERE SO FOCUSED ON TURNIN' ME INTO A DUMB ANIMAL THAT THEY FORGOT I ACTUALLY HAD A DAMN BRAIN.
I WAS WRONG.
TURNS OUT...
... I HAD SOME *HELP*.

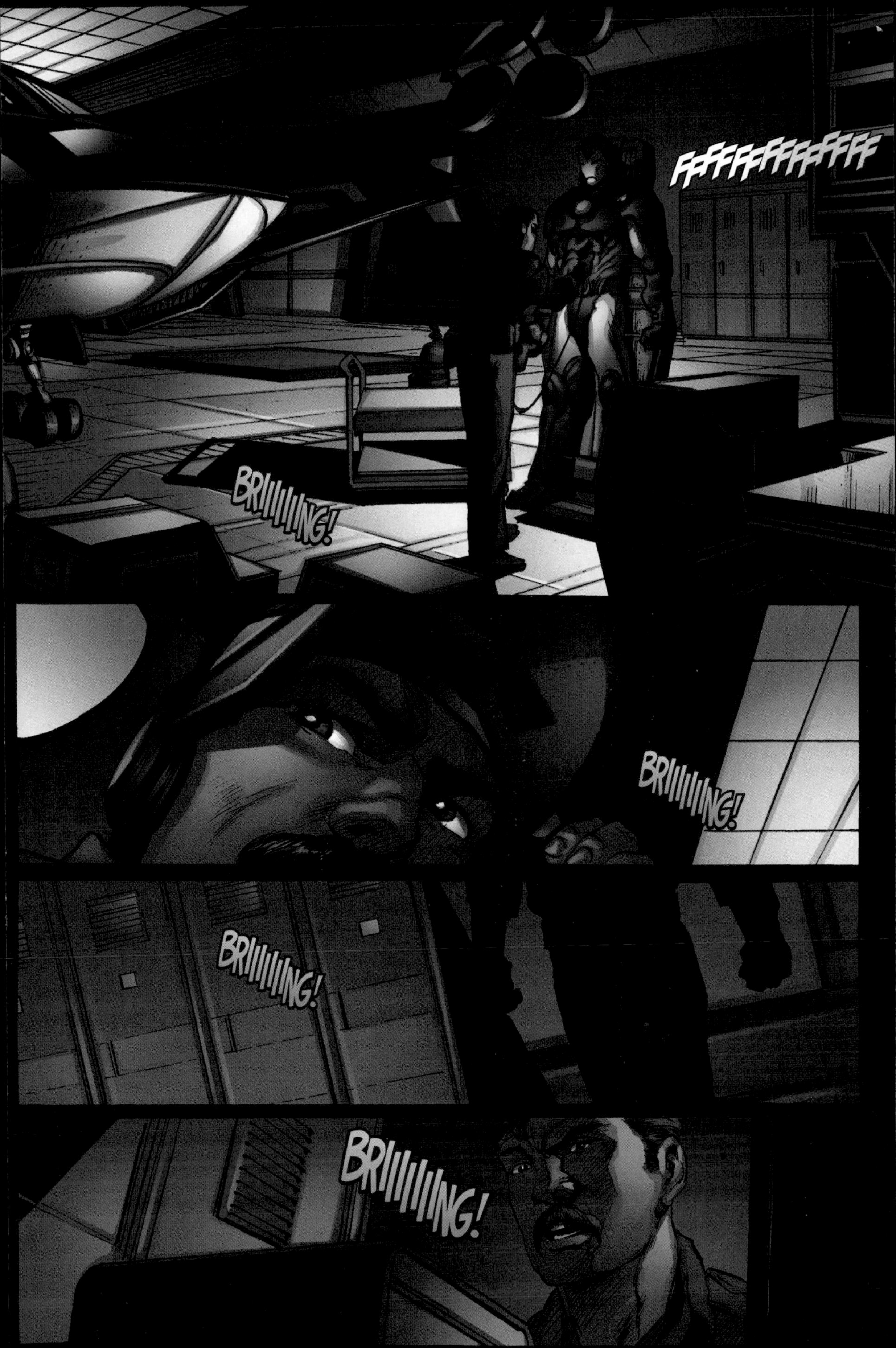
FFFFFFFFFFFFFF
BRIIIIIING!
BRIIIIIING!
BRIIIIIING!
BRIIIIIING!

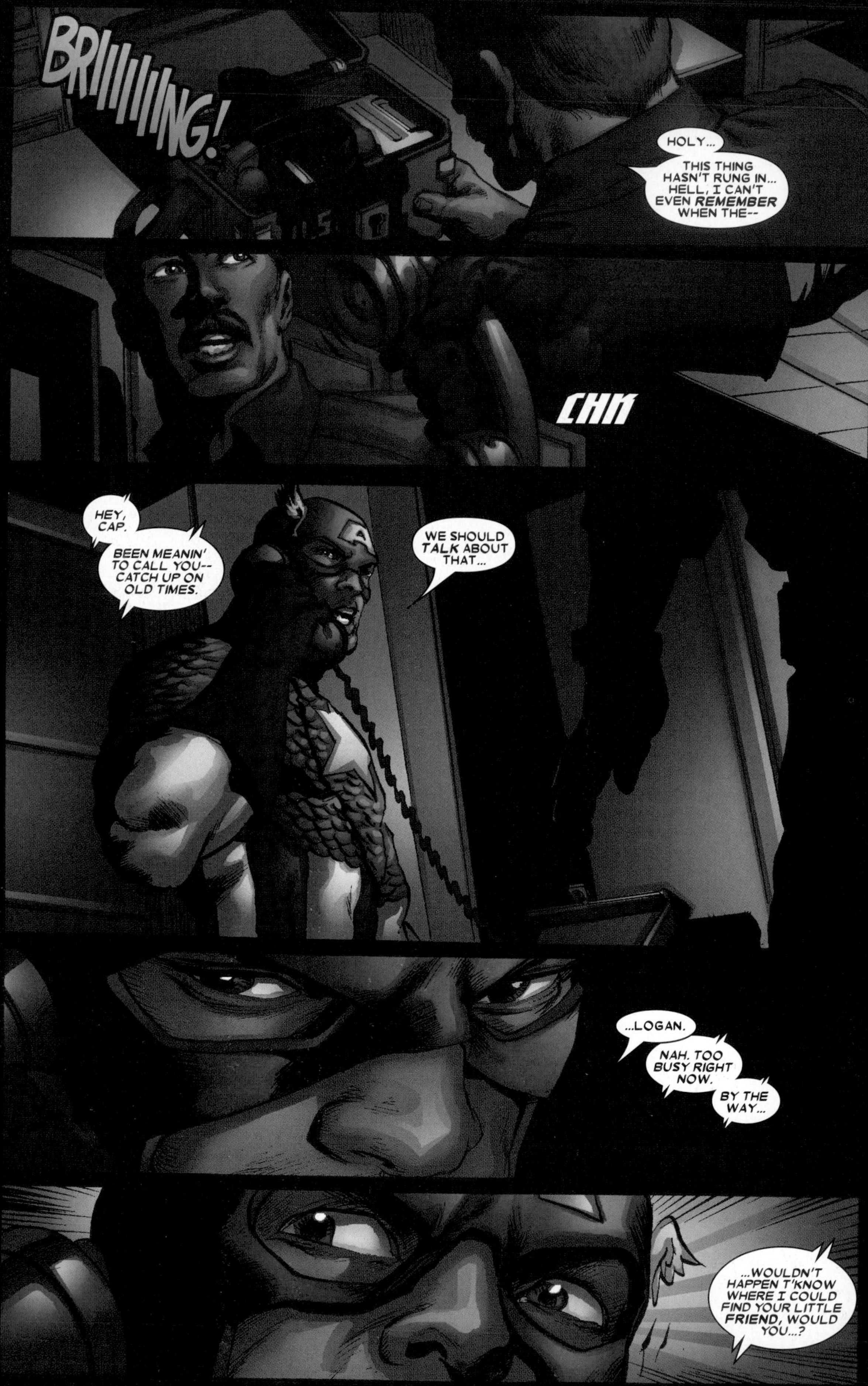
BRIIIIIING!
HOLY...
THIS THING HASN'T RUNG IN... HELL, I CAN'T EVEN REMEMBER WHEN THE--
CHK
HEY, CAP.
BEEN MEANIN' TO CALL YOU-- CATCH UP ON OLD TIMES.
WE SHOULD TALK ABOUT THAT...
...LOGAN.
NAH. TOO BUSY RIGHT NOW.
BY THE WAY...
...WOULDN'T HAPPEN T'KNOW WHERE I COULD FIND YOUR LITTLE FRIEND, WOULD YOU...?

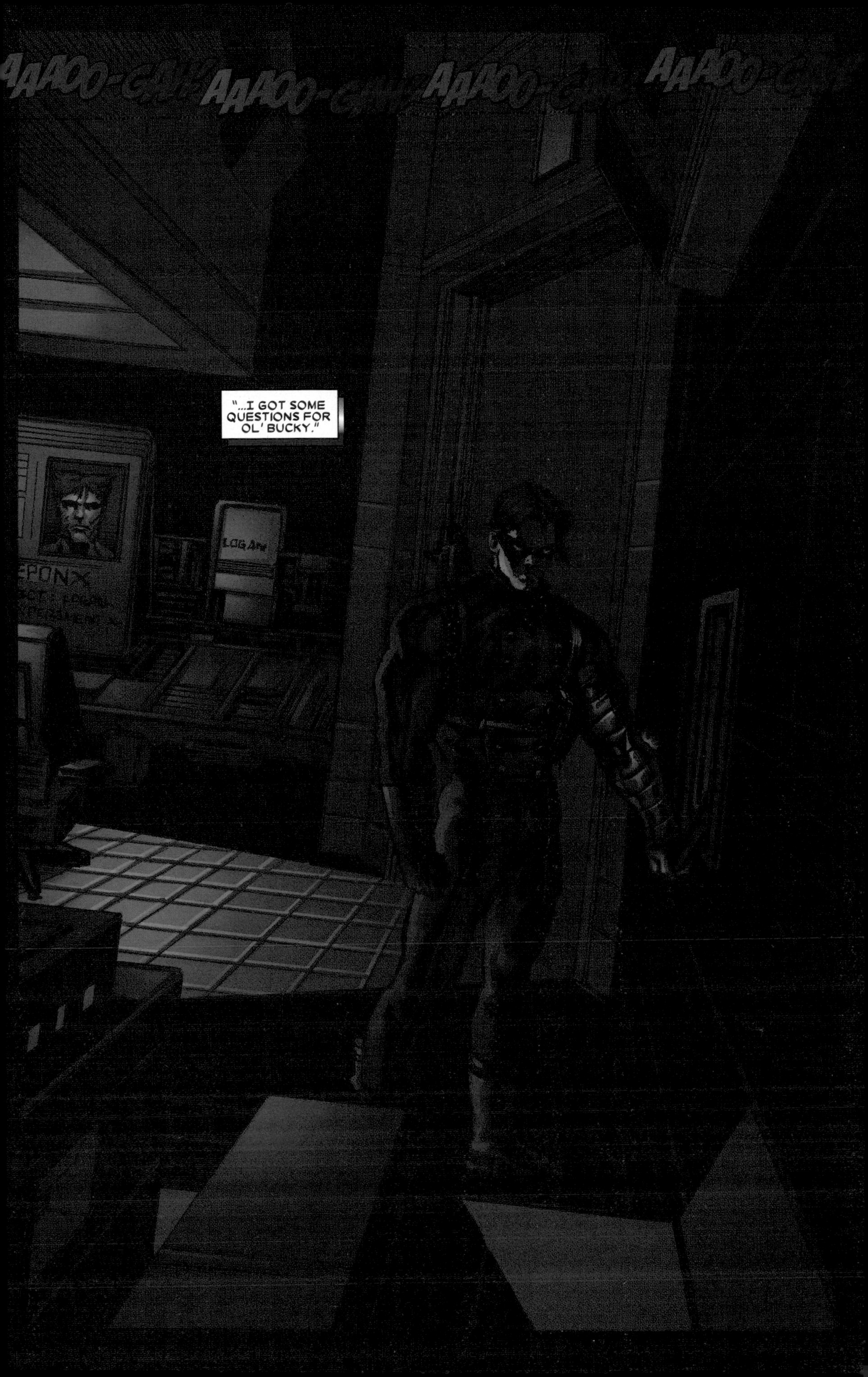
AAAOO-GAH! AAAOO-GAH! AAAOO-GAH! AAAOO-GAH!
"...I GOT SOME QUESTIONS FOR OL' BUCKY."

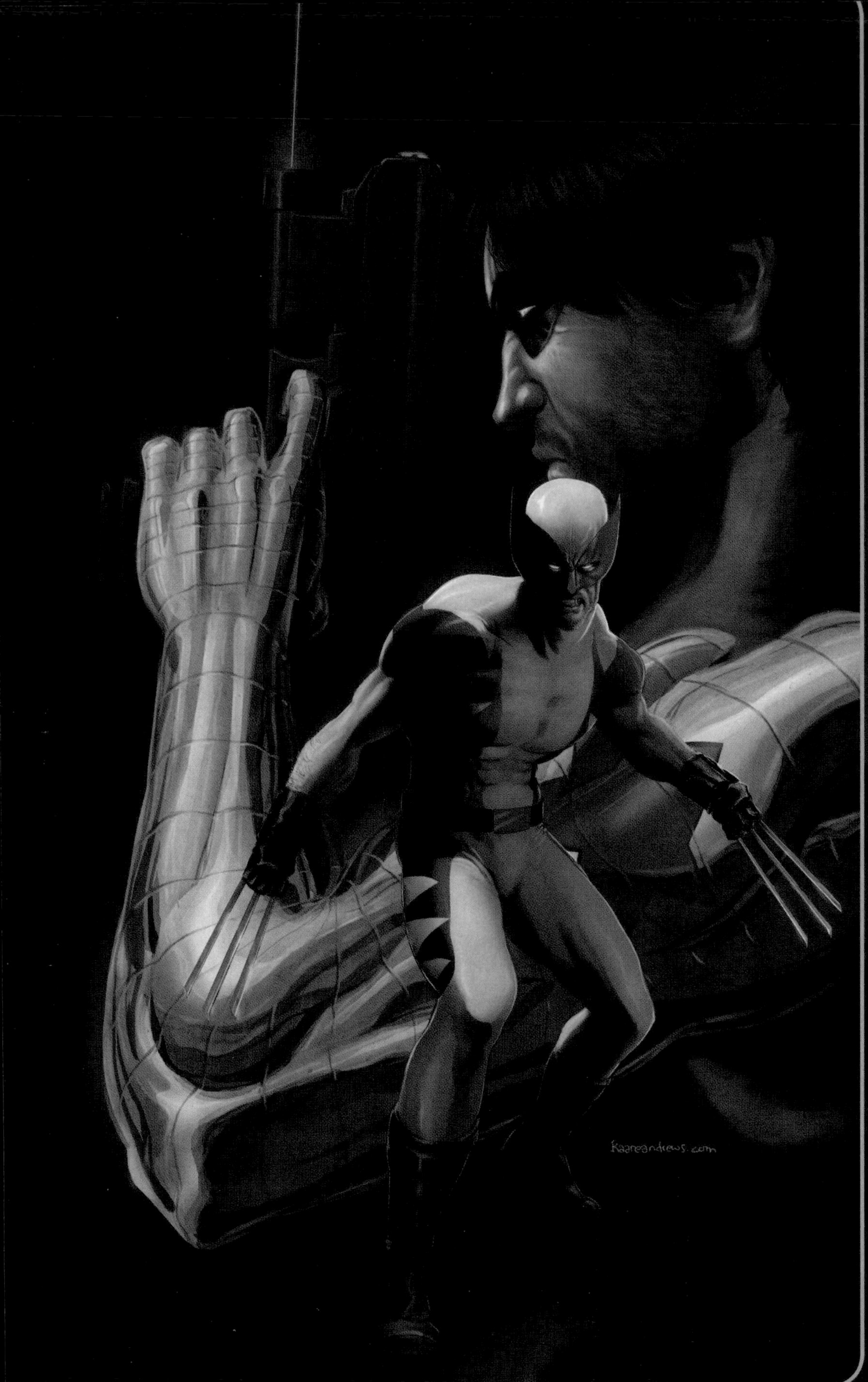
kaareandrews.com

ISSUE #39

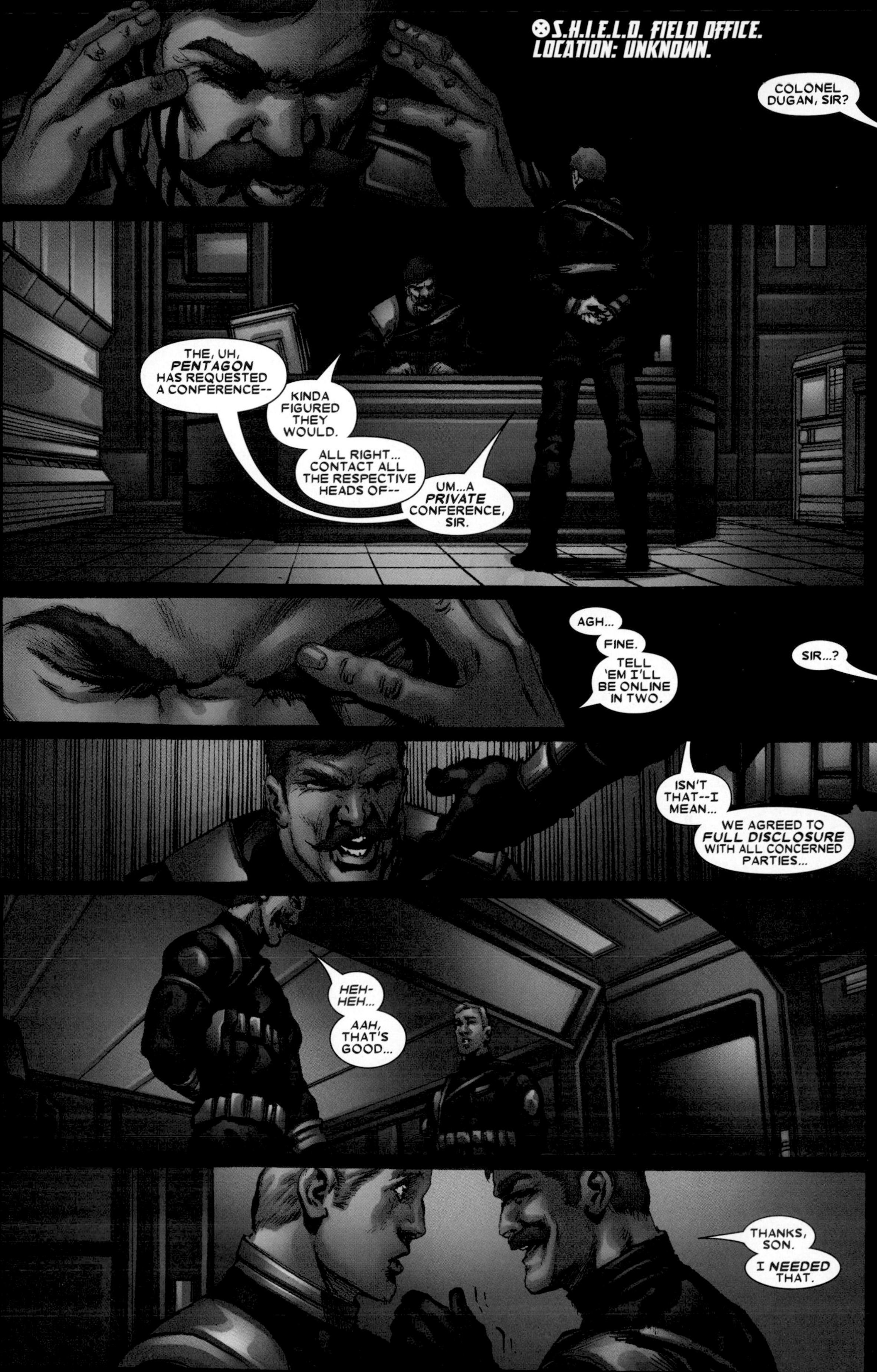
S.H.I.E.L.D. FIELD OFFICE. LOCATION: UNKNOWN.
COLONEL DUGAN, SIR?
THE, UH, PENTAGON HAS REQUESTED A CONFERENCE--
KINDA FIGURED THEY WOULD.
ALL RIGHT... CONTACT ALL THE RESPECTIVE HEADS OF--
UM...A PRIVATE CONFERENCE, SIR.
AGH...
FINE.
TELL 'EM I'LL BE ONLINE IN TWO.
SIR...?
ISN'T THAT--I MEAN...
WE AGREED TO FULL DISCLOSURE WITH ALL CONCERNED PARTIES...
HEH-HEH...
AAH, THAT'S GOOD...
THANKS, SON.
I NEEDED THAT.

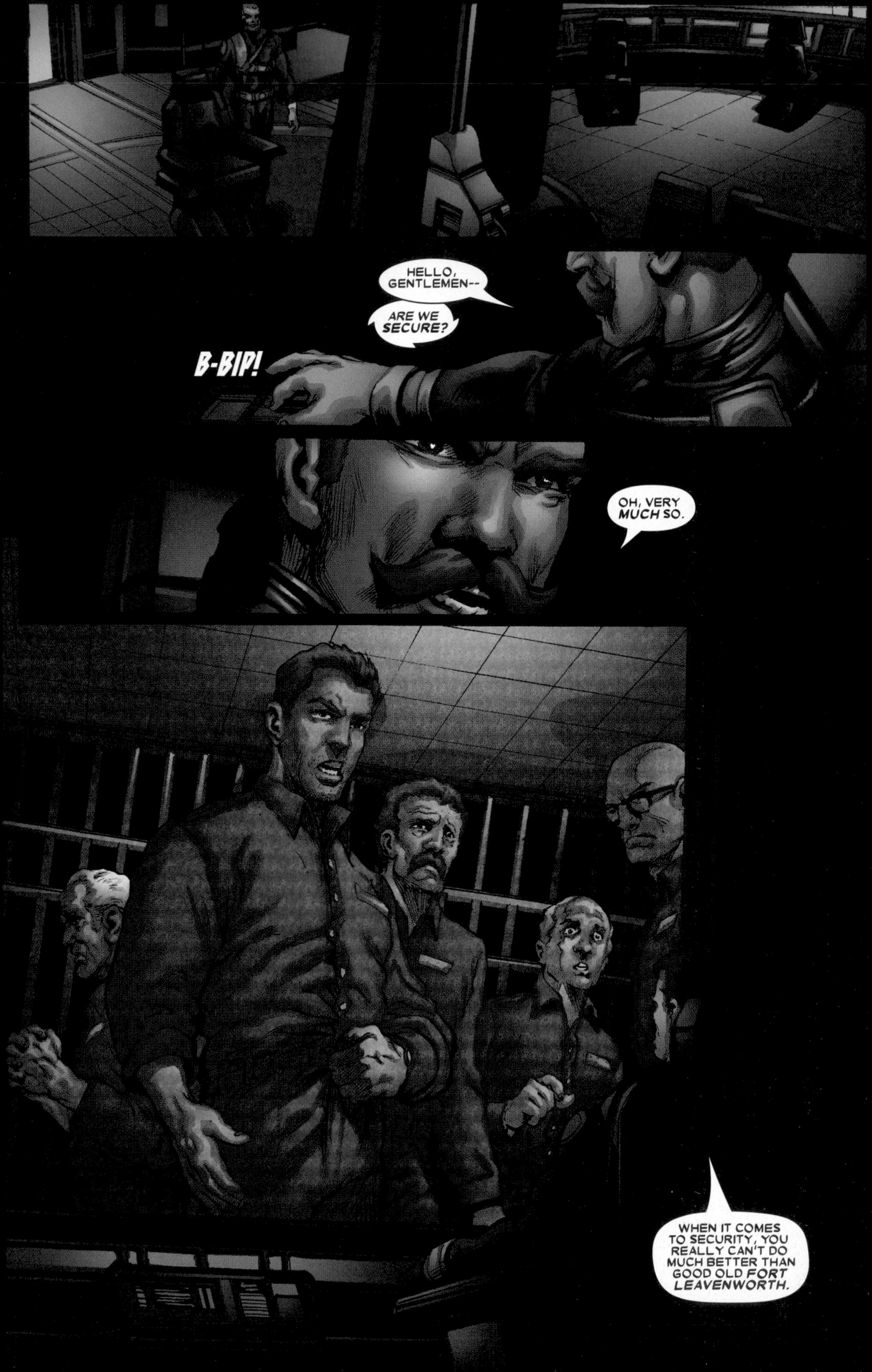
HELLO, GENTLEMEN--
ARE WE SECURE?
B-BIP!
OH, VERY MUCH SO.
WHEN IT COMES TO SECURITY, YOU REALLY CAN'T DO MUCH BETTER THAN GOOD OLD FORT LEAVENWORTH.

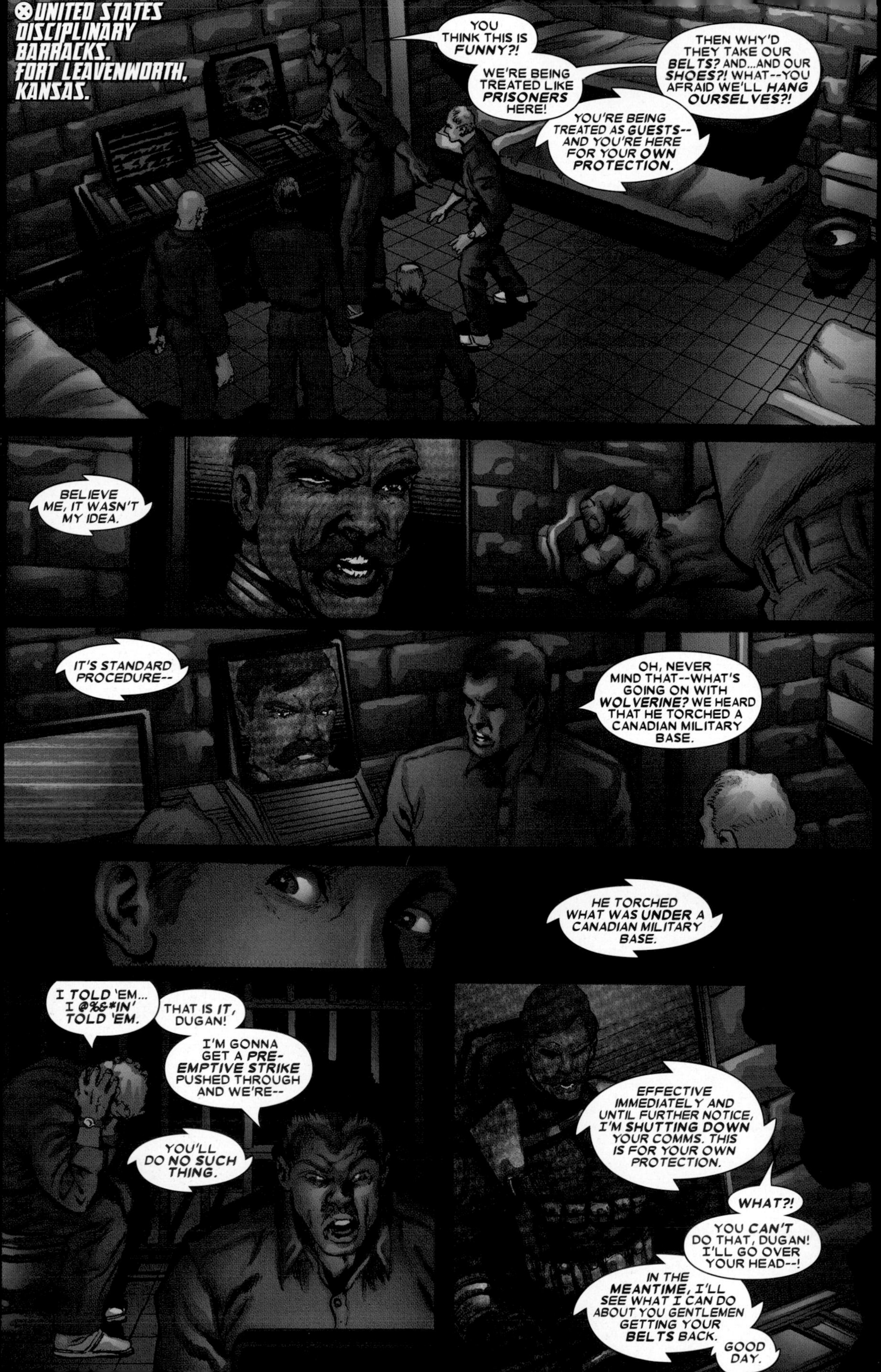
UNITED STATES DISCIPLINARY BARRACKS. FORT LEAVENWORTH, KANSAS.
YOU THINK THIS IS FUNNY?!
WE'RE BEING TREATED LIKE PRISONERS HERE!
THEN WHY'D THEY TAKE OUR BELTS? AND...AND OUR SHOES?! WHAT--YOU AFRAID WE'LL HANG OURSELVES?!
YOU'RE BEING TREATED AS GUESTS-- AND YOU'RE HERE FOR YOUR OWN PROTECTION.
BELIEVE ME, IT WASN'T MY IDEA.
IT'S STANDARD PROCEDURE--
OH, NEVER MIND THAT--WHAT'S GOING ON WITH WOLVERINE? WE HEARD THAT HE TORCHED A CANADIAN MILITARY BASE.
HE TORCHED WHAT WAS UNDER A CANADIAN MILITARY BASE.
I TOLD 'EM... I @%&*IN' TOLD 'EM.
THAT IS IT, DUGAN!
I'M GONNA GET A PRE-EMPTIVE STRIKE PUSHED THROUGH AND WE'RE--
YOU'LL DO NO SUCH THING.
EFFECTIVE IMMEDIATELY AND UNTIL FURTHER NOTICE, I'M SHUTTING DOWN YOUR COMMS. THIS IS FOR YOUR OWN PROTECTION.
WHAT?!
YOU CAN'T DO THAT, DUGAN! I'LL GO OVER YOUR HEAD--!
IN THE MEANTIME, I'LL SEE WHAT I CAN DO ABOUT YOU GENTLEMEN GETTING YOUR BELTS BACK.
GOOD DAY.

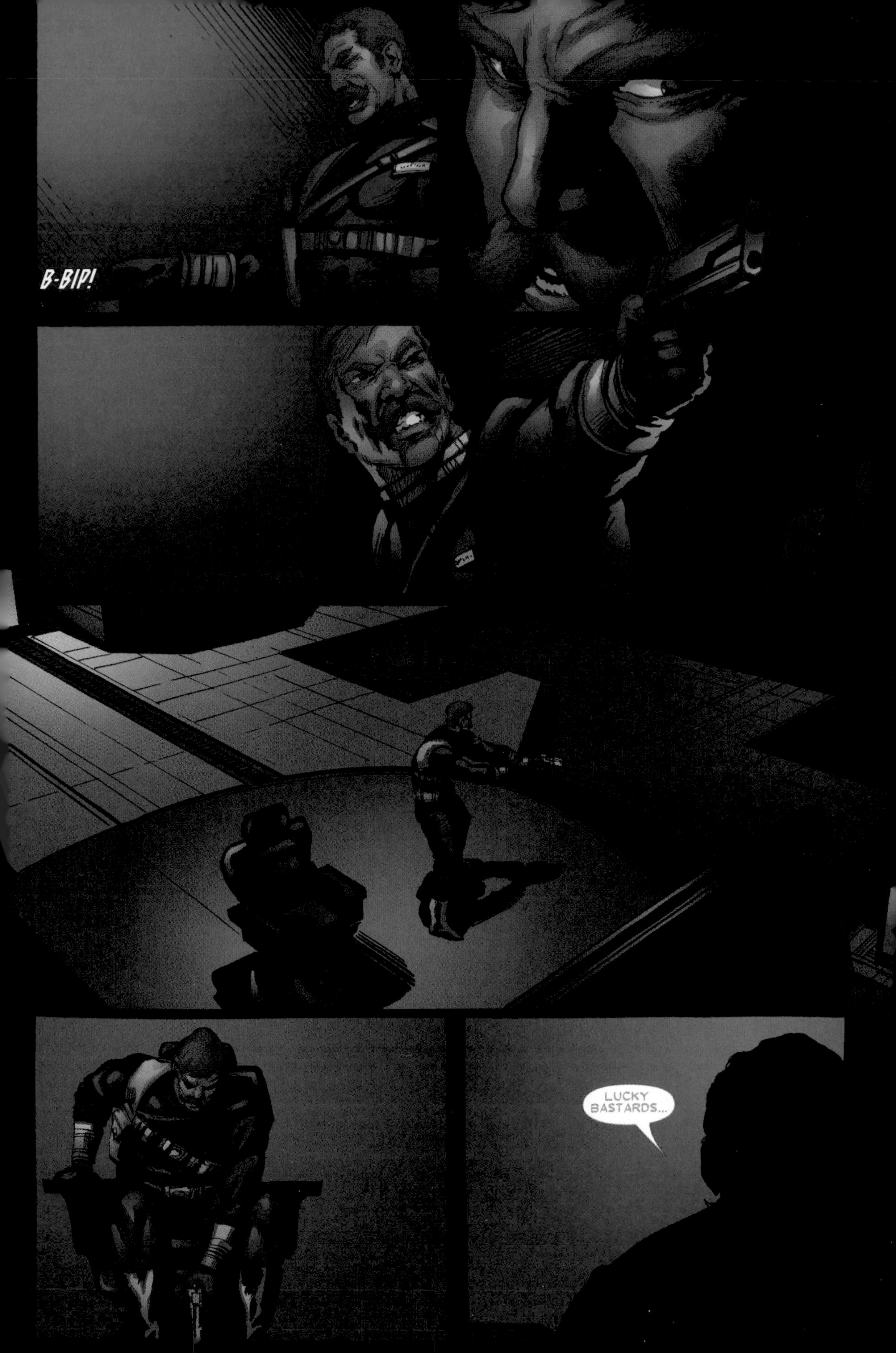
B-BIP!
LUCKY BASTARDS...

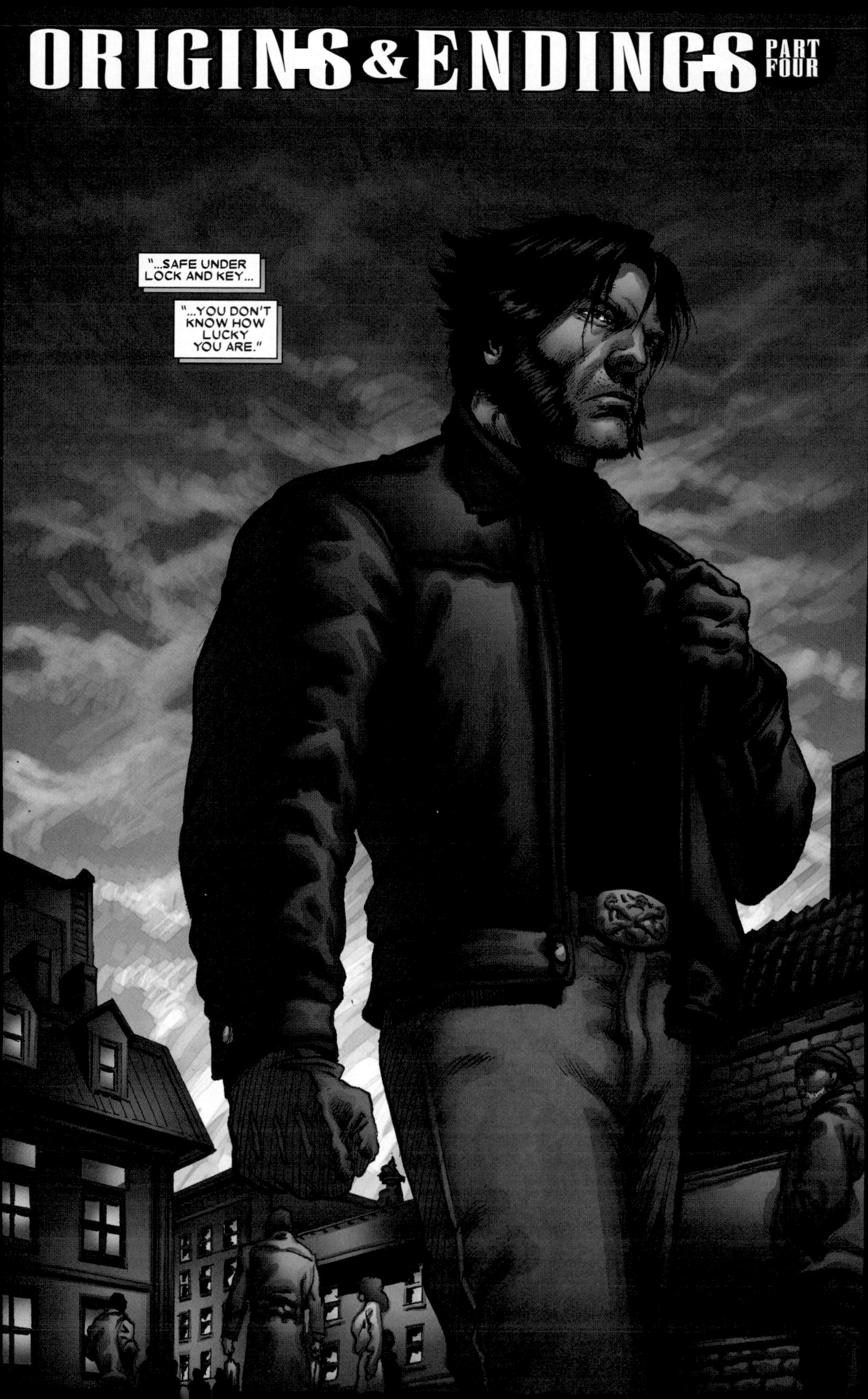
ORIGINS & ENDINGS PART FOUR
"...SAFE UNDER LOCK AND KEY...
"...YOU DON'T KNOW HOW LUCKY YOU ARE."

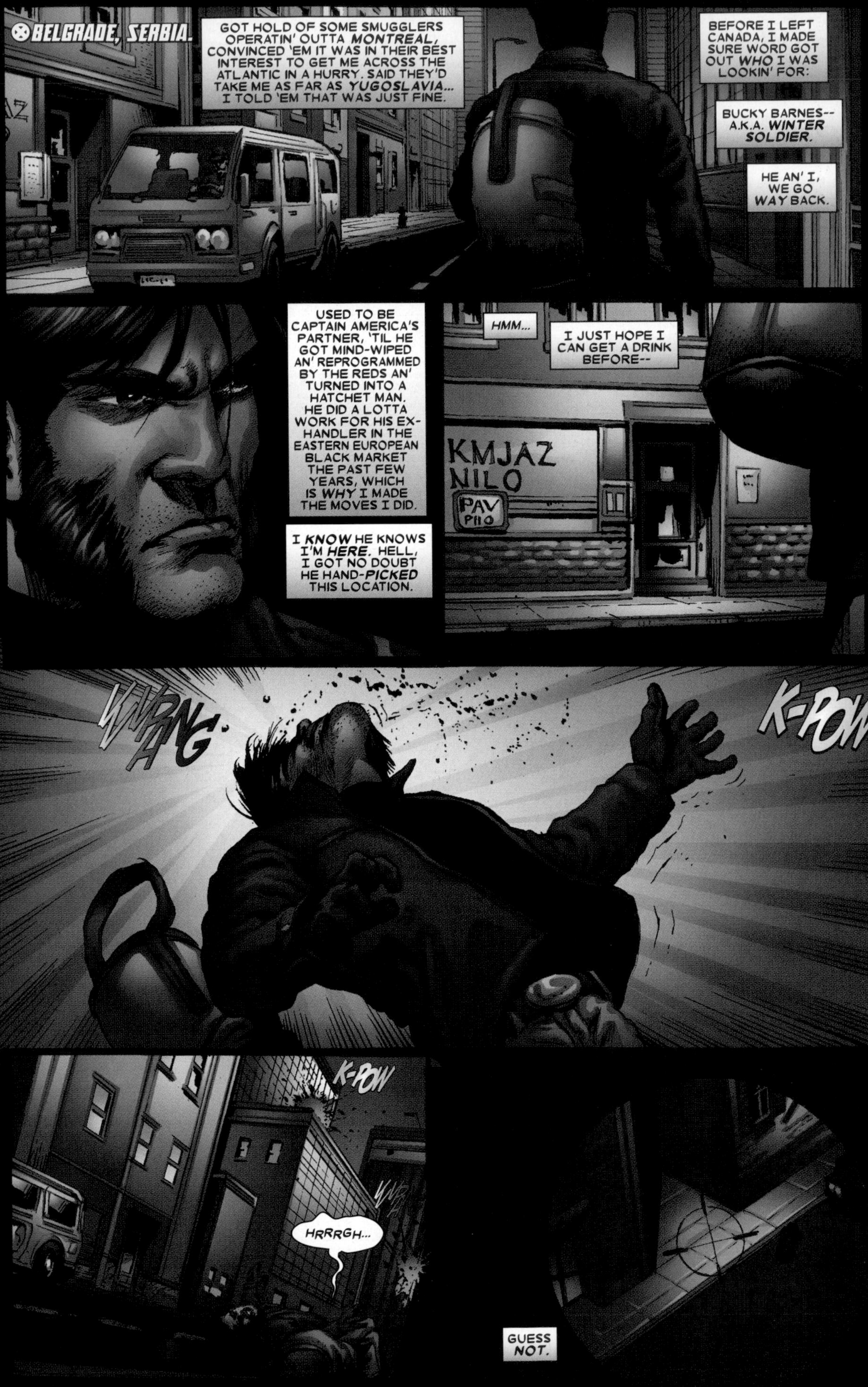
BELGRADE, SERBIA.
GOT HOLD OF SOME SMUGGLERS OPERATIN' OUTTA MONTREAL, CONVINCED 'EM IT WAS IN THEIR BEST INTEREST TO GET ME ACROSS THE ATLANTIC IN A HURRY. SAID THEY'D TAKE ME AS FAR AS YUGOSLAVIA... I TOLD 'EM THAT WAS JUST FINE.
BEFORE I LEFT CANADA, I MADE SURE WORD GOT OUT WHO I WAS LOOKIN' FOR:
BUCKY BARNES-- A.K.A. WINTER SOLDIER.
HE AN' I, WE GO WAY BACK.
USED TO BE CAPTAIN AMERICA'S PARTNER, 'TIL HE GOT MIND-WIPED AN' REPROGRAMMED BY THE REDS AN' TURNED INTO A HATCHET MAN. HE DID A LOTTA WORK FOR HIS EX-HANDLER IN THE EASTERN EUROPEAN BLACK MARKET THE PAST FEW YEARS, WHICH IS WHY I MADE THE MOVES I DID.
I KNOW HE KNOWS I'M HERE. HELL, I GOT NO DOUBT HE HAND-PICKED THIS LOCATION.
HMM...
I JUST HOPE I CAN GET A DRINK BEFORE--
KMJAZ
NILO
PAV
P110
WNRANG
K-POW
K-POW
HRRRGH...
GUESS NOT.

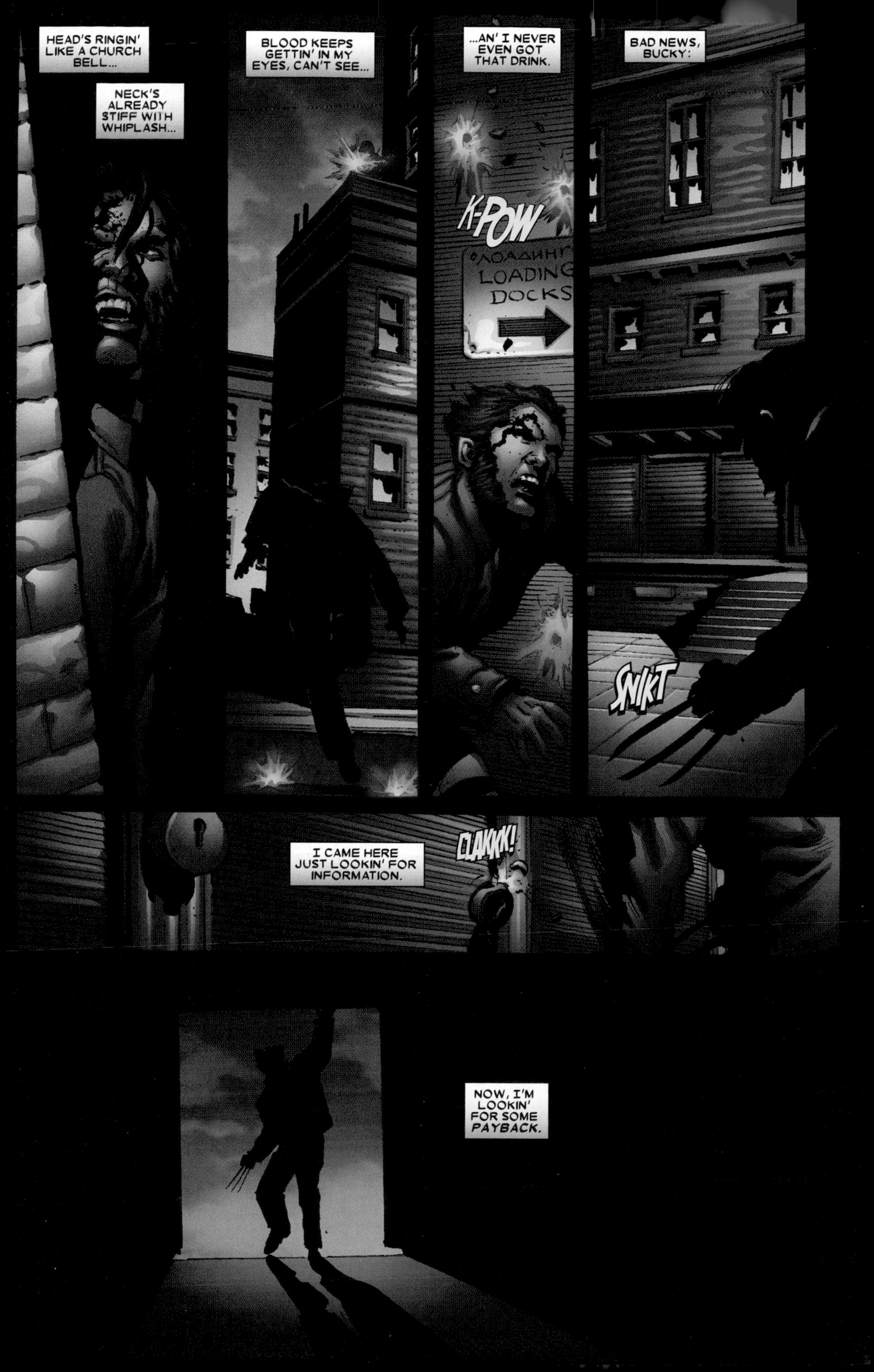

HEAD'S RINGIN' LIKE A CHURCH BELL...
NECK'S ALREADY STIFF WITH WHIPLASH...
BLOOD KEEPS GETTIN' IN MY EYES, CAN'T SEE...
...AN' I NEVER EVEN GOT THAT DRINK.
K-POW
LOADING DOCKS
BAD NEWS, BUCKY:
SNIKT
I CAME HERE JUST LOOKIN' FOR INFORMATION.
CLAKKK!
NOW, I'M LOOKIN' FOR SOME PAYBACK.

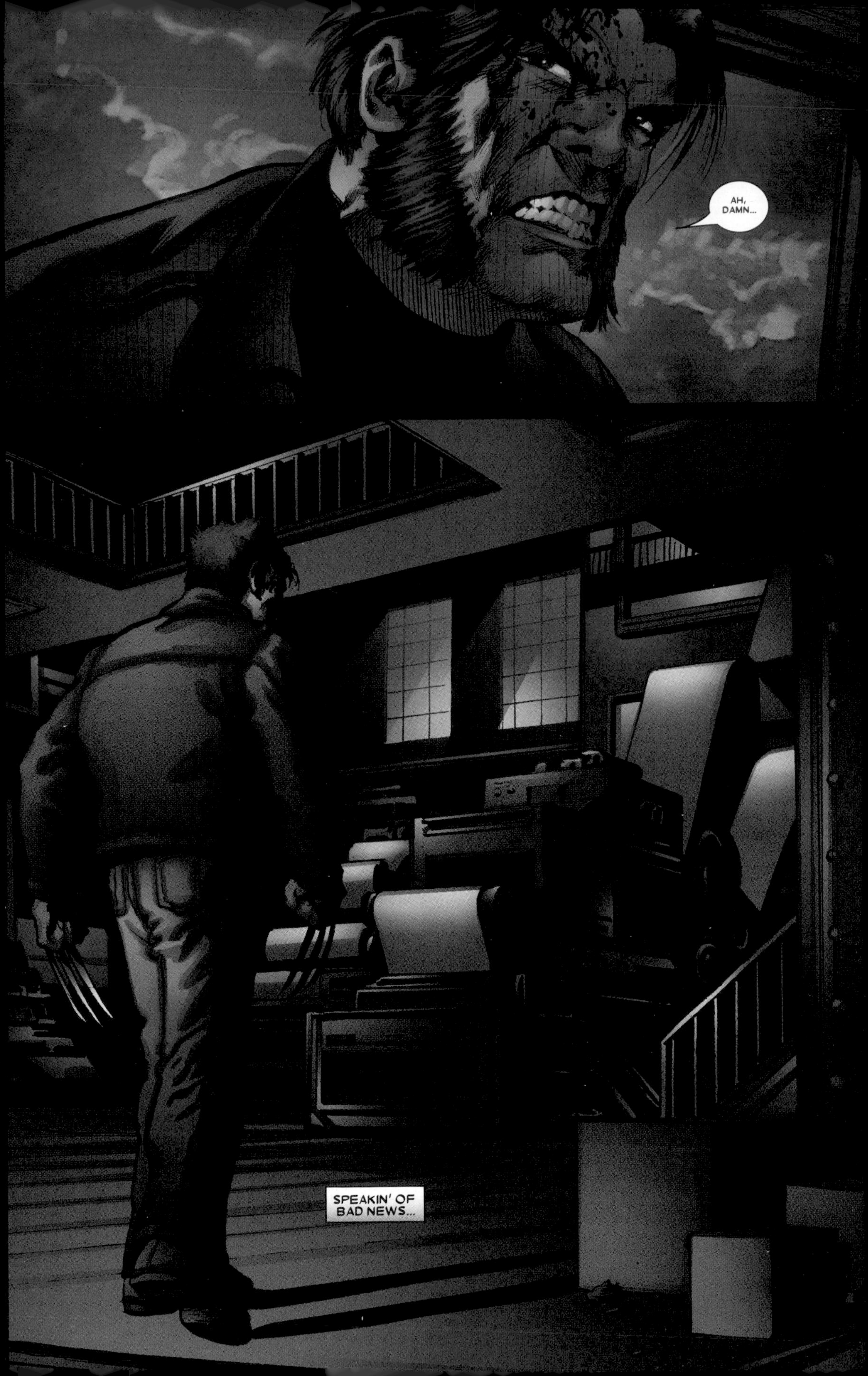
AH, DAMN...
SPEAKIN' OF BAD NEWS...

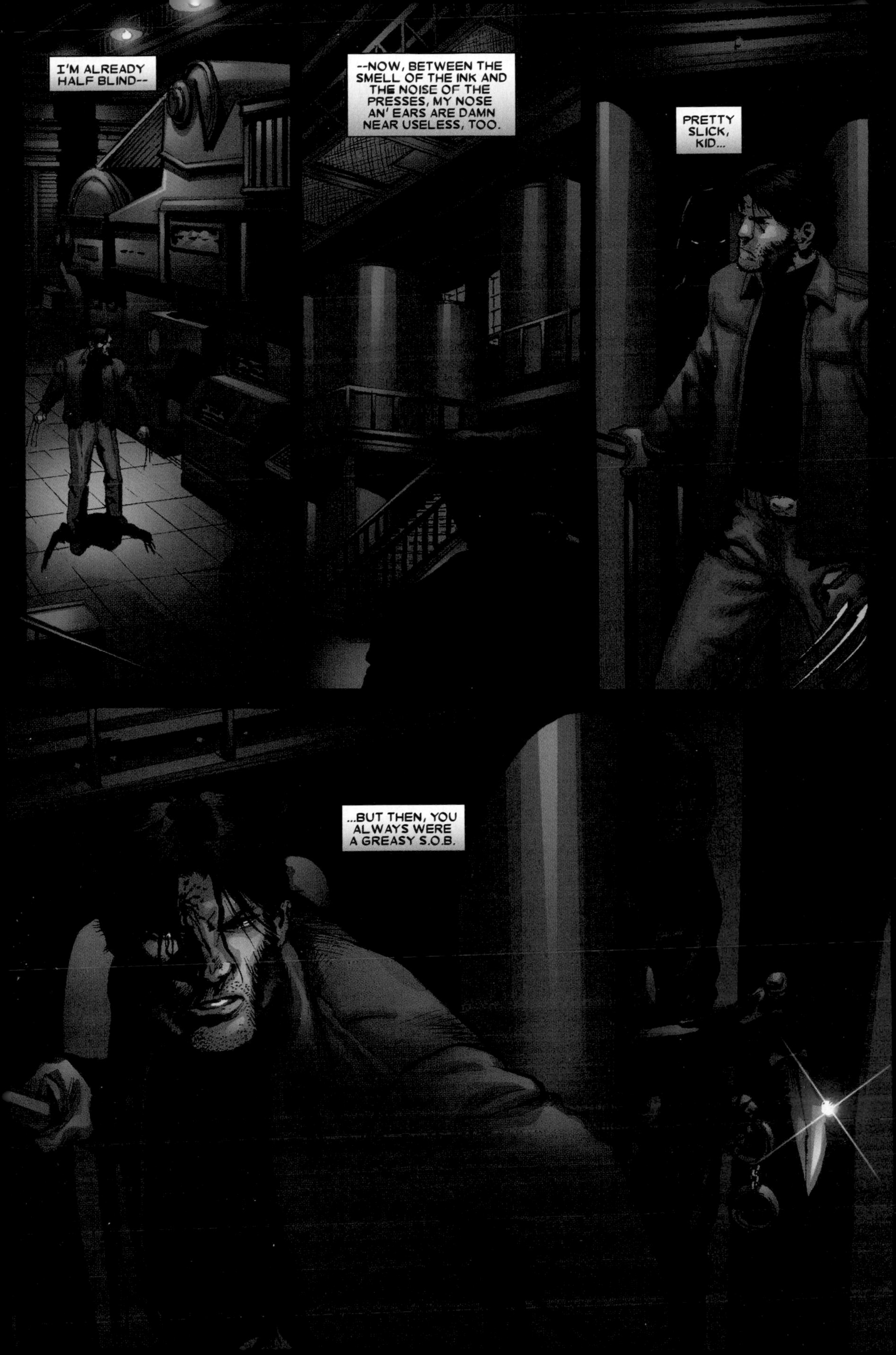
I'M ALREADY HALF BLIND--
--NOW, BETWEEN THE SMELL OF THE INK AND THE NOISE OF THE PRESSES, MY NOSE AN' EARS ARE DAMN NEAR USELESS, TOO.
PRETTY SLICK, KID...
...BUT THEN, YOU ALWAYS WERE A GREASY S.O.B.

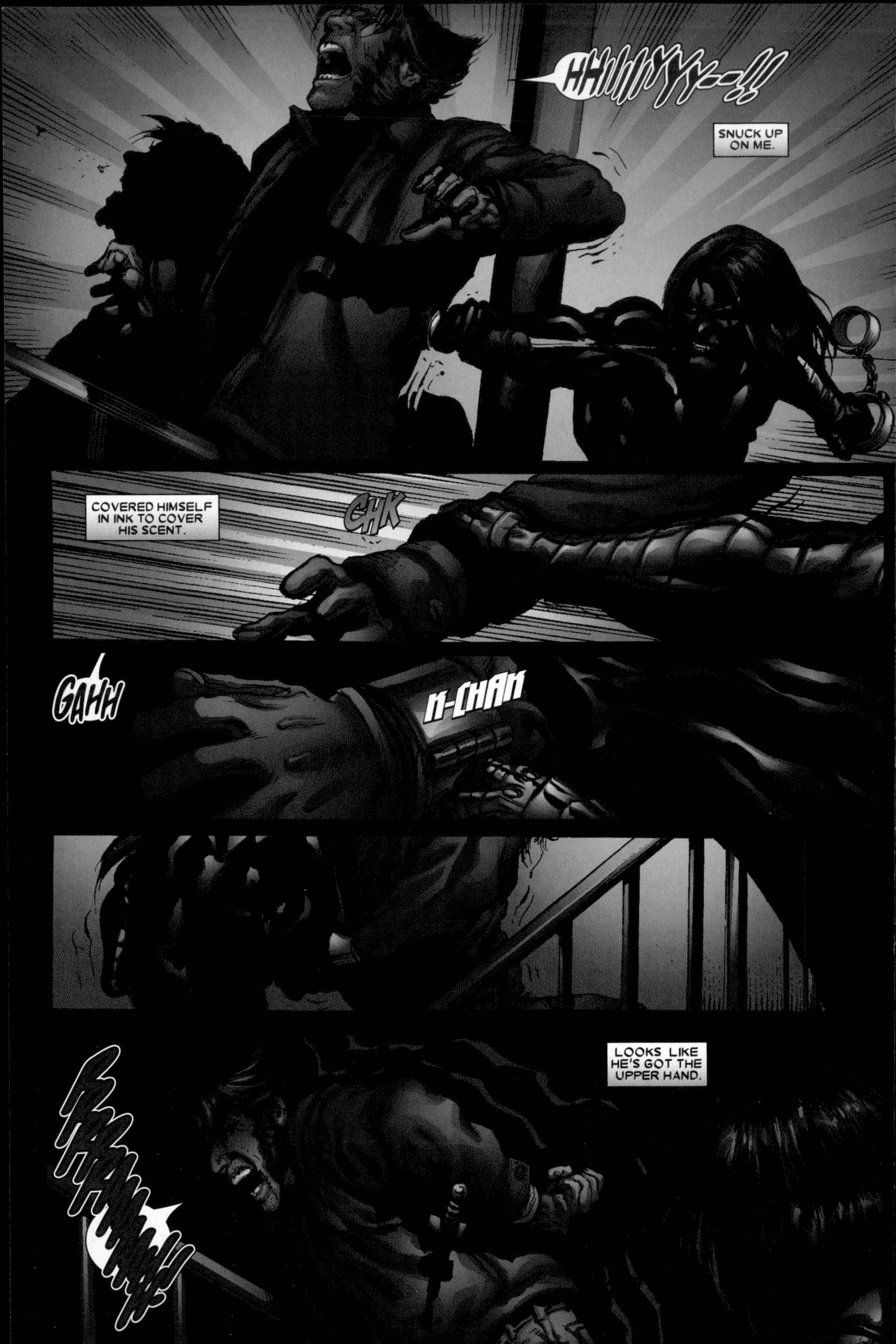
SNUCK UP ON ME.
COVERED HIMSELF IN INK TO COVER HIS SCENT.
CHK
GAHH
K-CHAK
LOOKS LIKE HE'S GOT THE UPPER HAND.

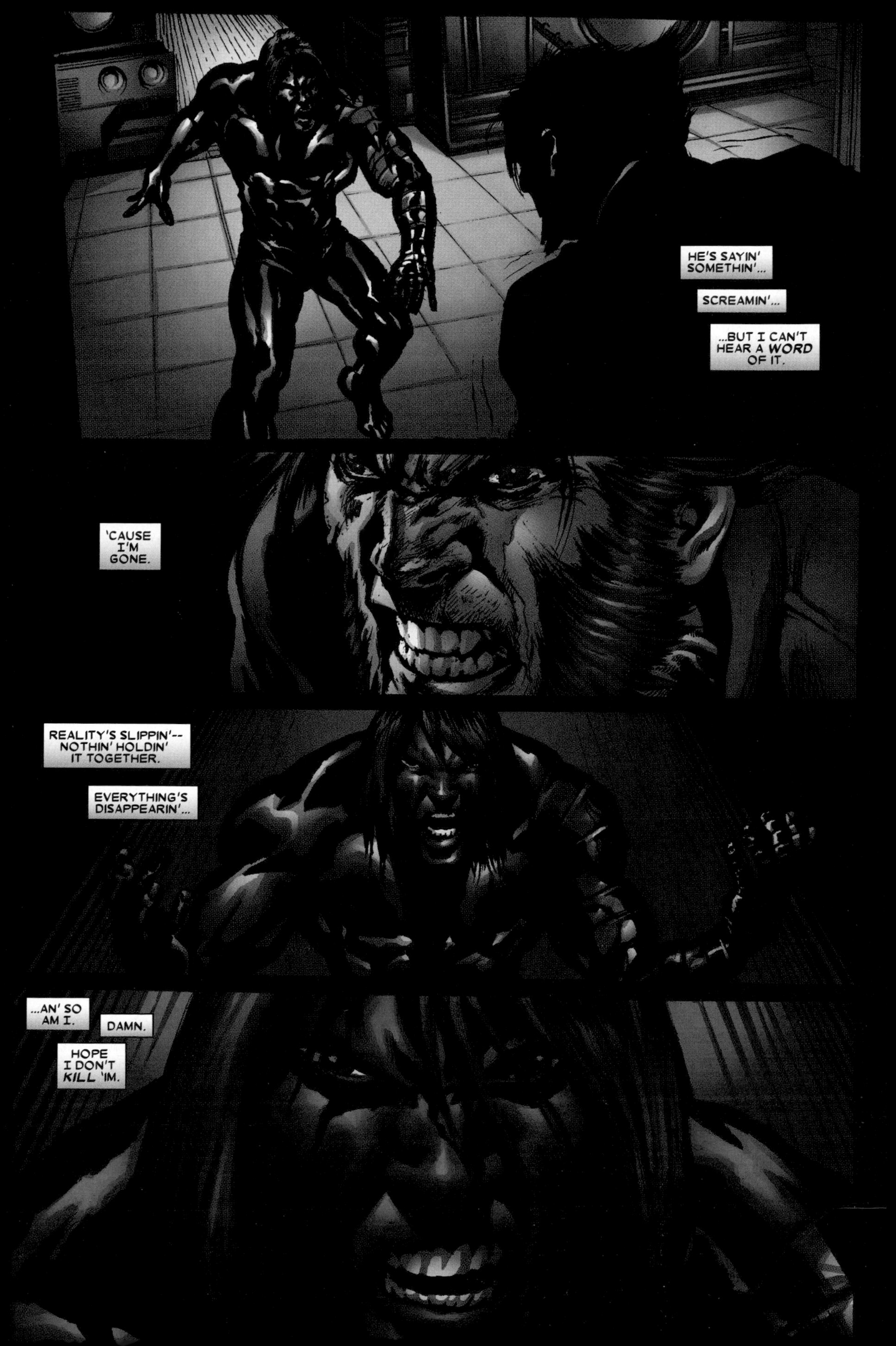

HE'S SAYIN' SOMETHIN'...
SCREAMIN'...
...BUT I CAN'T HEAR A WORD OF IT.
'CAUSE I'M GONE.
REALITY'S SLIPPIN'-- NOTHIN' HOLDIN' IT TOGETHER.
EVERYTHING'S DISAPPEARIN'...
...AN' SO AM I.
DAMN.
HOPE I DON'T KILL 'IM.

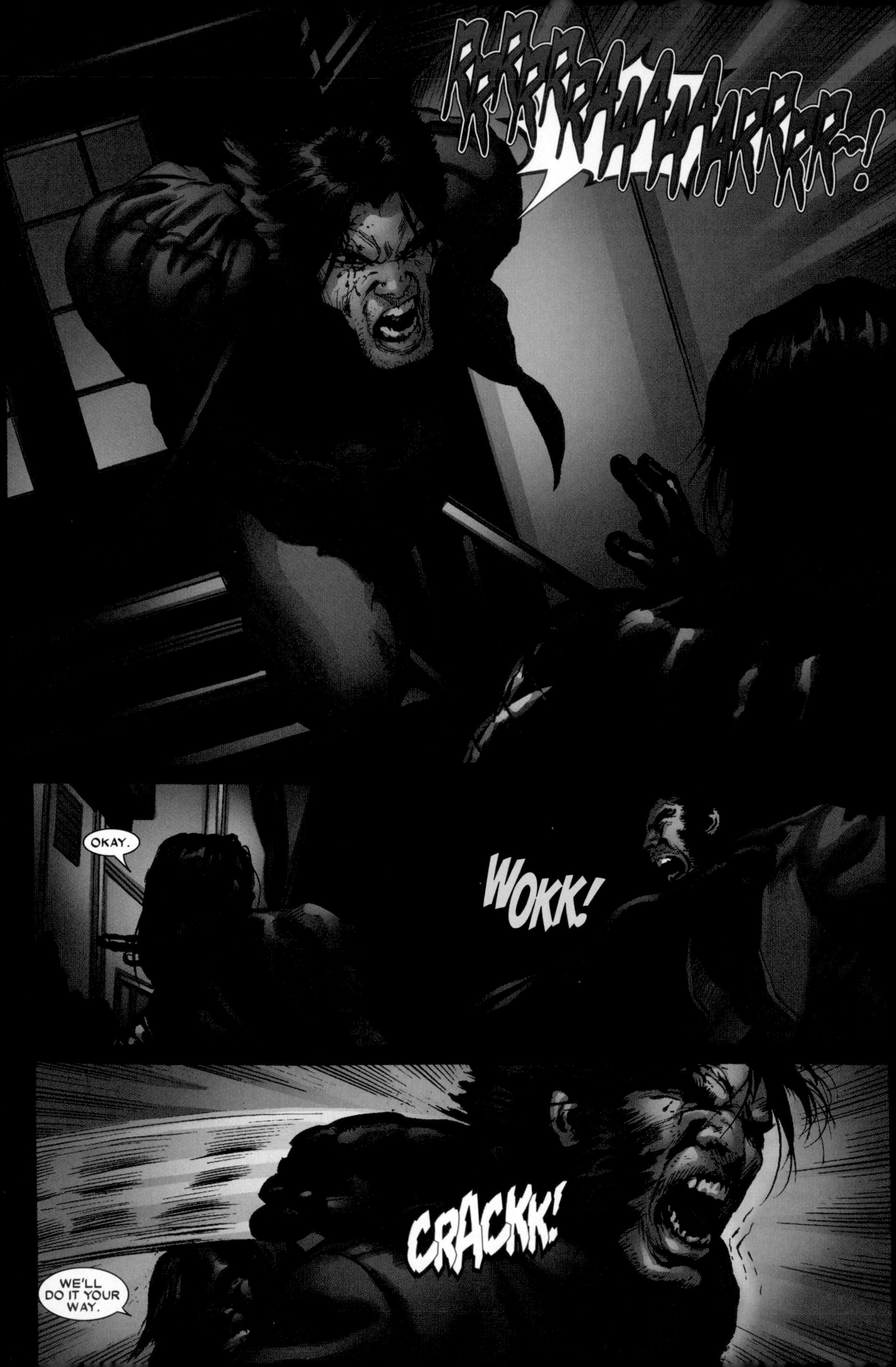
RRRRAAAAARRR~!
OKAY.
WOKK!
CRACKK!
WE'LL DO IT YOUR WAY.

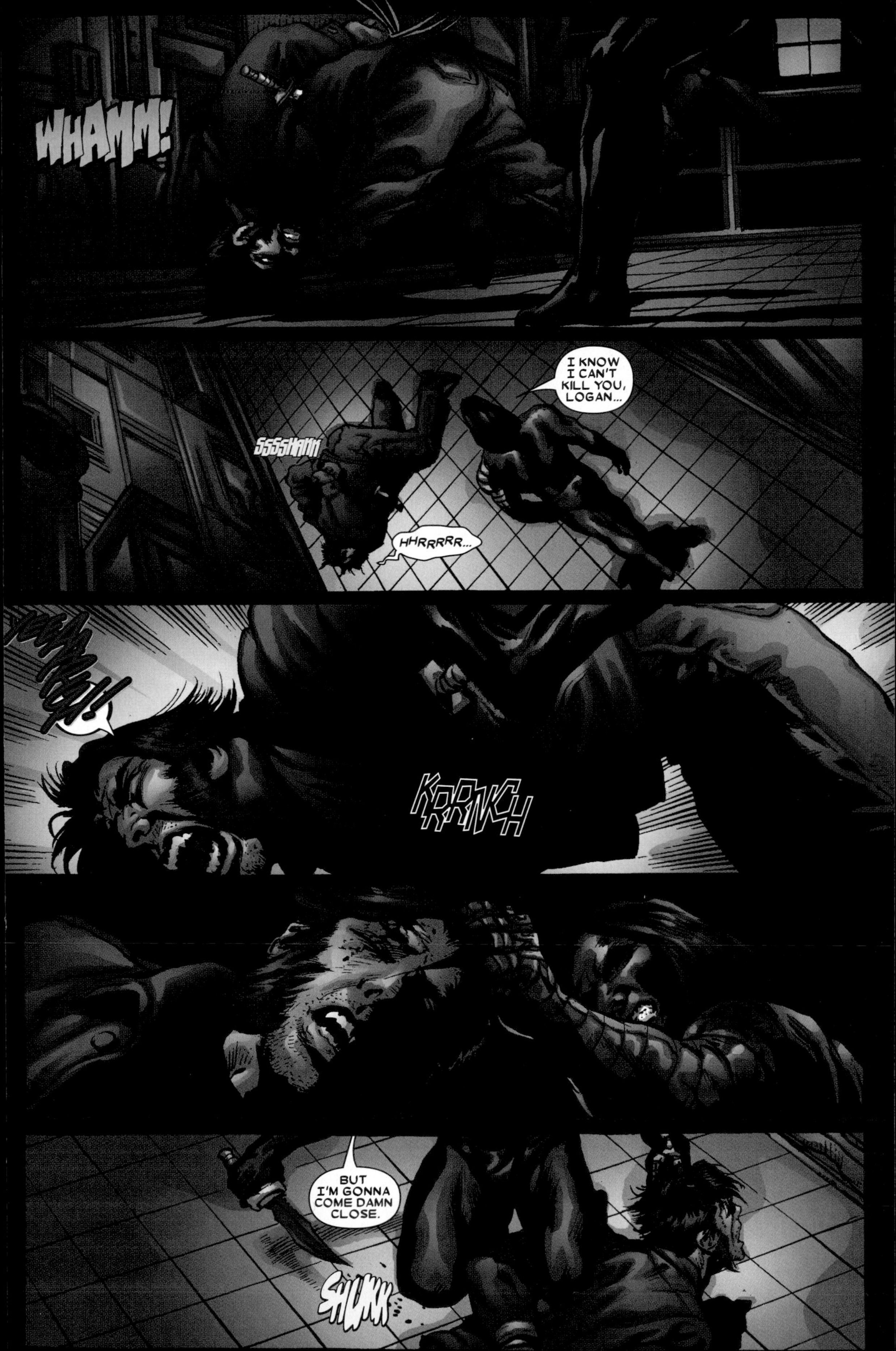
WHAMM!
I KNOW I CAN'T KILL YOU, LOGAN...
SSSSHANK
HHRRRRR...
KRRRNCH
BUT I'M GONNA COME DAMN CLOSE.
SHUNK

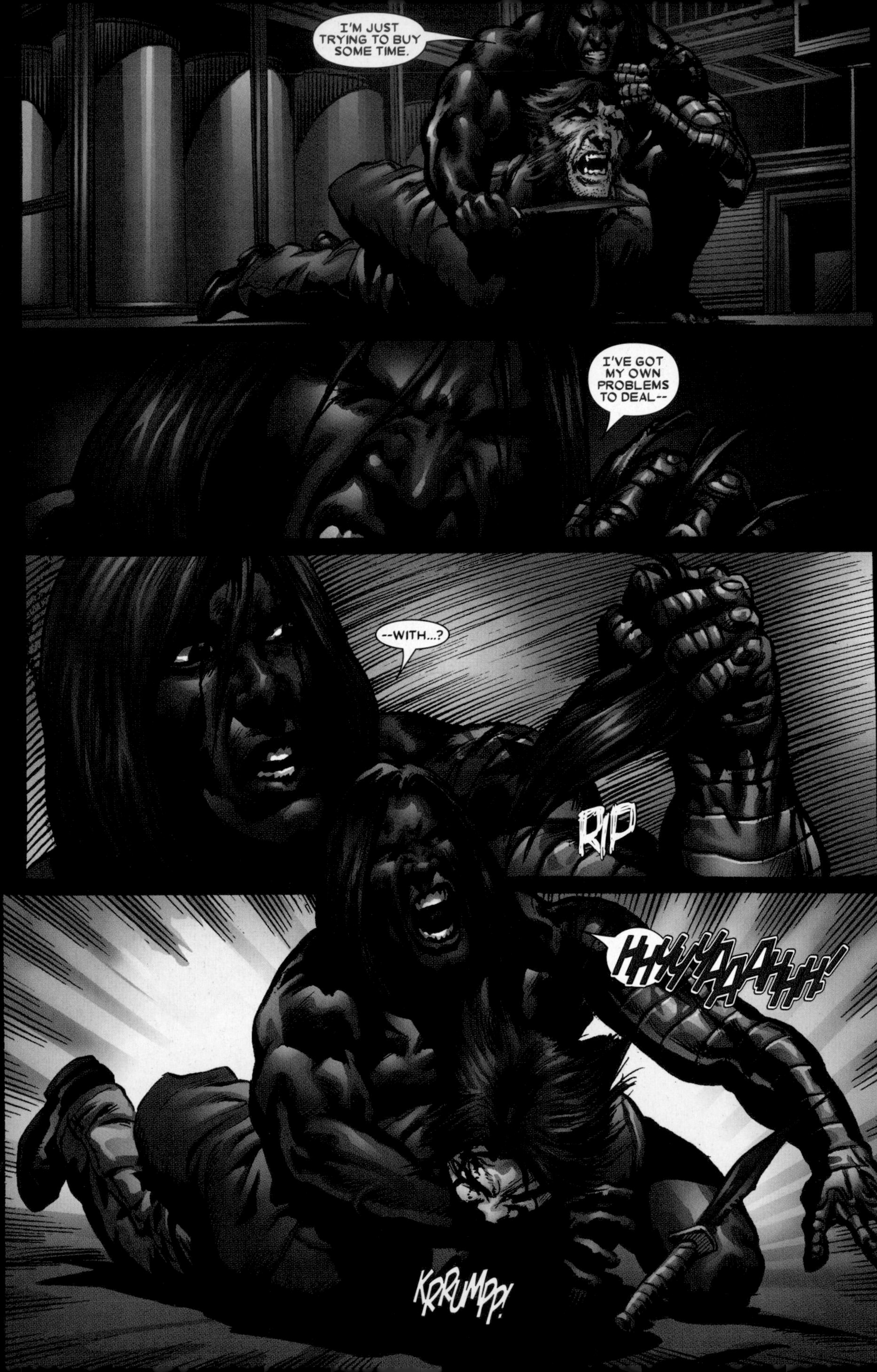
I'M JUST TRYING TO BUY SOME TIME.
I'VE GOT MY OWN PROBLEMS TO DEAL--
--WITH...?
RIP
HHYYAAAHHH!
KRRUMPP!

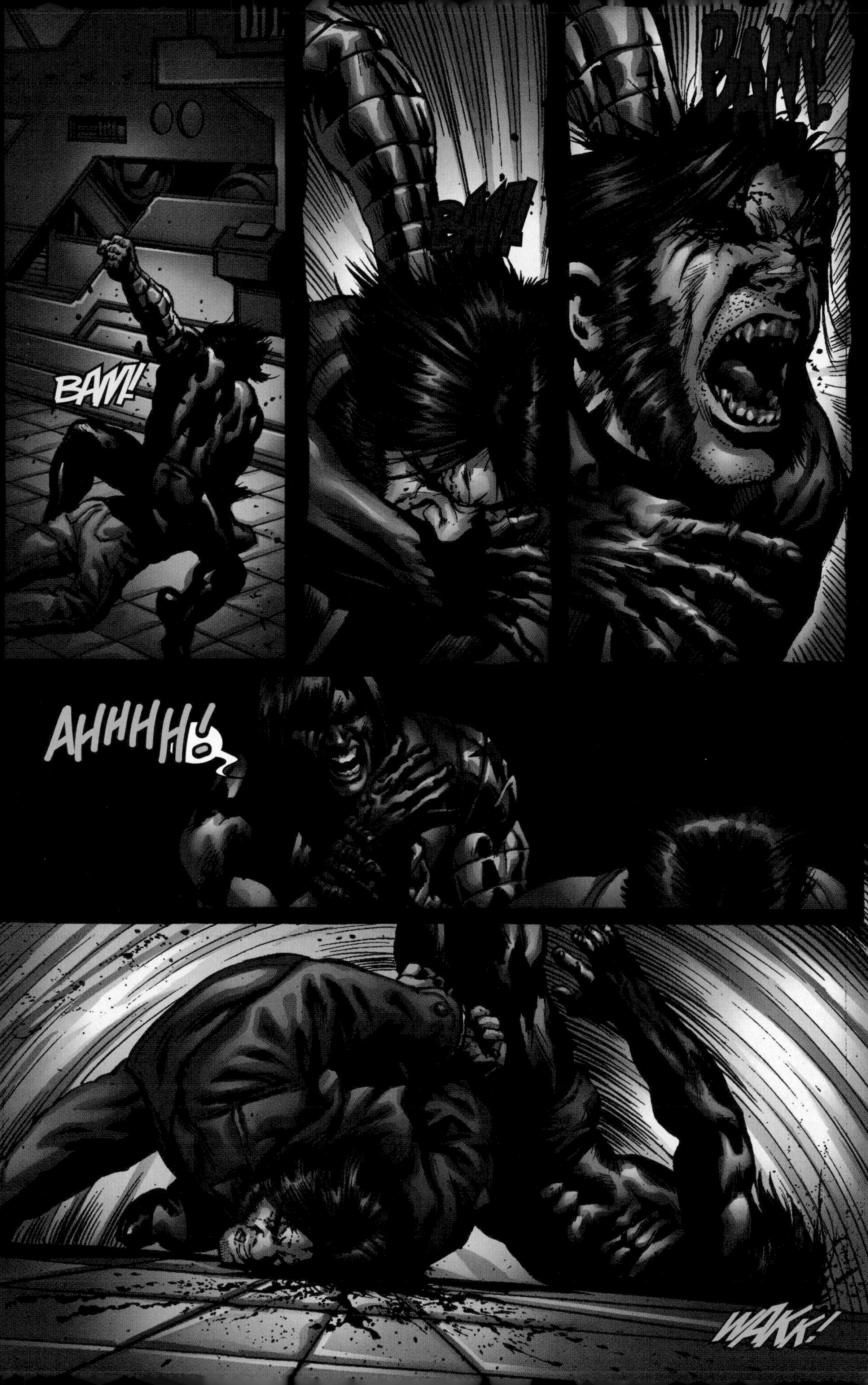
BAM!
BAM!
BAM!
AHHHHHH!
WAKK!

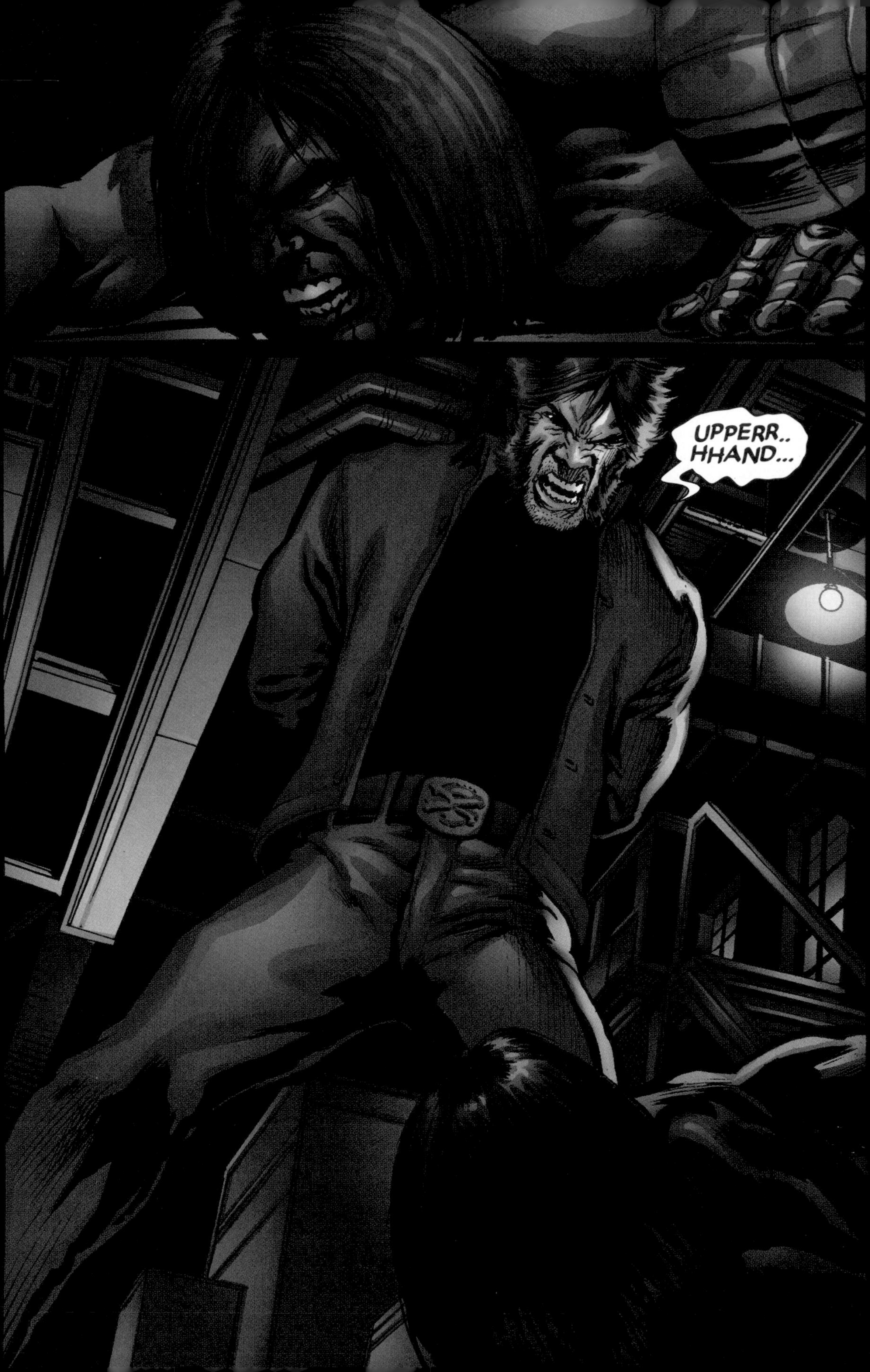
UPPERR.. HHAND...

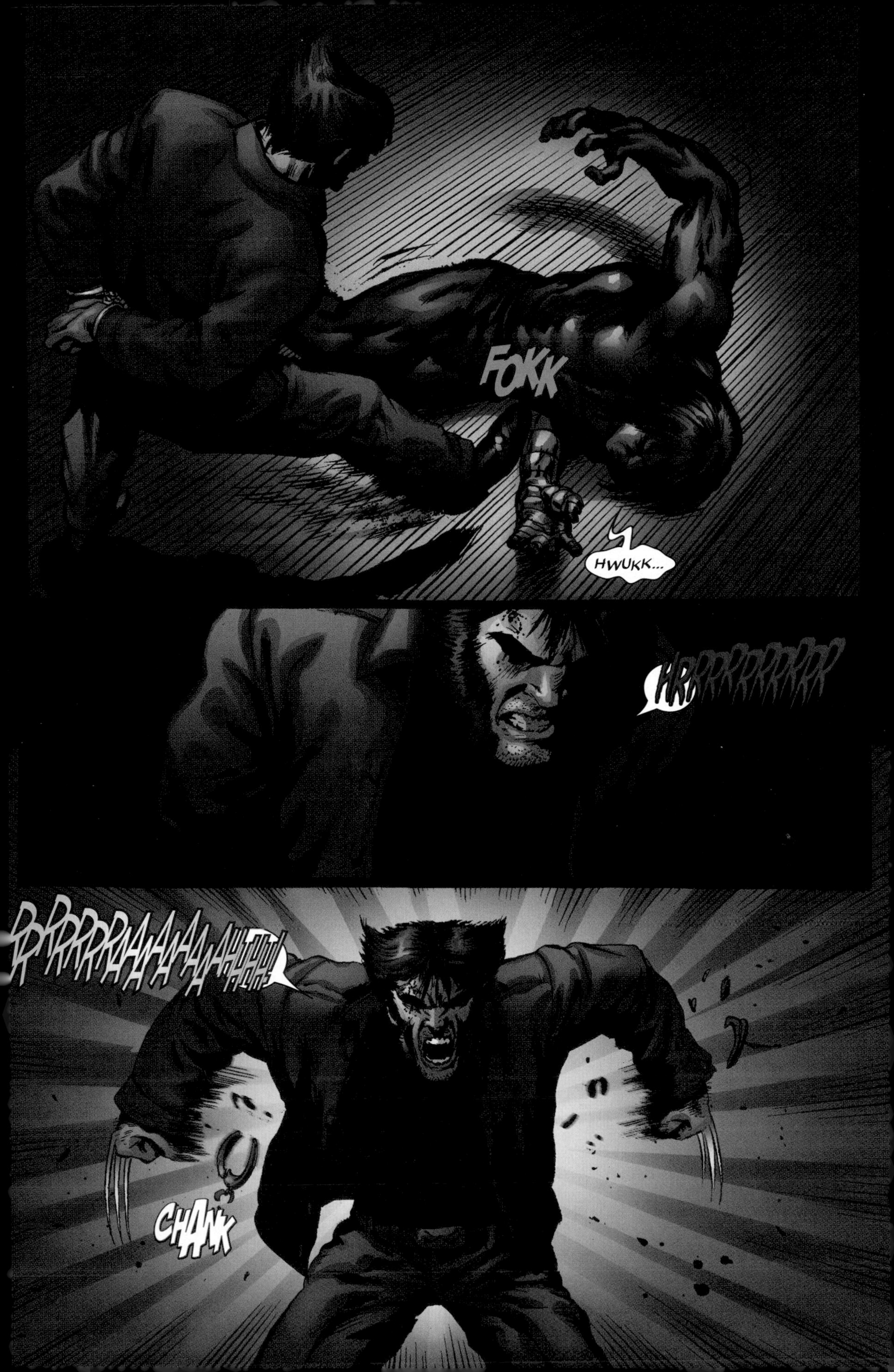

FOKK
HWUKK...
HRRRRRRRRRRR
RRRRRRRRAAAAAAAHHHH!
CHANK

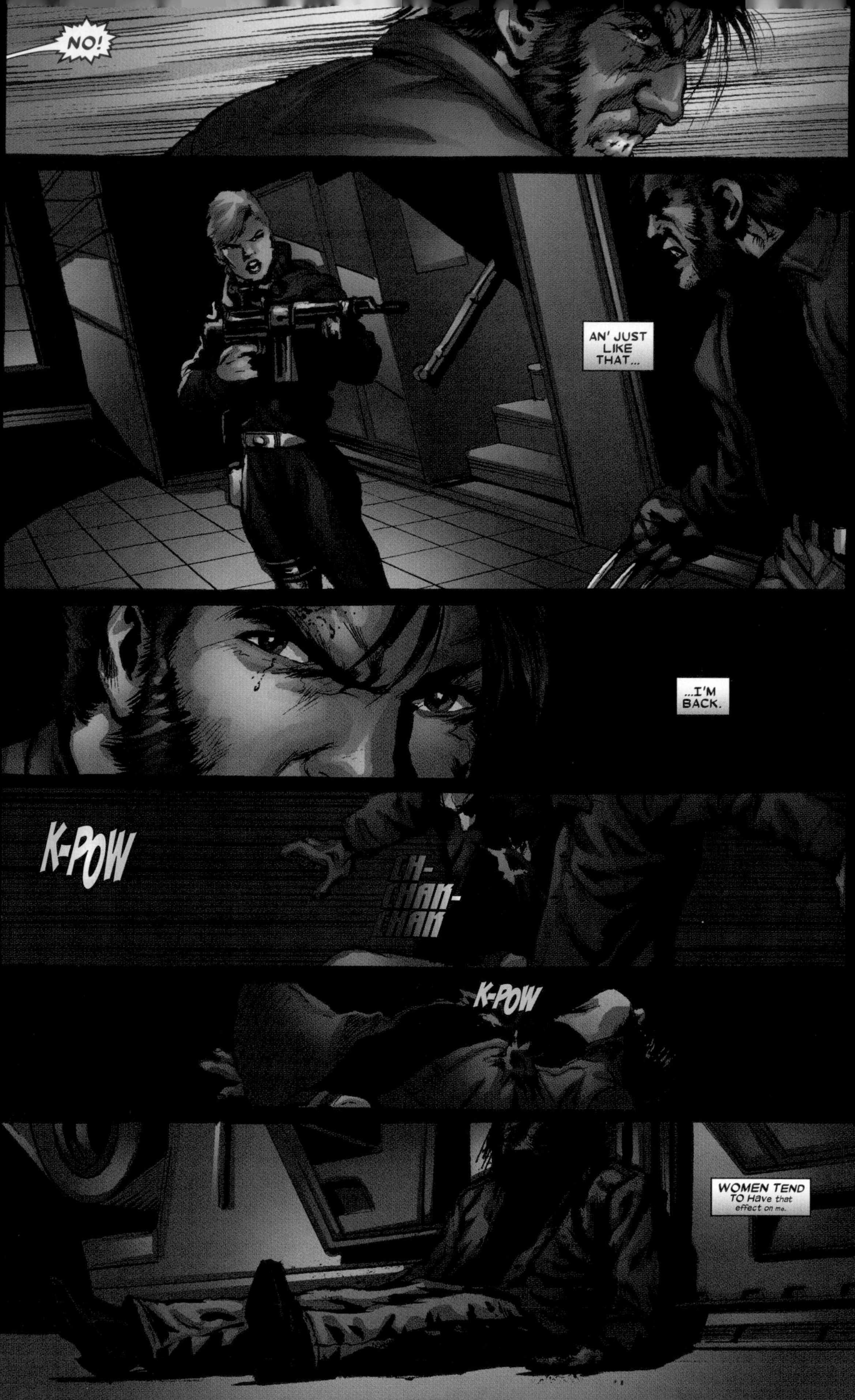
NO!
AN' JUST LIKE THAT...
...I'M BACK.
K-POW
K-POW
WOMEN TEND TO HAVE THAT EFFECT ON ME.

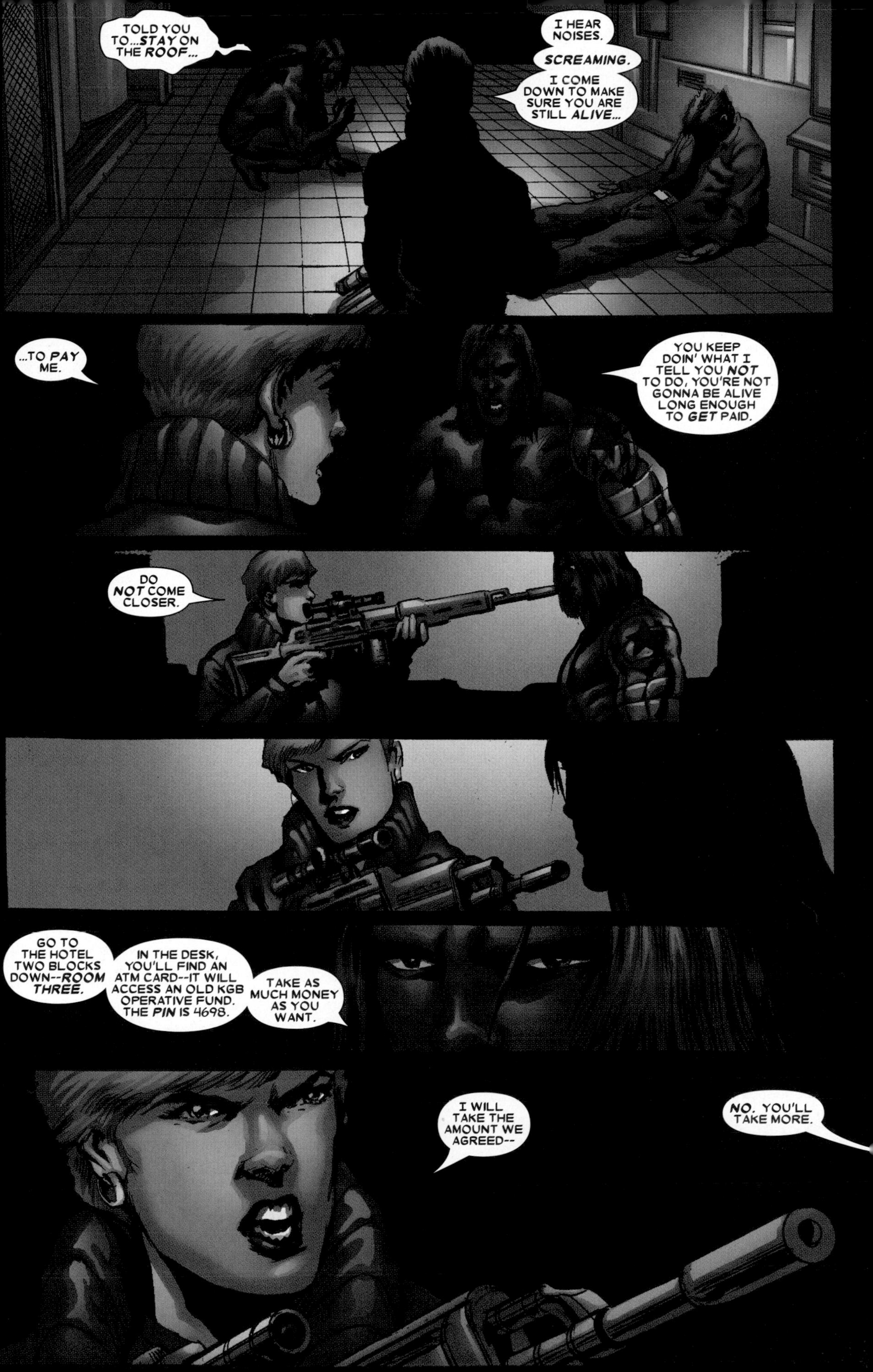
TOLD YOU TO...STAY ON THE ROOF...
I HEAR NOISES.
SCREAMING.
I COME DOWN TO MAKE SURE YOU ARE STILL ALIVE...
...TO PAY ME.
YOU KEEP DOIN' WHAT I TELL YOU NOT TO DO, YOU'RE NOT GONNA BE ALIVE LONG ENOUGH TO GET PAID.
DO NOT COME CLOSER.
GO TO THE HOTEL TWO BLOCKS DOWN--ROOM THREE.
IN THE DESK, YOU'LL FIND AN ATM CARD--IT WILL ACCESS AN OLD KGB OPERATIVE FUND. THE PIN IS 4698.
TAKE AS MUCH MONEY AS YOU WANT.
I WILL TAKE THE AMOUNT WE AGREED--
NO. YOU'LL TAKE MORE.

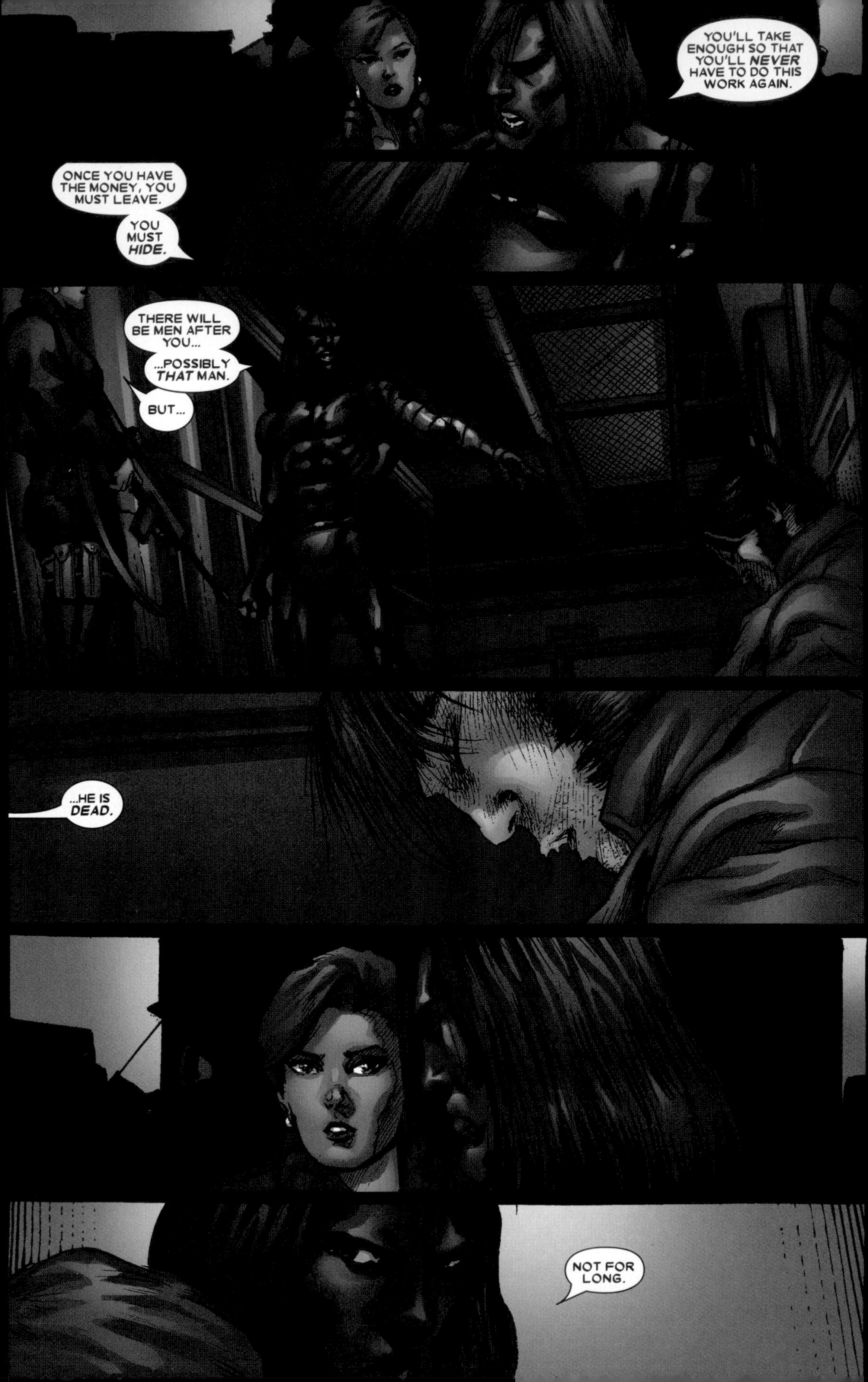
YOU'LL TAKE ENOUGH SO THAT YOU'LL *NEVER* HAVE TO DO THIS WORK AGAIN.
ONCE YOU HAVE THE MONEY, YOU MUST LEAVE.
YOU MUST *HIDE*.
THERE WILL BE MEN AFTER YOU...
...POSSIBLY *THAT* MAN.
BUT...
...HE IS *DEAD*.
NOT FOR LONG.

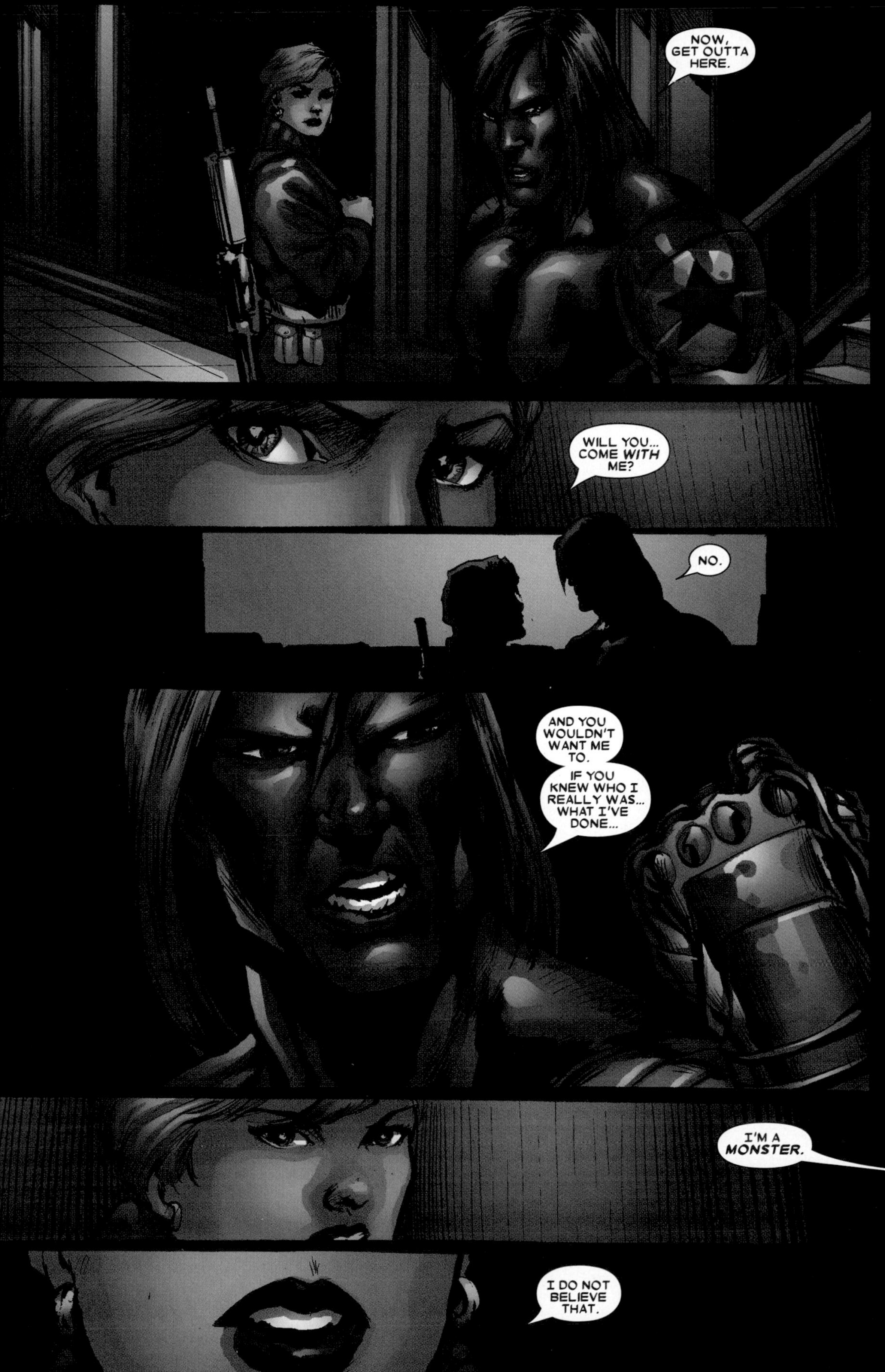
NOW, GET OUTTA HERE.
WILL YOU... COME WITH ME?
NO.
AND YOU WOULDN'T WANT ME TO.
IF YOU KNEW WHO I REALLY WAS... WHAT I'VE DONE...
I'M A MONSTER.
I DO NOT BELIEVE THAT.

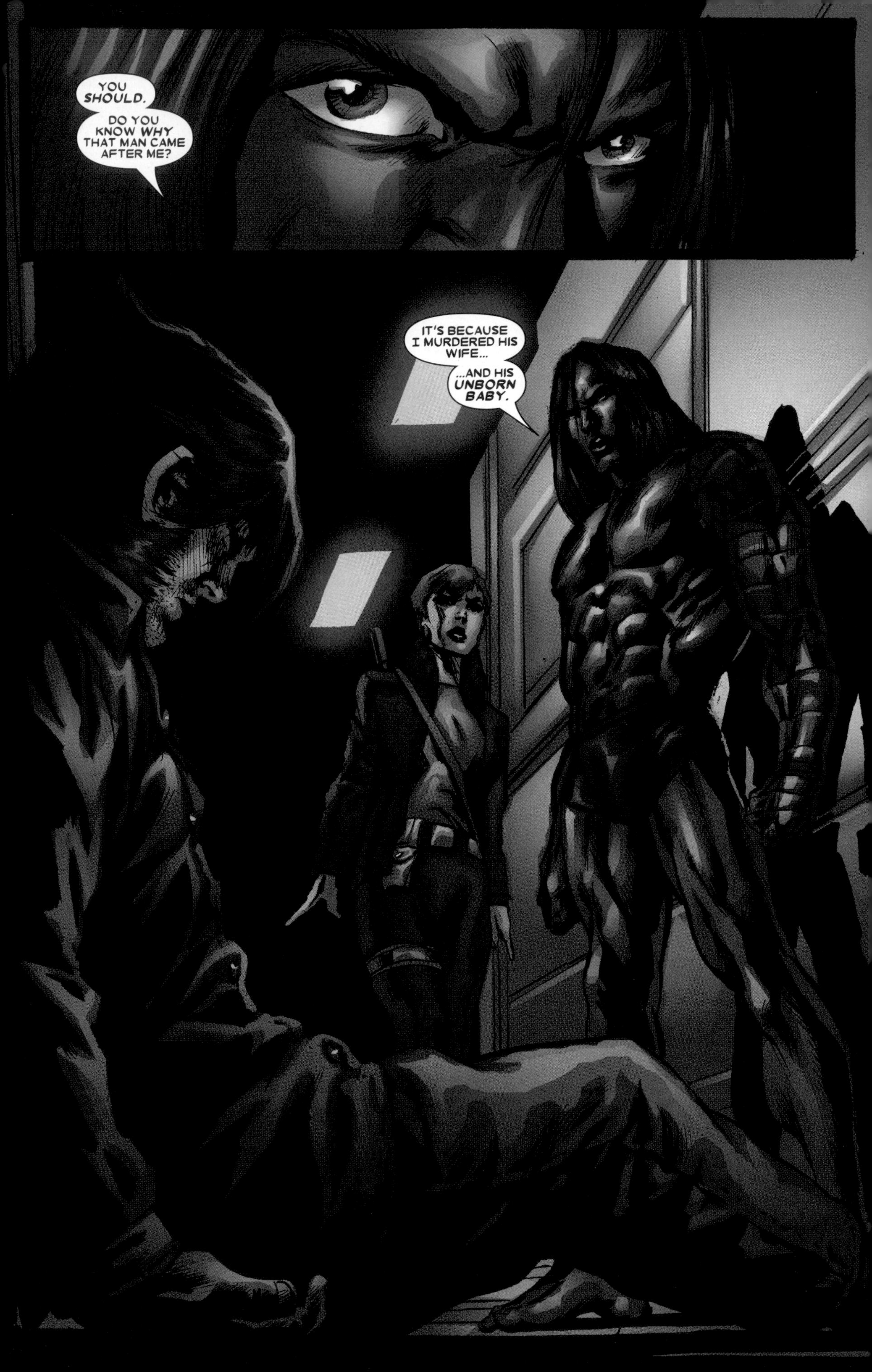
YOU SHOULD.
DO YOU KNOW WHY THAT MAN CAME AFTER ME?
IT'S BECAUSE I MURDERED HIS WIFE...
...AND HIS UNBORN BABY.

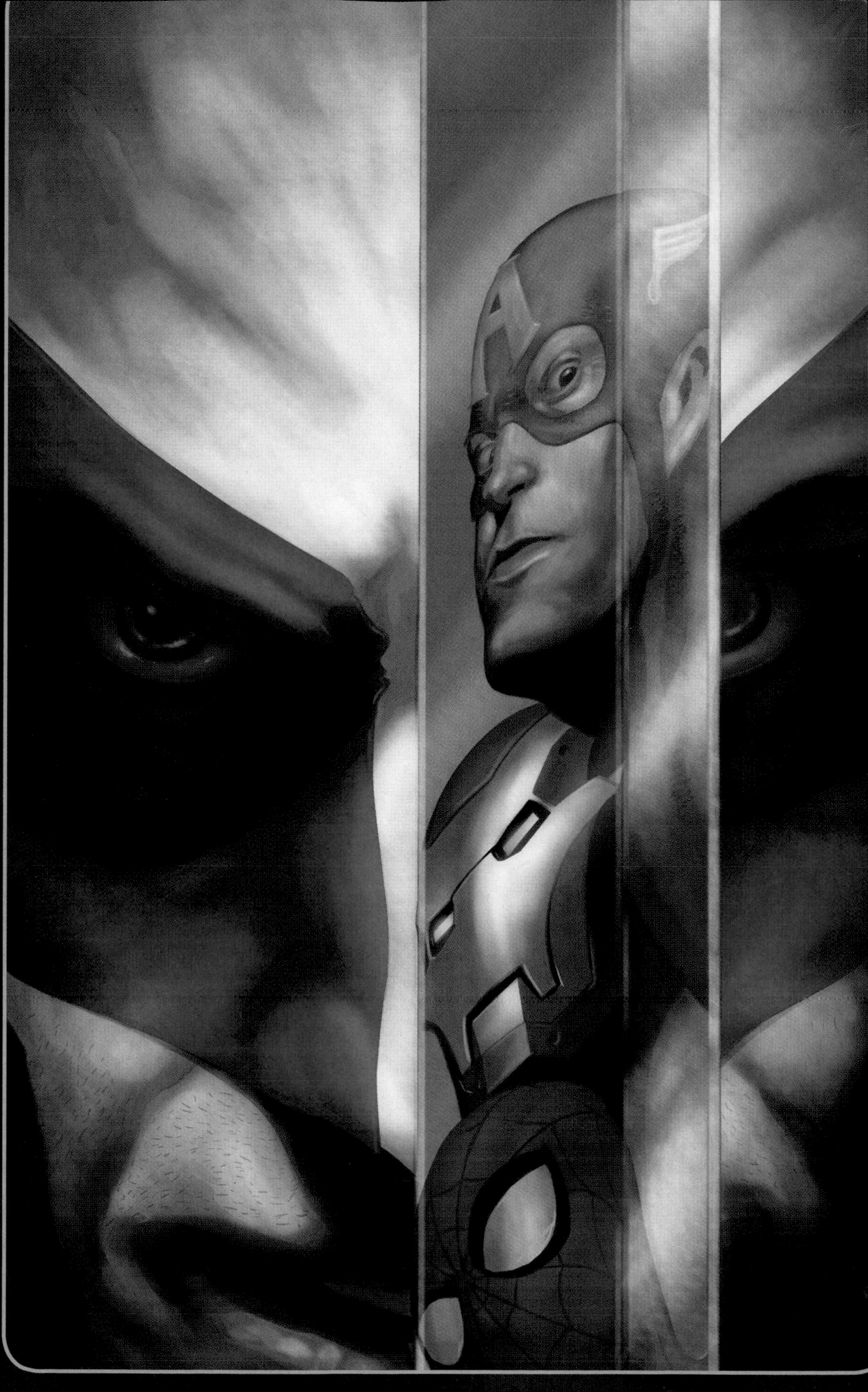

ISSUE #40

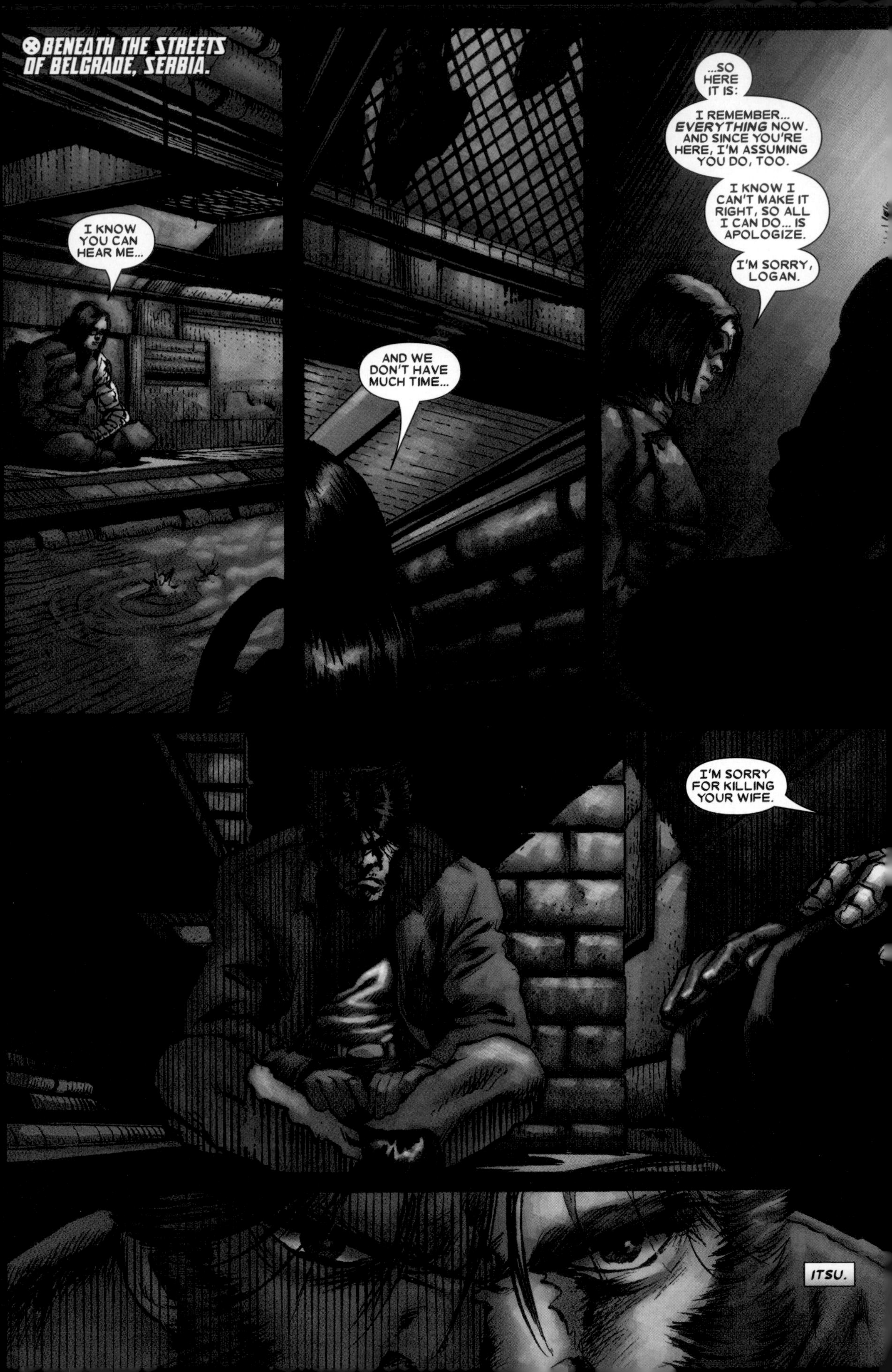

BENEATH THE STREETS OF BELGRADE, SERBIA.
I KNOW YOU CAN HEAR ME...
AND WE DON'T HAVE MUCH TIME...
...SO HERE IT IS:
I REMEMBER... EVERYTHING NOW. AND SINCE YOU'RE HERE, I'M ASSUMING YOU DO, TOO.
I KNOW I CAN'T MAKE IT RIGHT, SO ALL I CAN DO... IS APOLOGIZE.
I'M SORRY, LOGAN.
I'M SORRY FOR KILLING YOUR WIFE.
ITSU.

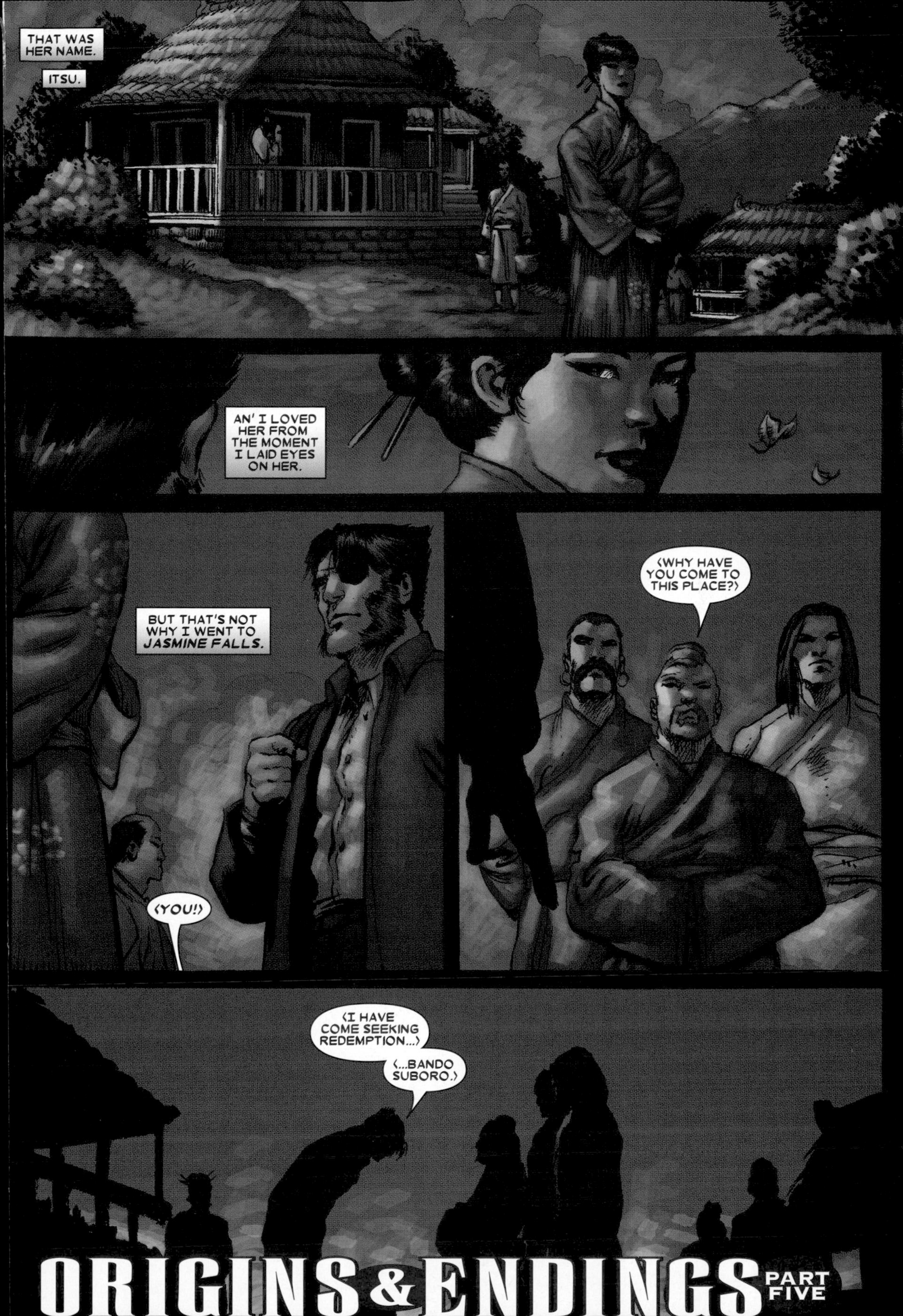

THAT WAS HER NAME.
ITSU.
AN' I LOVED HER FROM THE MOMENT I LAID EYES ON HER.
BUT THAT'S NOT WHY I WENT TO *JASMINE FALLS.*
‹YOU!›
‹WHY HAVE YOU COME TO THIS PLACE?›
‹I HAVE COME SEEKING REDEMPTION...›
‹...BANDO SUBORO.›
ORIGINS & ENDINGS PART FIVE

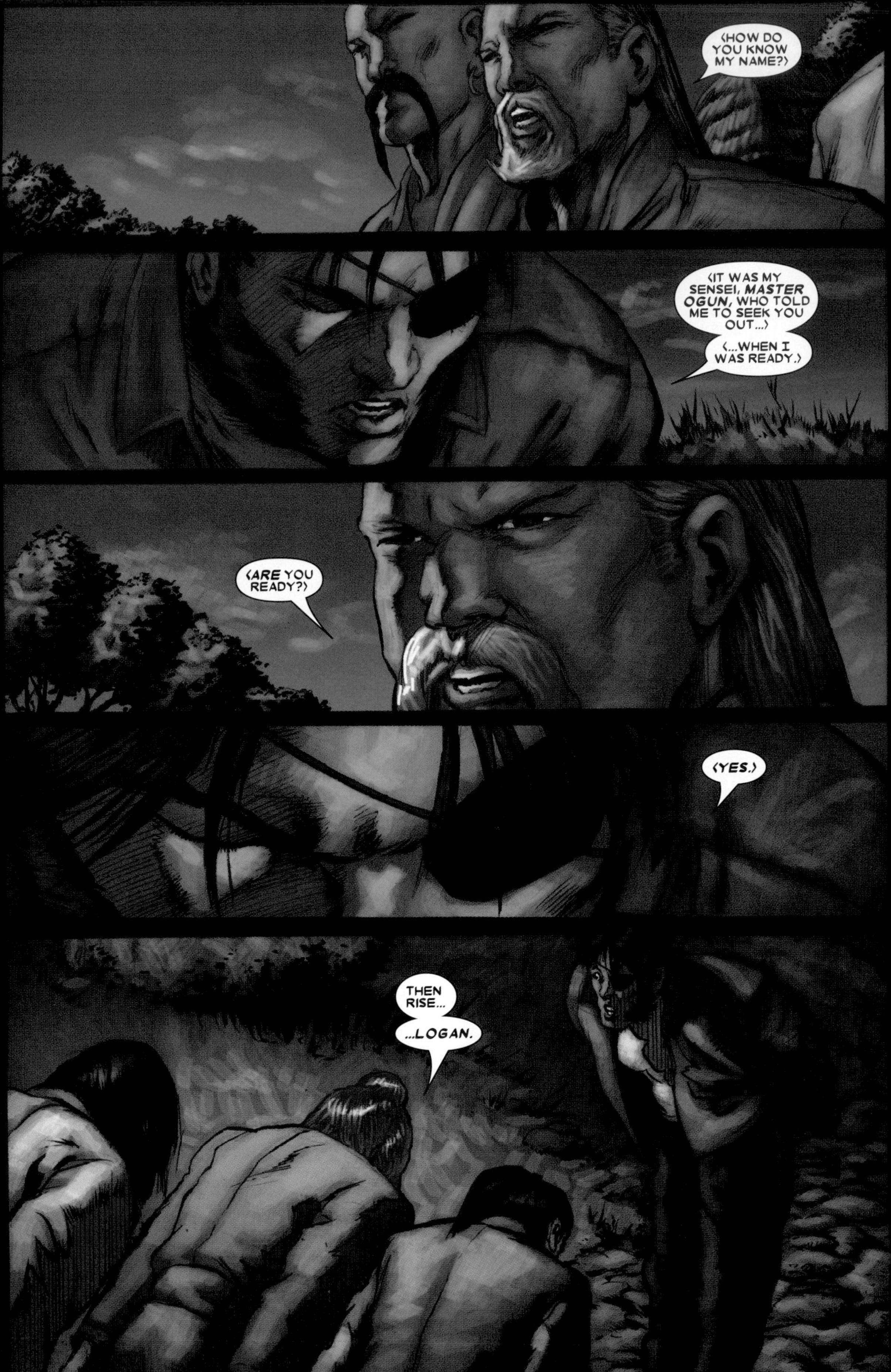
‹HOW DO YOU KNOW MY NAME?›
‹IT WAS MY SENSEI, MASTER OGUN, WHO TOLD ME TO SEEK YOU OUT...›
‹...WHEN I WAS READY.›
‹ARE YOU READY?›
‹YES.›
THEN RISE...
...LOGAN.

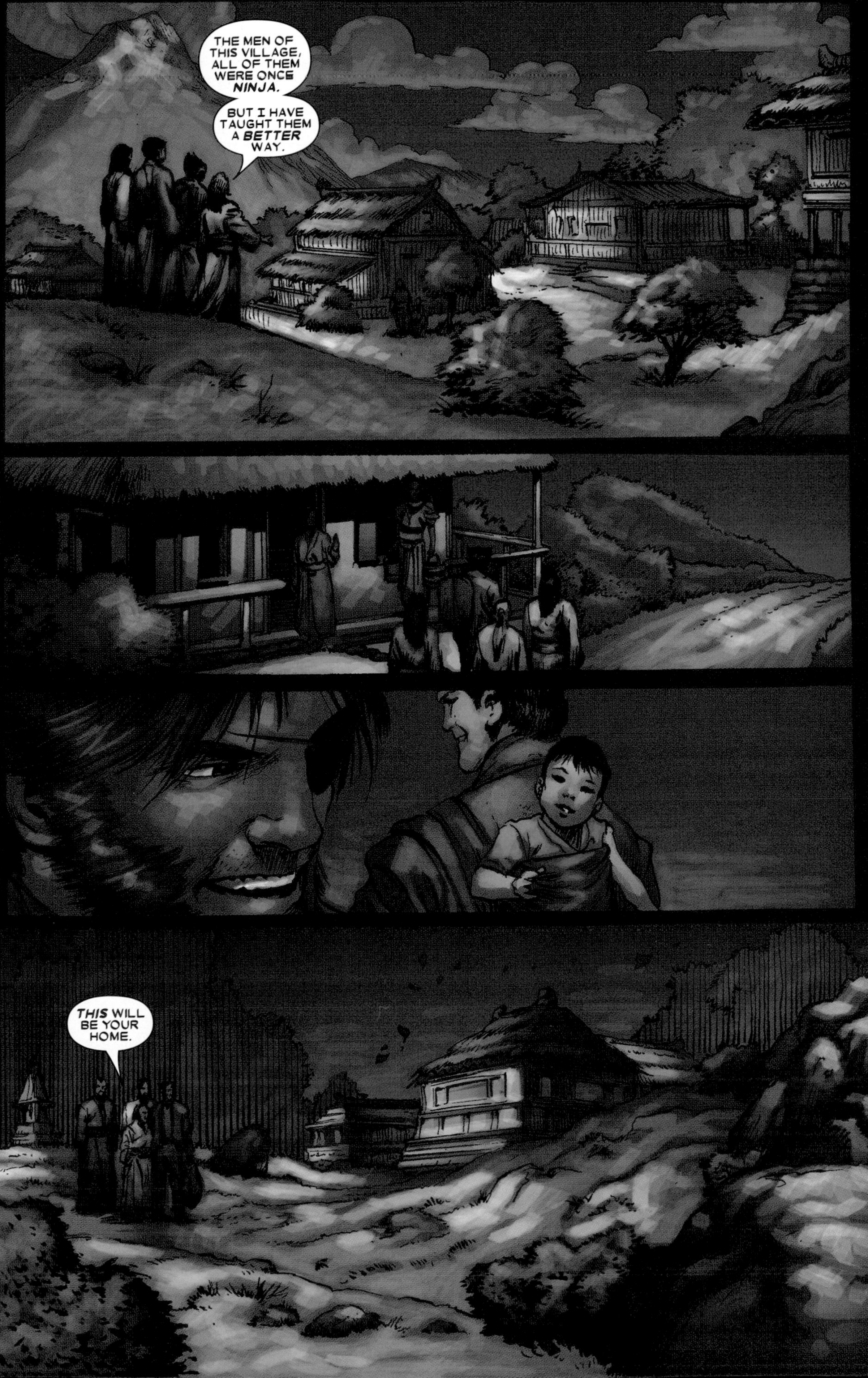
THE MEN OF THIS VILLAGE, ALL OF THEM WERE ONCE NINJA.
BUT I HAVE TAUGHT THEM A BETTER WAY.
THIS WILL BE YOUR HOME.

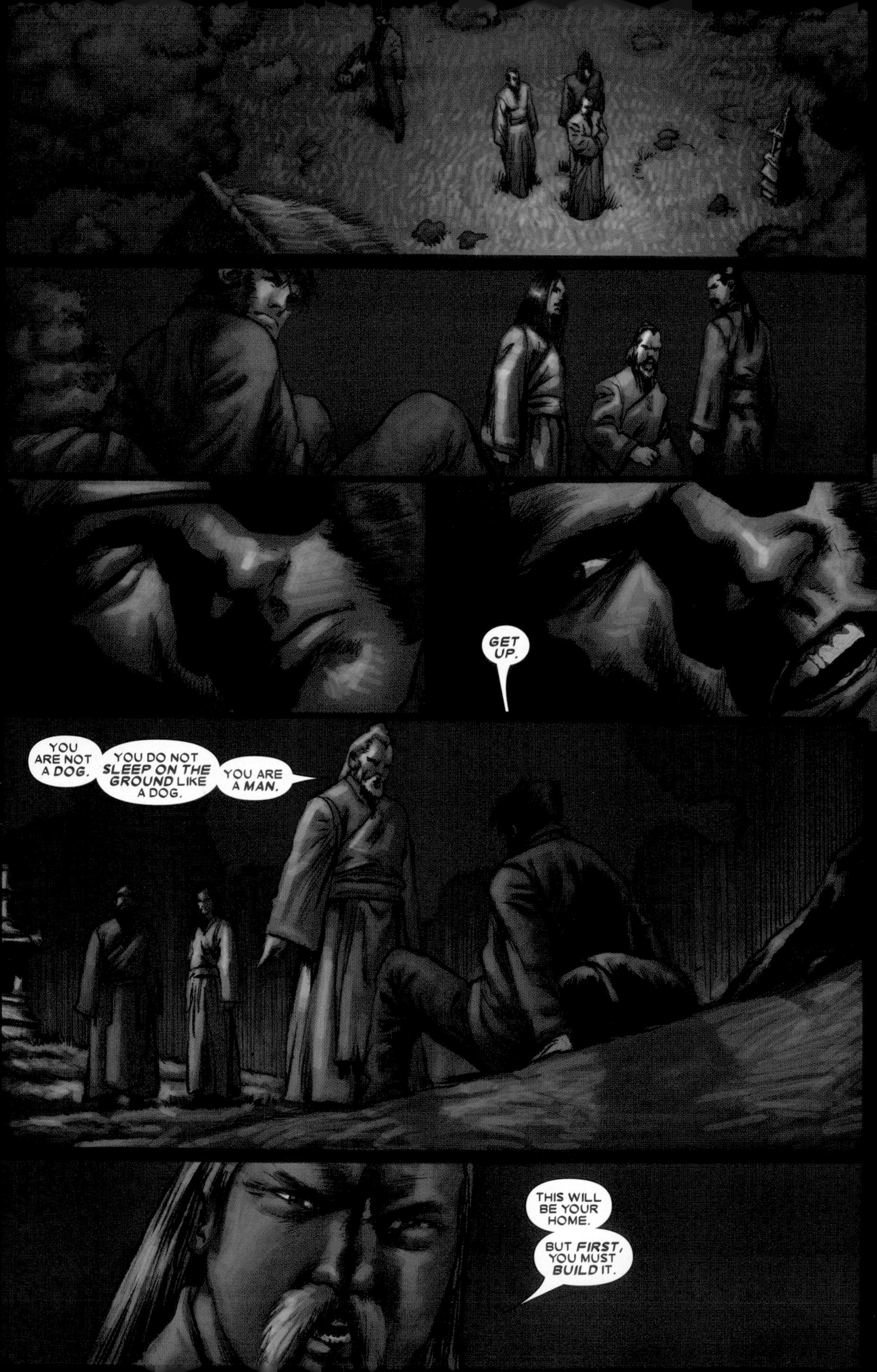
GET UP.
YOU ARE NOT A DOG.
YOU DO NOT SLEEP ON THE GROUND LIKE A DOG.
YOU ARE A MAN.
THIS WILL BE YOUR HOME.
BUT FIRST, YOU MUST BUILD IT.

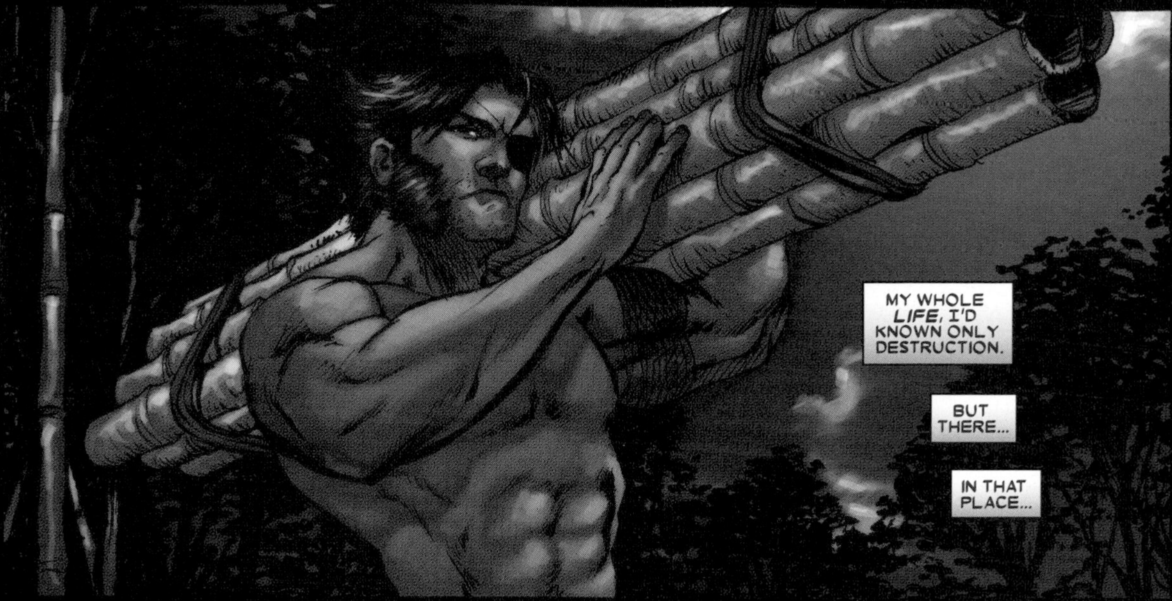
MY WHOLE LIFE, I'D KNOWN ONLY DESTRUCTION.
BUT THERE...
IN THAT PLACE...

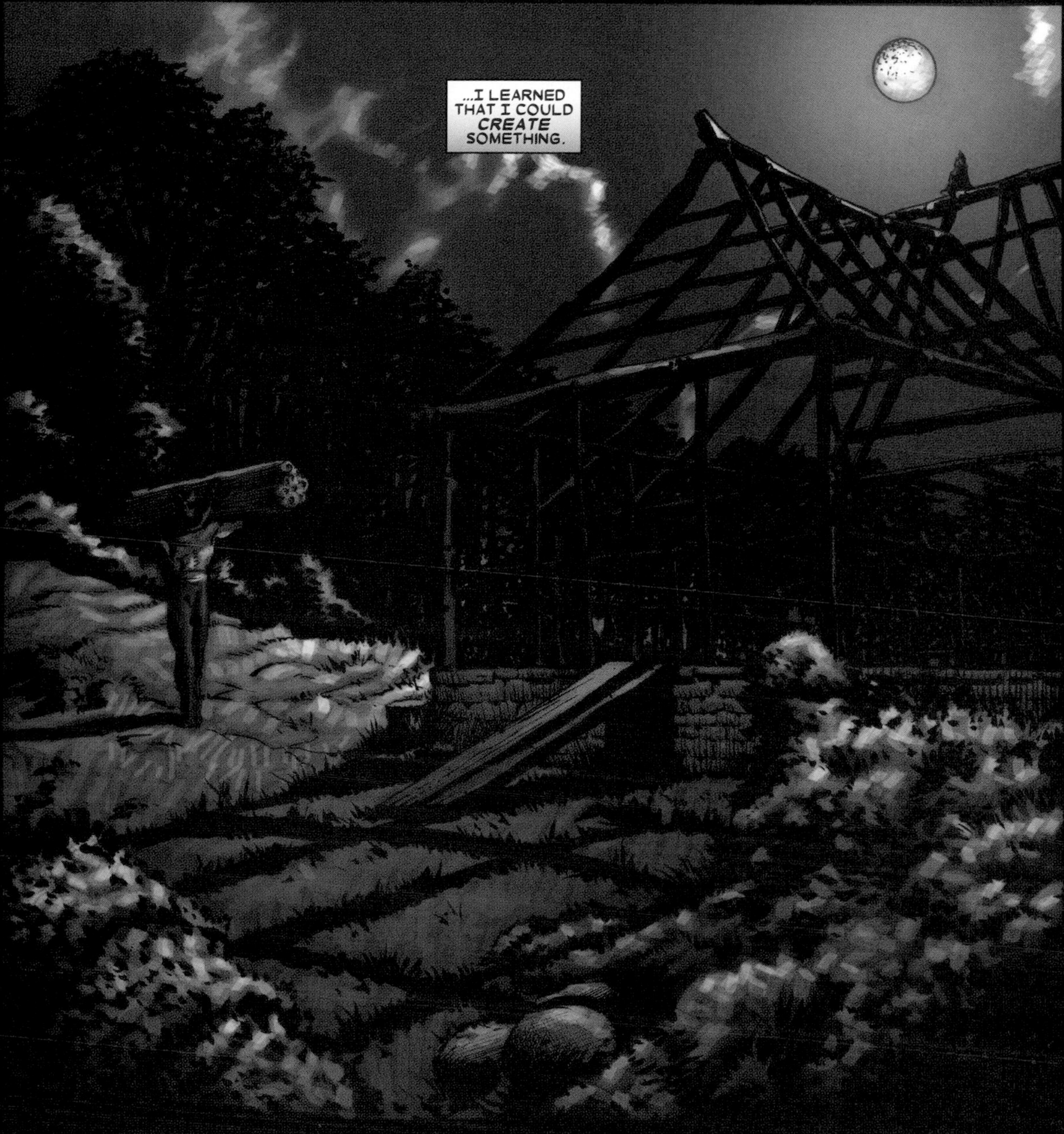
...I LEARNED THAT I COULD CREATE SOMETHING.

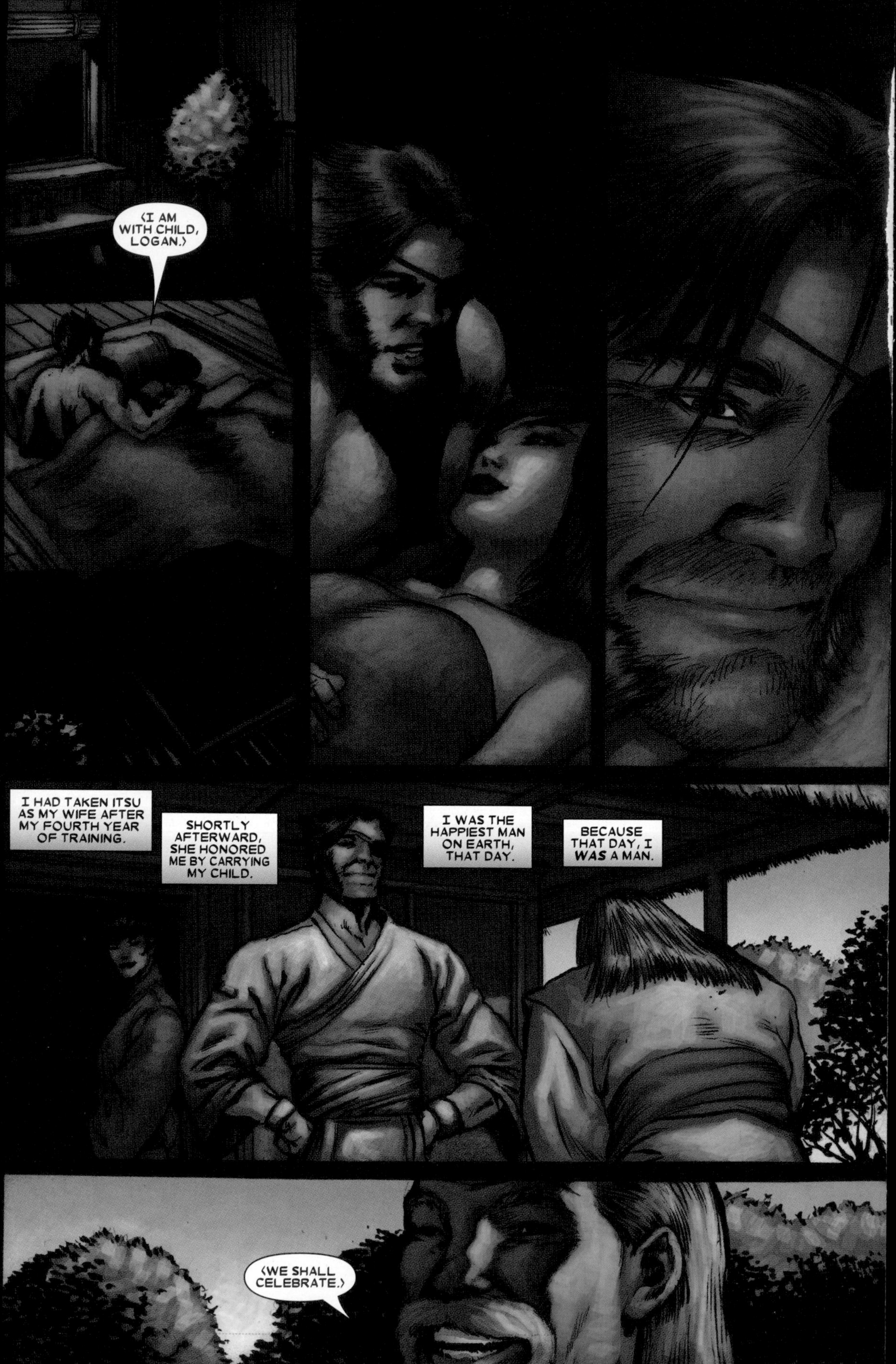

‹I AM WITH CHILD, LOGAN.›
I HAD TAKEN ITSU AS MY WIFE AFTER MY FOURTH YEAR OF TRAINING.
SHORTLY AFTERWARD, SHE HONORED ME BY CARRYING MY CHILD.
I WAS THE HAPPIEST MAN ON EARTH, THAT DAY.
BECAUSE THAT DAY, I *WAS* A MAN.
‹WE SHALL CELEBRATE.›

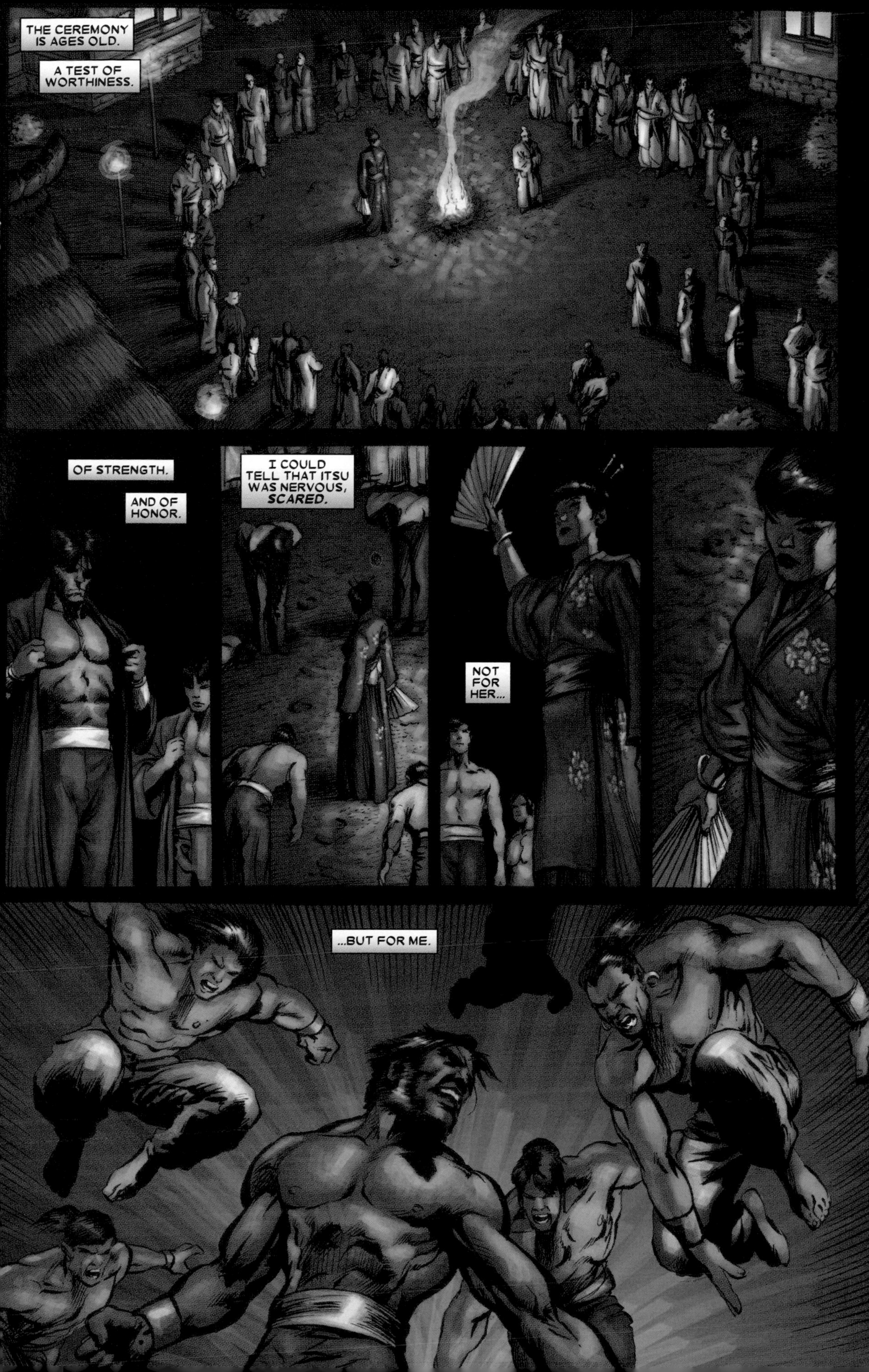
THE CEREMONY IS AGES OLD.
A TEST OF WORTHINESS.
OF STRENGTH.
AND OF HONOR.
I COULD TELL THAT ITSU WAS NERVOUS, *SCARED*.
NOT FOR HER...
...BUT FOR ME.

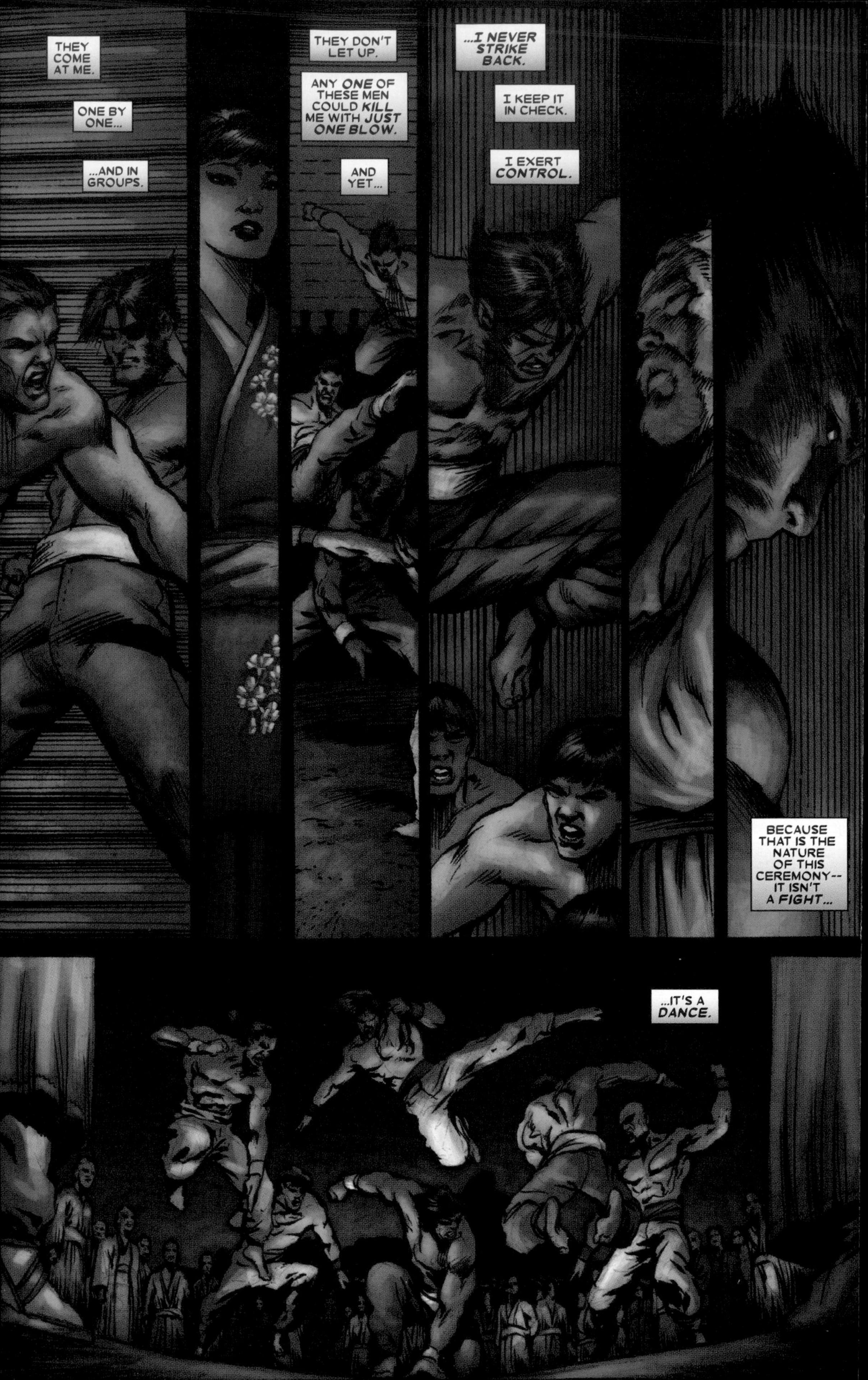

THEY COME AT ME.
ONE BY ONE...
...AND IN GROUPS.
THEY DON'T LET UP.
ANY ONE OF THESE MEN COULD KILL ME WITH JUST ONE BLOW.
AND YET...
...I NEVER STRIKE BACK.
I KEEP IT IN CHECK.
I EXERT CONTROL.
BECAUSE THAT IS THE NATURE OF THIS CEREMONY-- IT ISN'T A FIGHT...
...IT'S A DANCE.

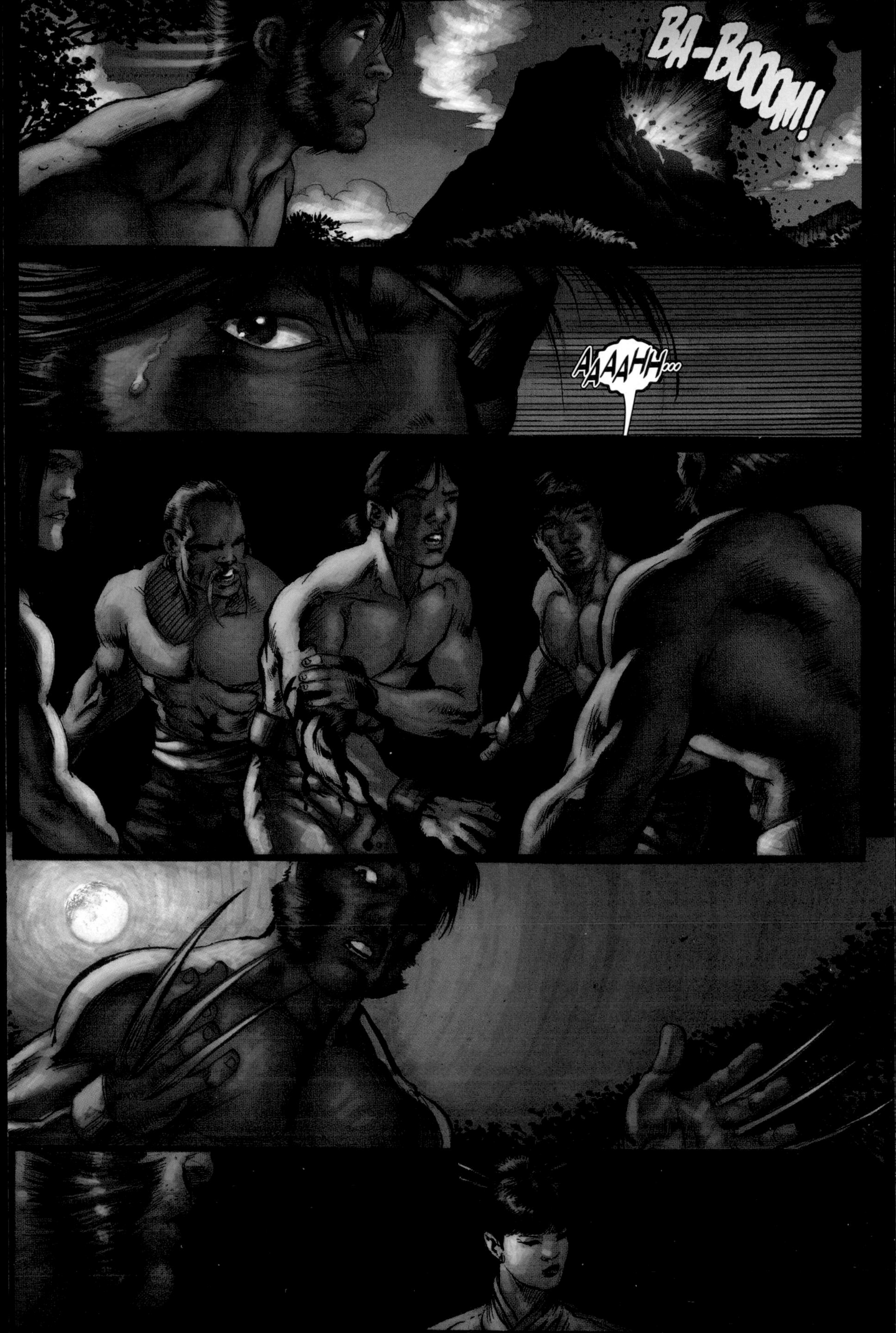
BA-BOOOM!
AAAAHH...

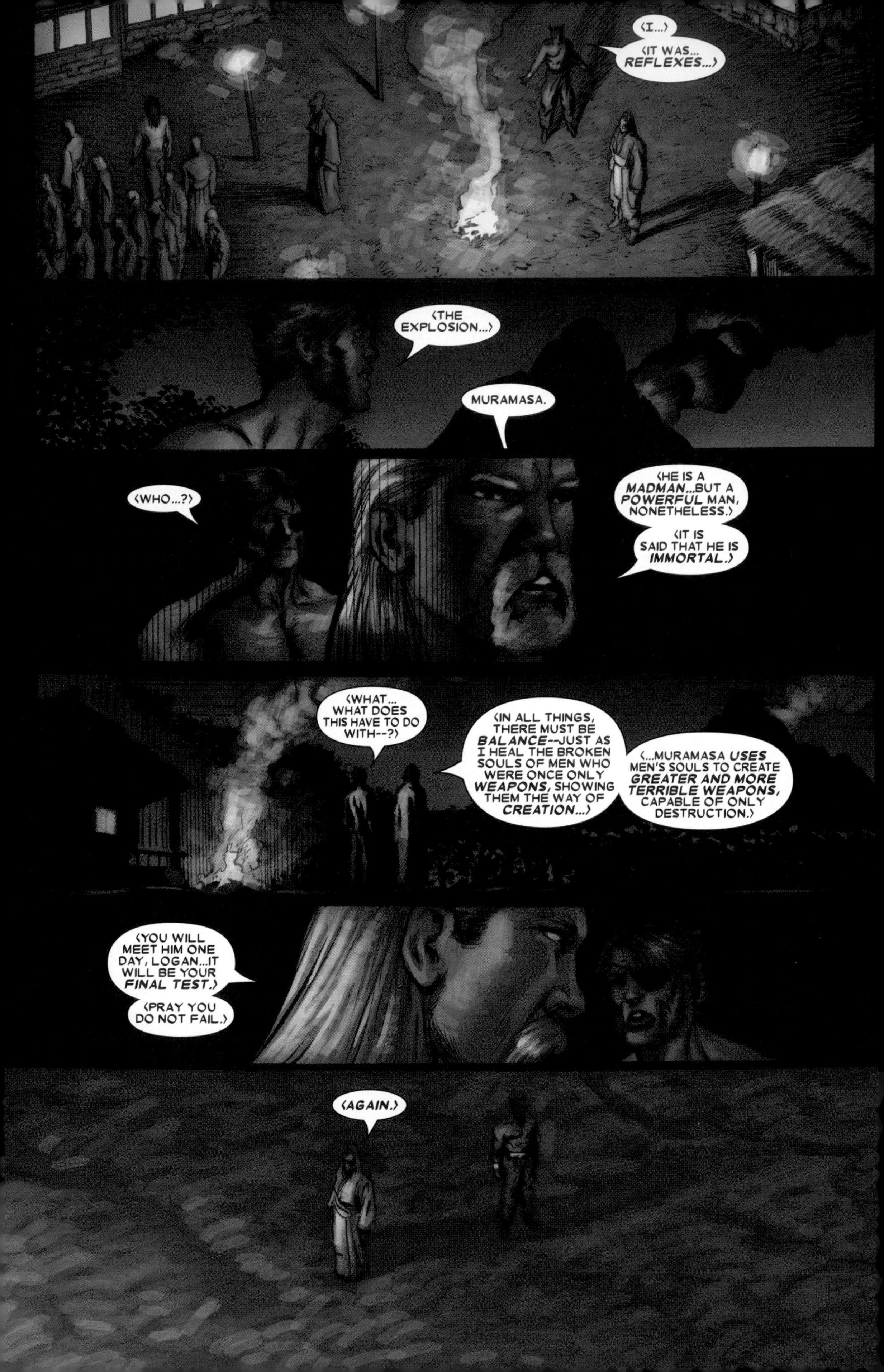

‹I...›
‹IT WAS... REFLEXES...›
‹THE EXPLOSION...›
MURAMASA.
‹WHO...?›
‹HE IS A MADMAN...BUT A POWERFUL MAN, NONETHELESS.›
‹IT IS SAID THAT HE IS IMMORTAL.›
‹WHAT... WHAT DOES THIS HAVE TO DO WITH--?›
‹IN ALL THINGS, THERE MUST BE BALANCE--JUST AS I HEAL THE BROKEN SOULS OF MEN WHO WERE ONCE ONLY WEAPONS, SHOWING THEM THE WAY OF CREATION...›
‹...MURAMASA USES MEN'S SOULS TO CREATE GREATER AND MORE TERRIBLE WEAPONS, CAPABLE OF ONLY DESTRUCTION.›
‹YOU WILL MEET HIM ONE DAY, LOGAN...IT WILL BE YOUR FINAL TEST.›
‹PRAY YOU DO NOT FAIL.›
‹AGAIN.›

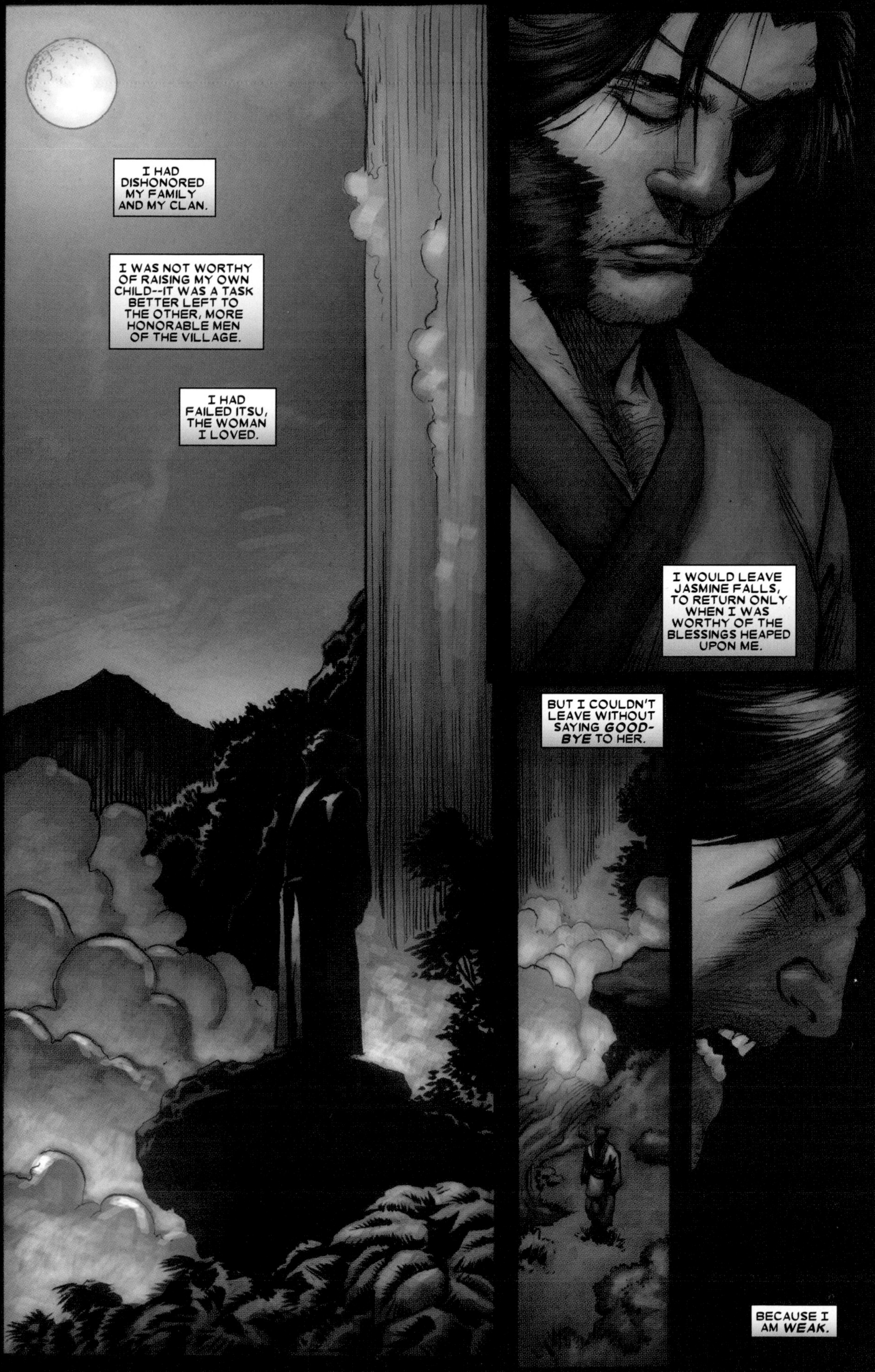
I HAD DISHONORED MY FAMILY AND MY CLAN.
I WAS NOT WORTHY OF RAISING MY OWN CHILD--IT WAS A TASK BETTER LEFT TO THE OTHER, MORE HONORABLE MEN OF THE VILLAGE.
I HAD FAILED ITSU, THE WOMAN I LOVED.
I WOULD LEAVE JASMINE FALLS, TO RETURN ONLY WHEN I WAS WORTHY OF THE BLESSINGS HEAPED UPON ME.
BUT I COULDN'T LEAVE WITHOUT SAYING GOOD-BYE TO HER.
BECAUSE I AM WEAK.

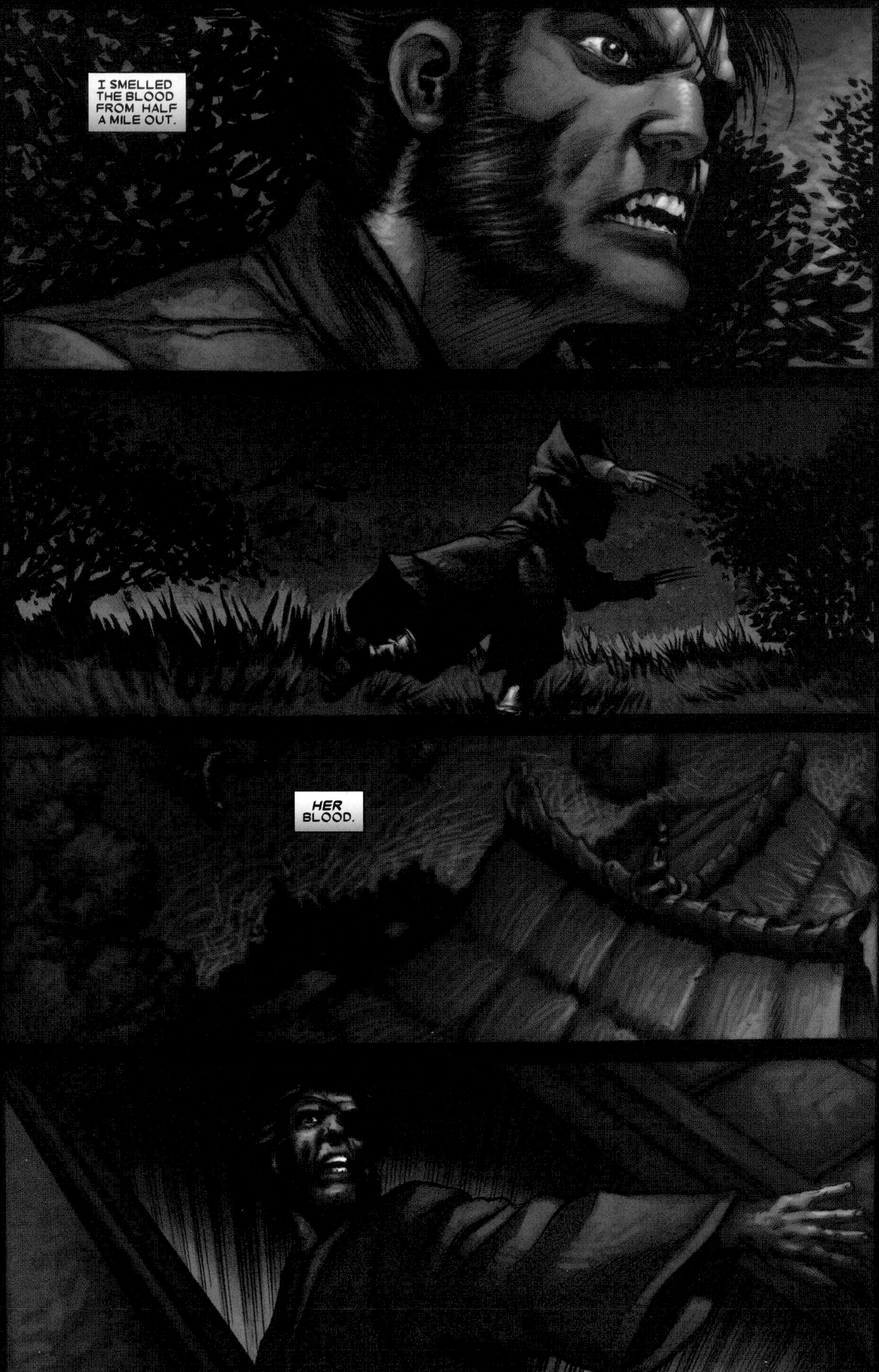
I SMELLED THE BLOOD FROM HALF A MILE OUT.
HER BLOOD.

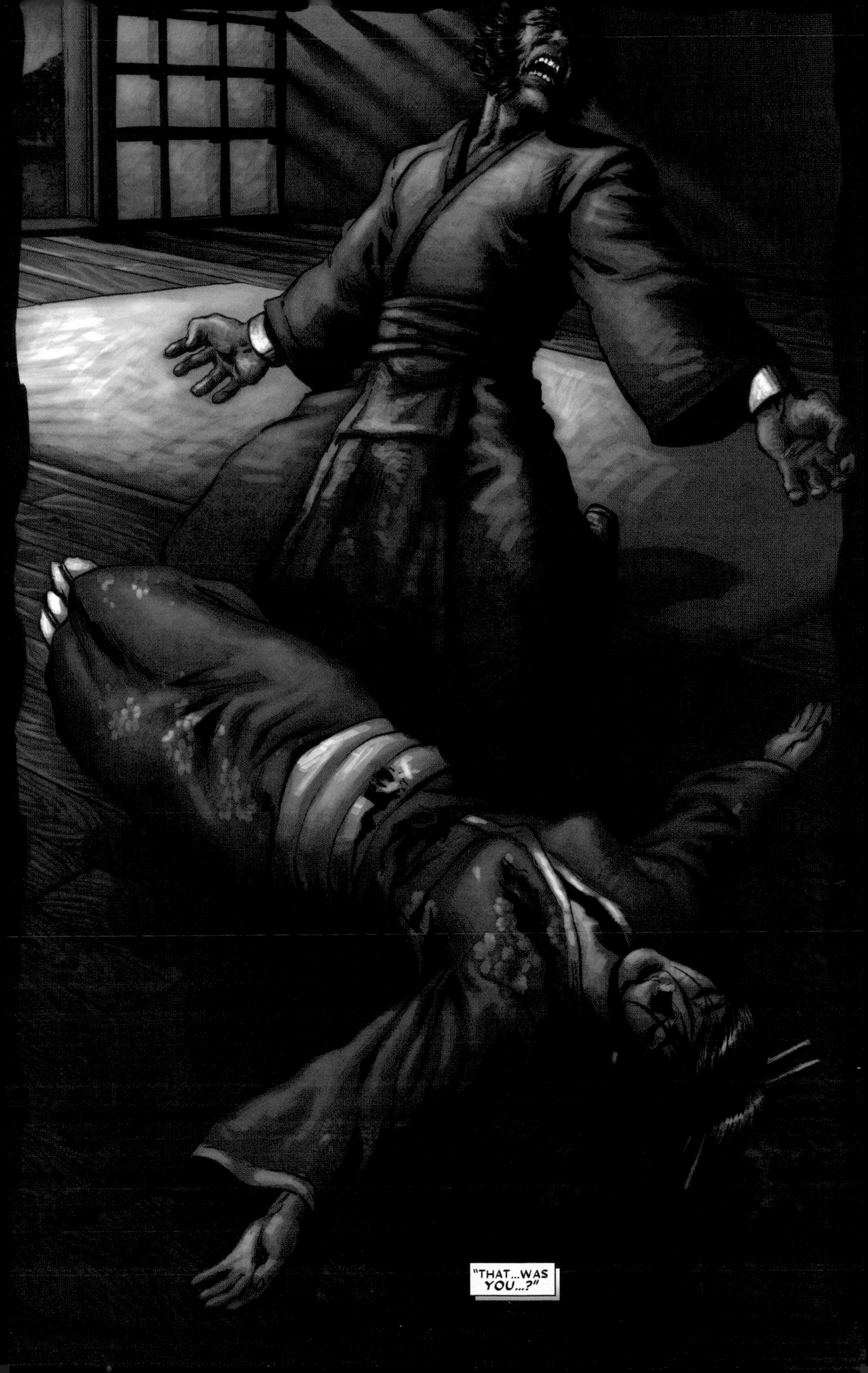
"THAT...WAS YOU...?"

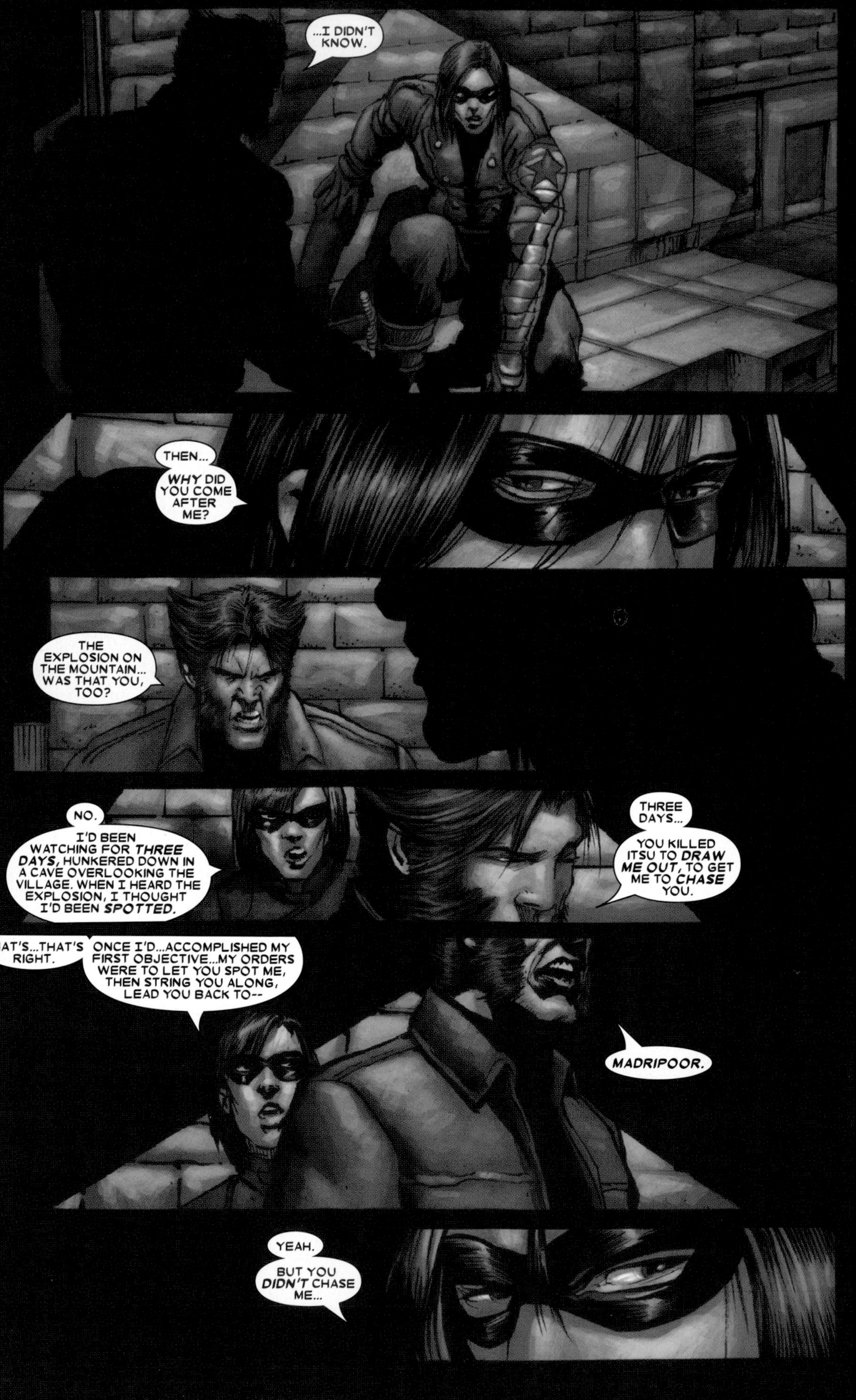
...I DIDN'T KNOW.
THEN... WHY DID YOU COME AFTER ME?
THE EXPLOSION ON THE MOUNTAIN... WAS THAT YOU, TOO?
NO.
I'D BEEN WATCHING FOR THREE DAYS, HUNKERED DOWN IN A CAVE OVERLOOKING THE VILLAGE. WHEN I HEARD THE EXPLOSION, I THOUGHT I'D BEEN SPOTTED.
THREE DAYS...
YOU KILLED ITSU TO DRAW ME OUT, TO GET ME TO CHASE YOU.
THAT'S...THAT'S RIGHT.
ONCE I'D...ACCOMPLISHED MY FIRST OBJECTIVE...MY ORDERS WERE TO LET YOU SPOT ME, THEN STRING YOU ALONG, LEAD YOU BACK TO--
MADRIPOOR.
YEAH.
BUT YOU DIDN'T CHASE ME...

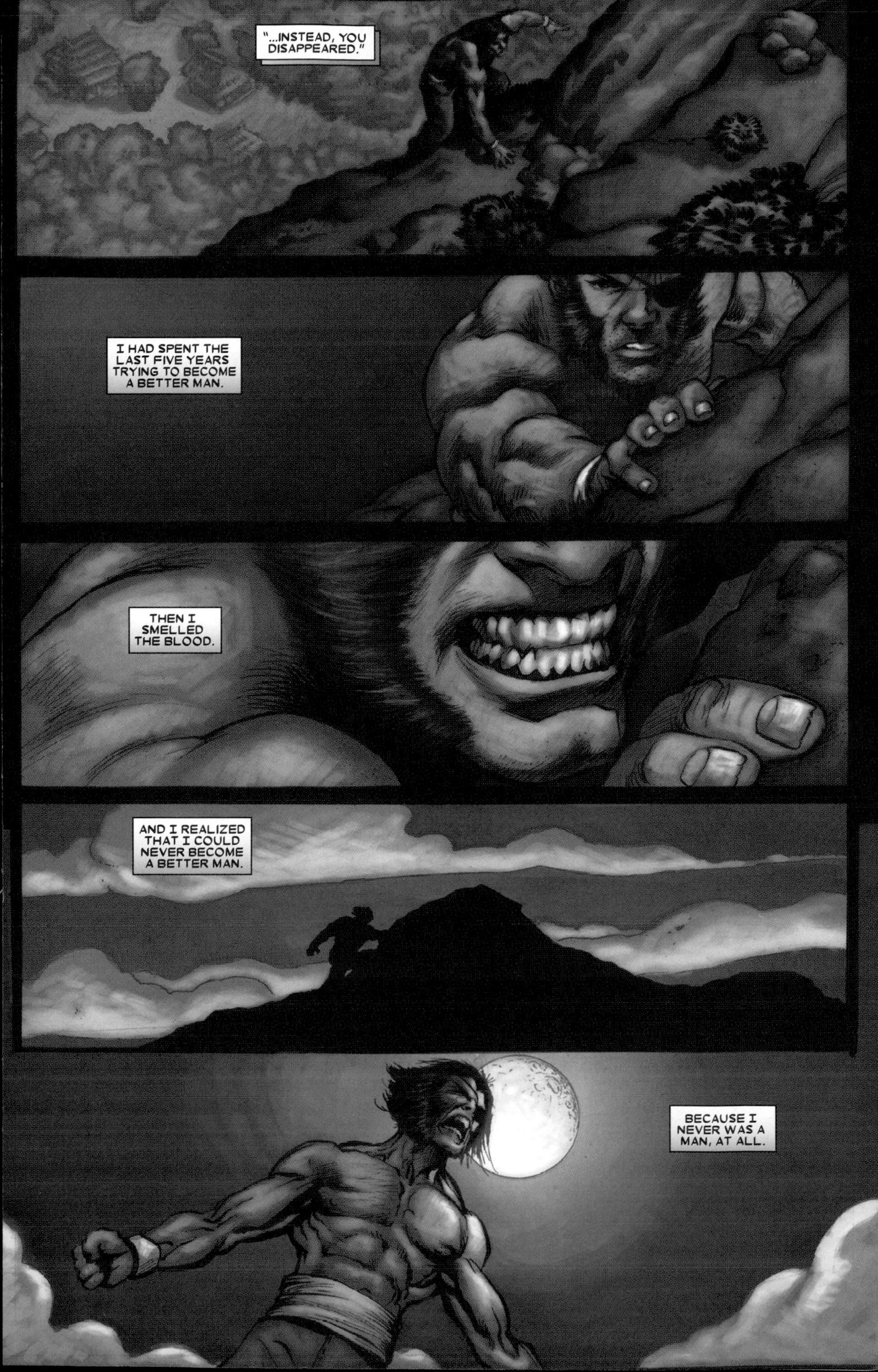
"...INSTEAD, YOU DISAPPEARED."
I HAD SPENT THE LAST FIVE YEARS TRYING TO BECOME A BETTER MAN.
THEN I SMELLED THE BLOOD.
AND I REALIZED THAT I COULD NEVER BECOME A BETTER MAN.
BECAUSE I NEVER WAS A MAN, AT ALL.

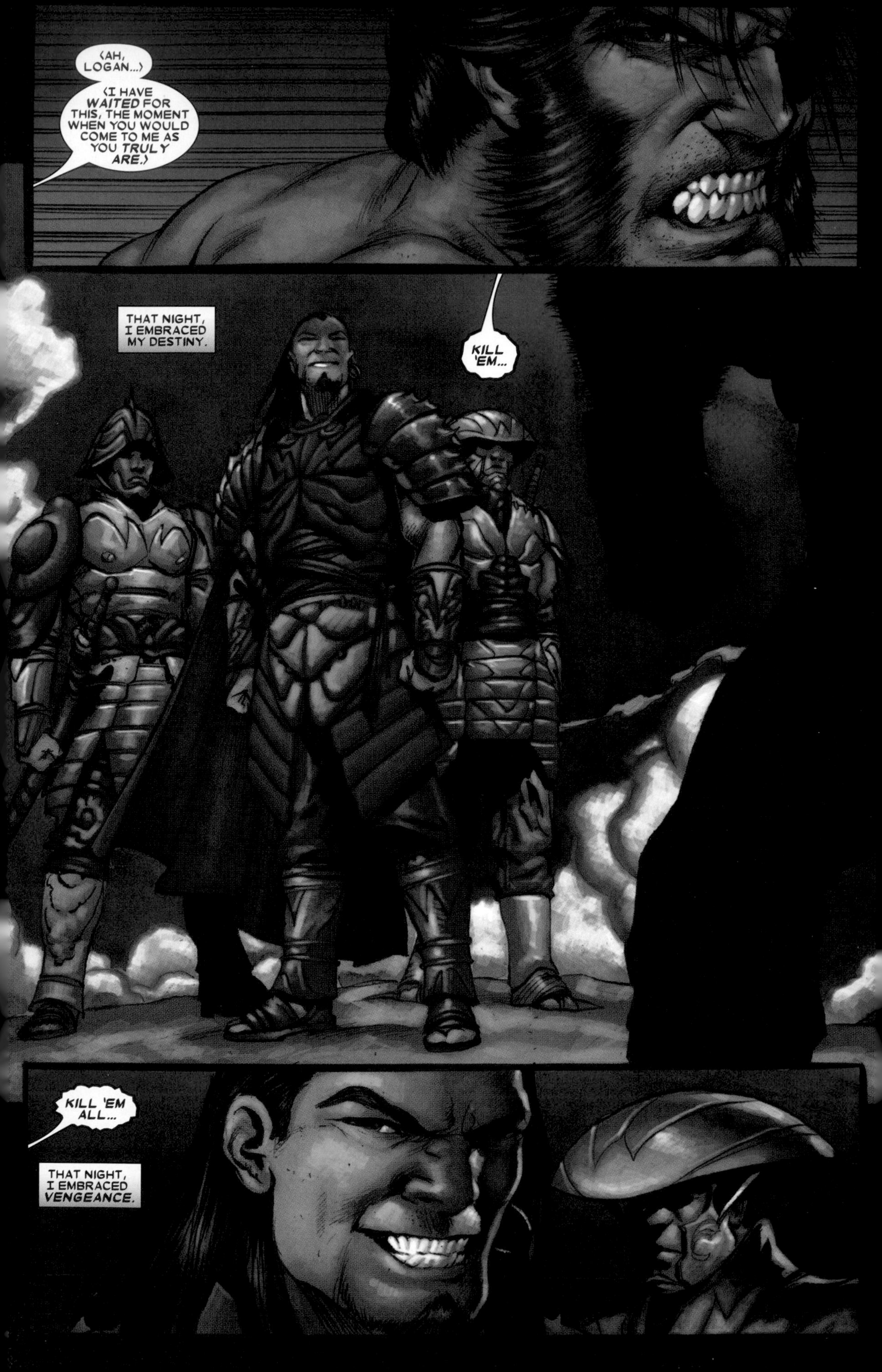

‹AH, LOGAN...›
‹I HAVE WAITED FOR THIS, THE MOMENT WHEN YOU WOULD COME TO ME AS YOU TRULY ARE.›
THAT NIGHT, I EMBRACED MY DESTINY.
KILL 'EM...
KILL 'EM ALL...
THAT NIGHT, I EMBRACED VENGEANCE.

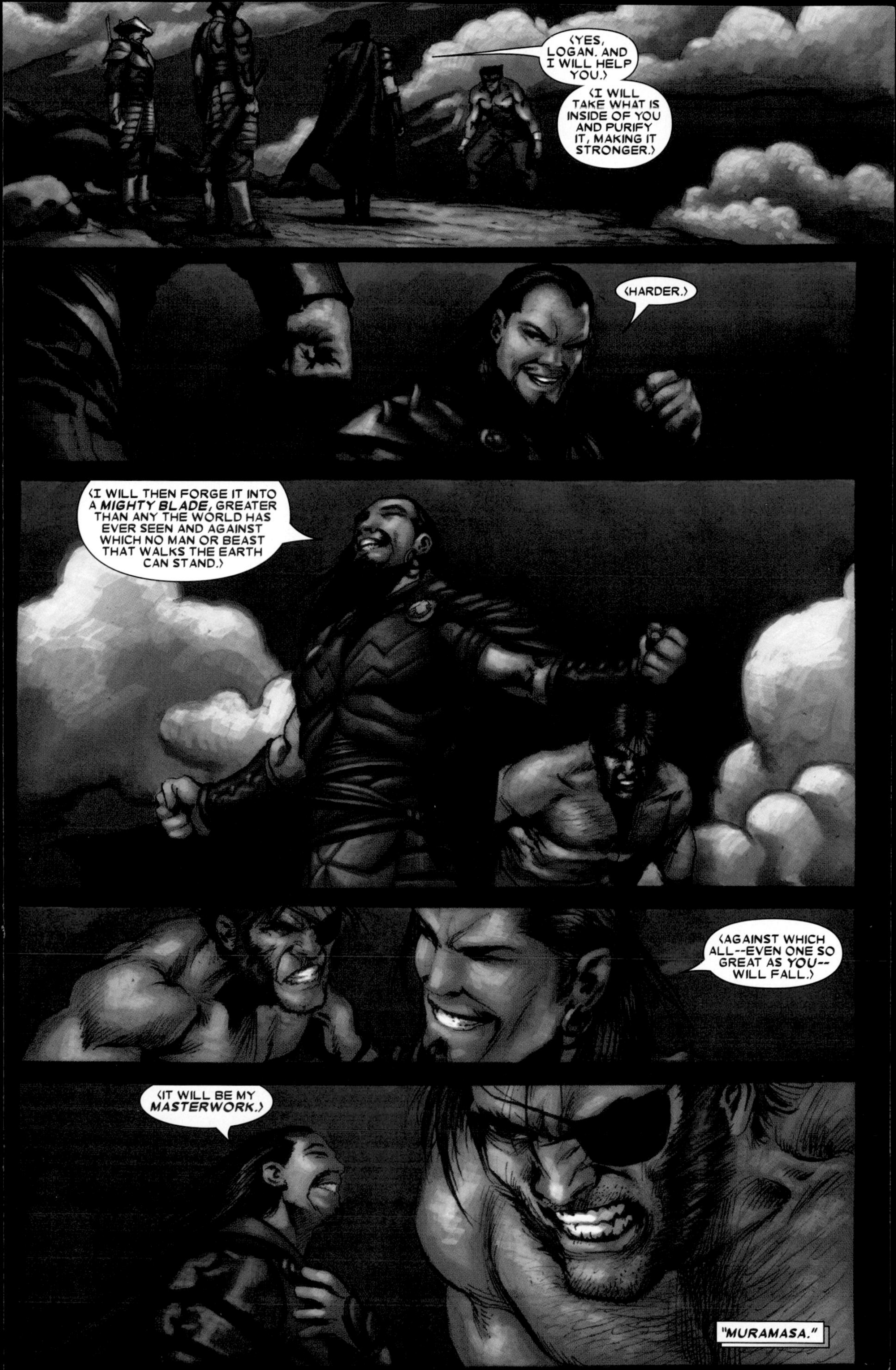
‹YES, LOGAN, AND I WILL HELP YOU.›
‹I WILL TAKE WHAT IS INSIDE OF YOU AND PURIFY IT, MAKING IT STRONGER.›
‹HARDER.›
‹I WILL THEN FORGE IT INTO A *MIGHTY BLADE*, GREATER THAN ANY THE WORLD HAS EVER SEEN AND AGAINST WHICH NO MAN OR BEAST THAT WALKS THE EARTH CAN STAND.›
‹AGAINST WHICH ALL--EVEN ONE SO GREAT AS *YOU*-- WILL FALL.›
‹IT WILL BE MY *MASTERWORK*.›
"*MURAMASA*."

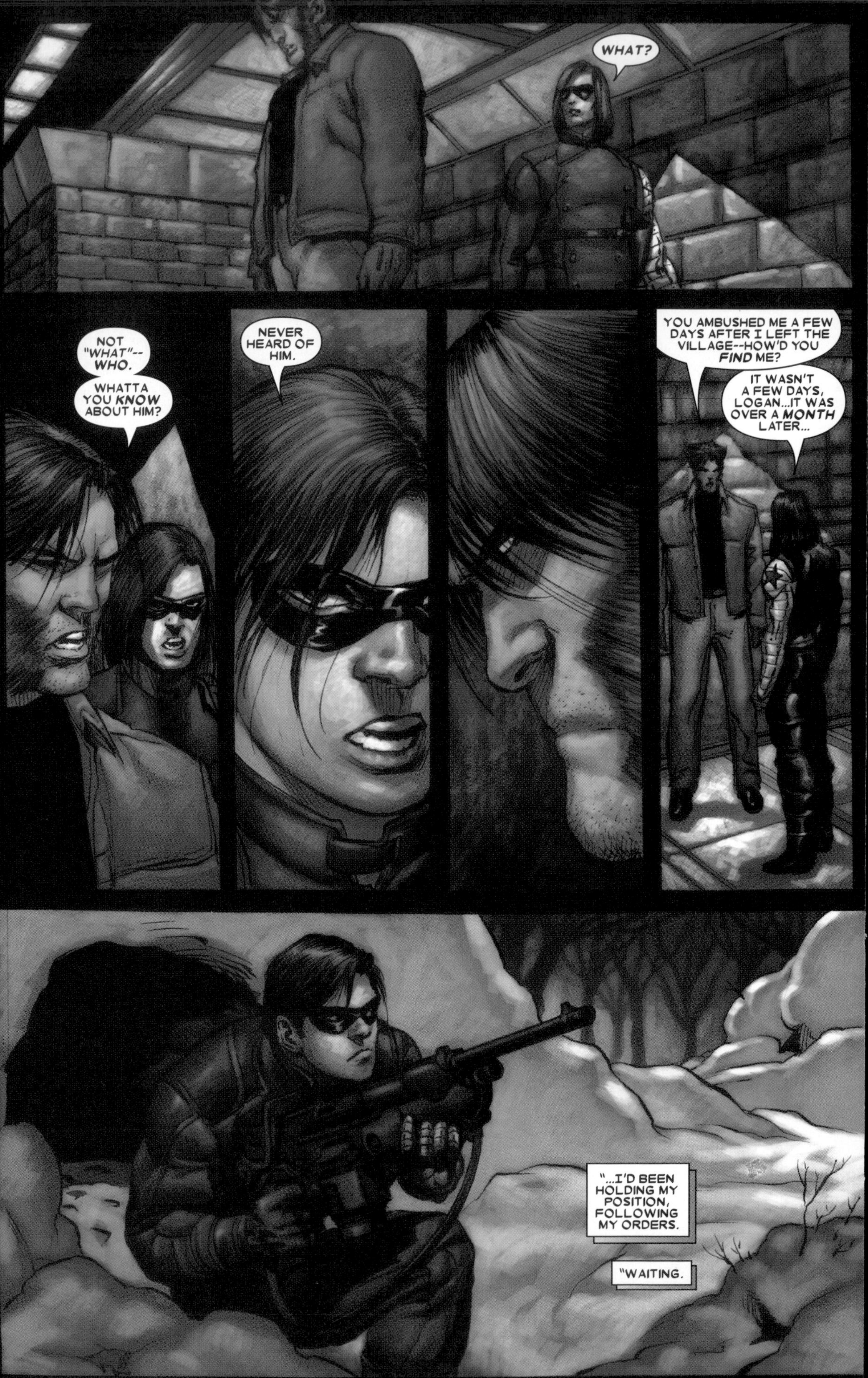
WHAT?
NOT "WHAT"-- WHO.
WHATTA YOU KNOW ABOUT HIM?
NEVER HEARD OF HIM.
YOU AMBUSHED ME A FEW DAYS AFTER I LEFT THE VILLAGE--HOW'D YOU FIND ME?
IT WASN'T A FEW DAYS, LOGAN...IT WAS OVER A MONTH LATER...
"...I'D BEEN HOLDING MY POSITION, FOLLOWING MY ORDERS.
"WAITING.

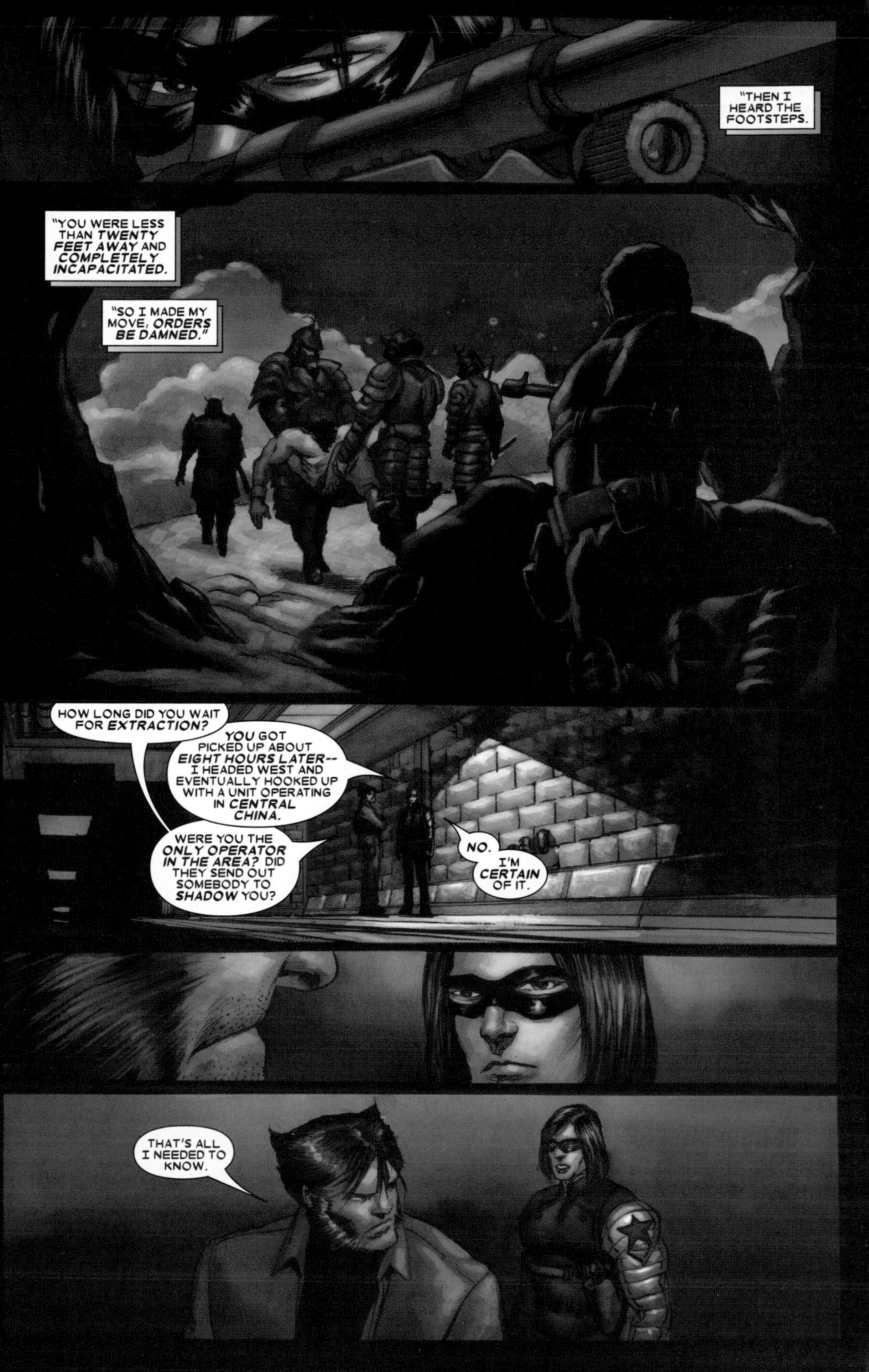
"THEN I HEARD THE FOOTSTEPS.
"YOU WERE LESS THAN TWENTY FEET AWAY AND COMPLETELY INCAPACITATED.
"SO I MADE MY MOVE, ORDERS BE DAMNED."
HOW LONG DID YOU WAIT FOR EXTRACTION?
YOU GOT PICKED UP ABOUT EIGHT HOURS LATER-- I HEADED WEST AND EVENTUALLY HOOKED UP WITH A UNIT OPERATING IN CENTRAL CHINA.
WERE YOU THE ONLY OPERATOR IN THE AREA? DID THEY SEND OUT SOMEBODY TO SHADOW YOU?
NO.
I'M CERTAIN OF IT.
THAT'S ALL I NEEDED TO KNOW.

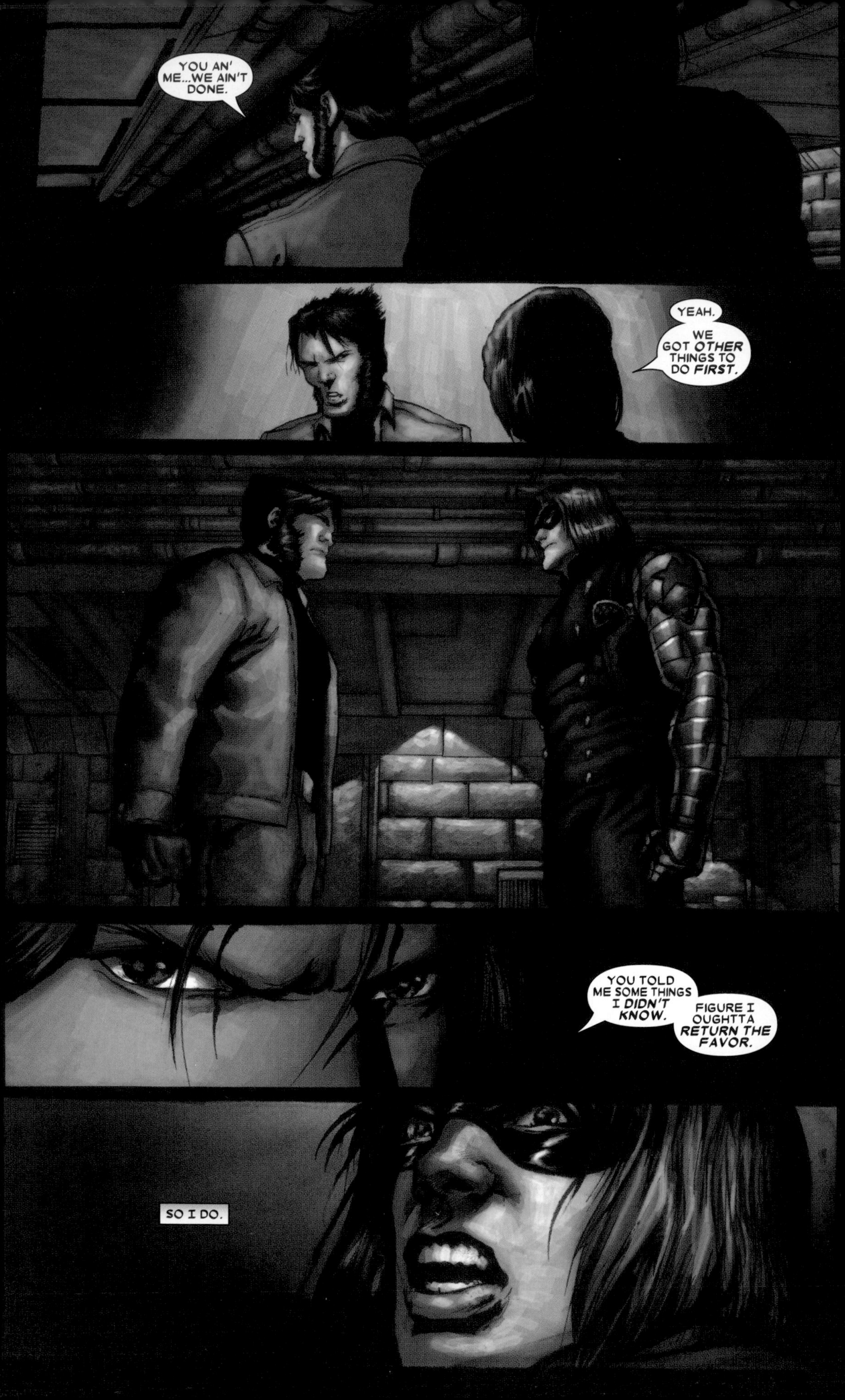
YOU AN' ME...WE AIN'T DONE.
YEAH.
WE GOT *OTHER* THINGS TO DO *FIRST*.
YOU TOLD ME SOME THINGS *I DIDN'T KNOW*.
FIGURE I OUGHTTA *RETURN THE FAVOR*.
SO I DO.

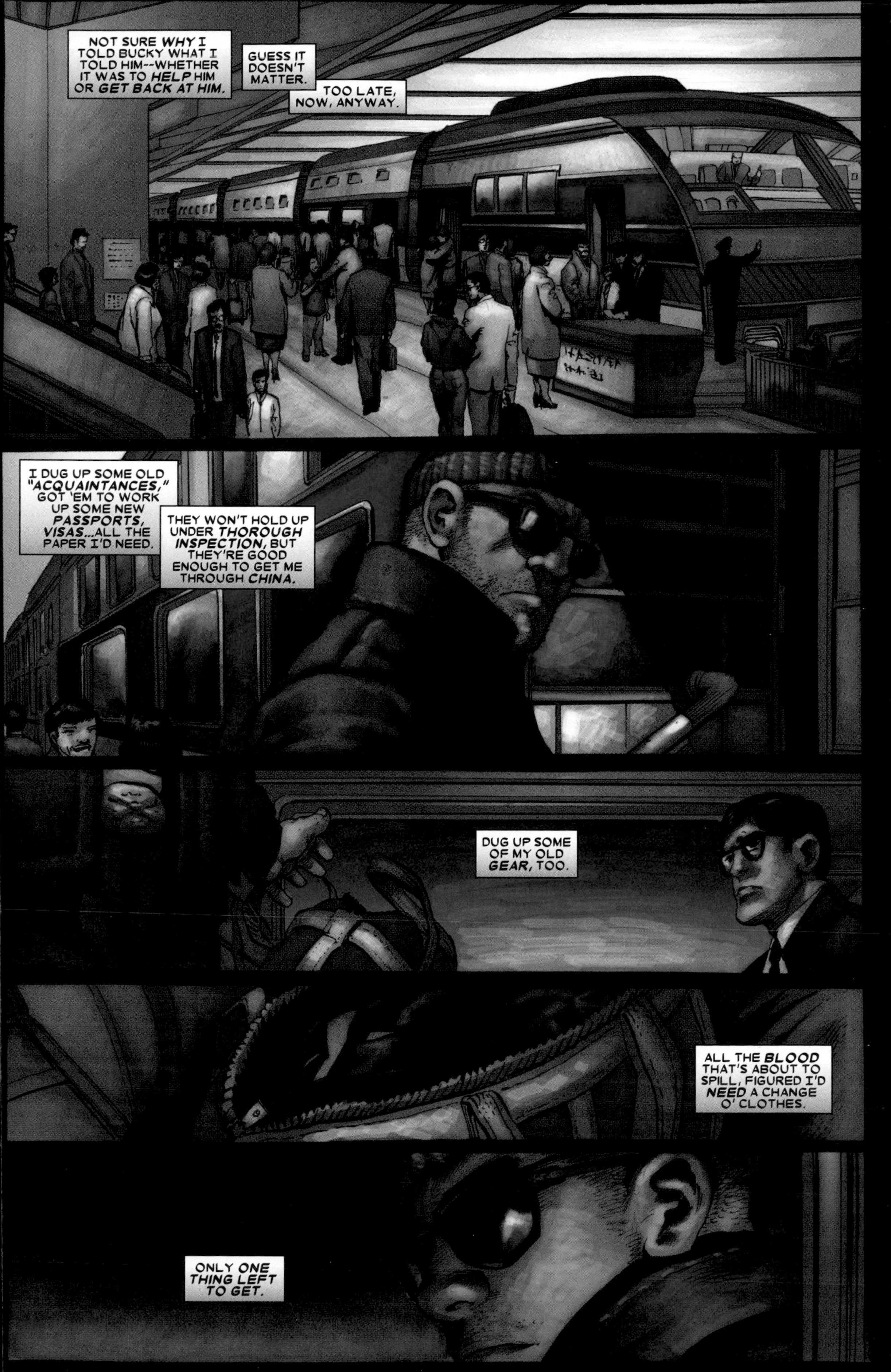
NOT SURE WHY I TOLD BUCKY WHAT I TOLD HIM--WHETHER IT WAS TO HELP HIM OR GET BACK AT HIM.
GUESS IT DOESN'T MATTER.
TOO LATE, NOW, ANYWAY.
I DUG UP SOME OLD "ACQUAINTANCES," GOT 'EM TO WORK UP SOME NEW PASSPORTS, VISAS...ALL THE PAPER I'D NEED.
THEY WON'T HOLD UP UNDER THOROUGH INSPECTION, BUT THEY'RE GOOD ENOUGH TO GET ME THROUGH CHINA.
DUG UP SOME OF MY OLD GEAR, TOO.
ALL THE BLOOD THAT'S ABOUT TO SPILL, FIGURED I'D NEED A CHANGE O' CLOTHES.
ONLY ONE THING LEFT TO GET.

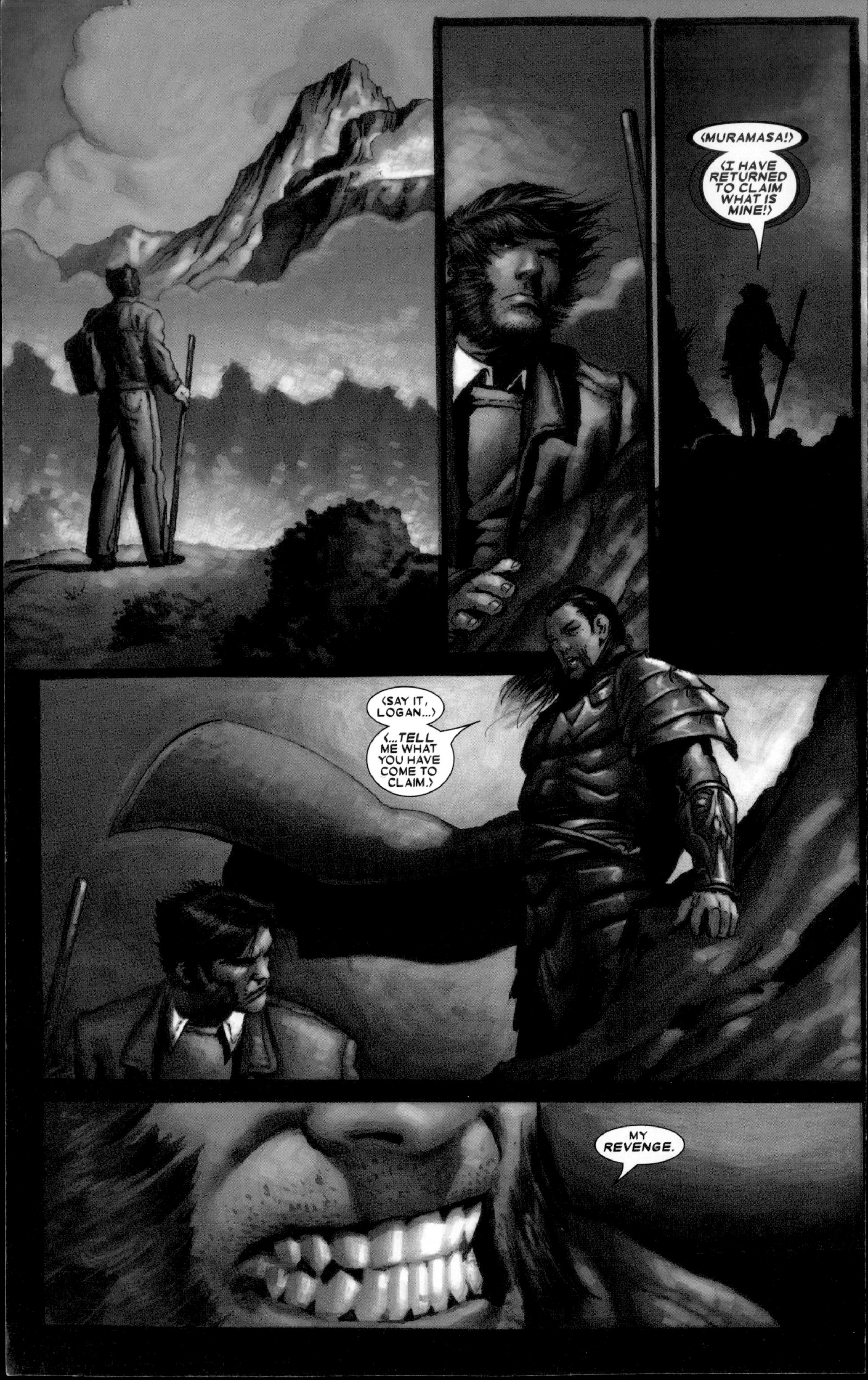
‹MURAMASA!›
‹I HAVE RETURNED TO CLAIM WHAT IS MINE!›
‹SAY IT, LOGAN...›
‹...TELL ME WHAT YOU HAVE COME TO CLAIM.›
MY REVENGE.

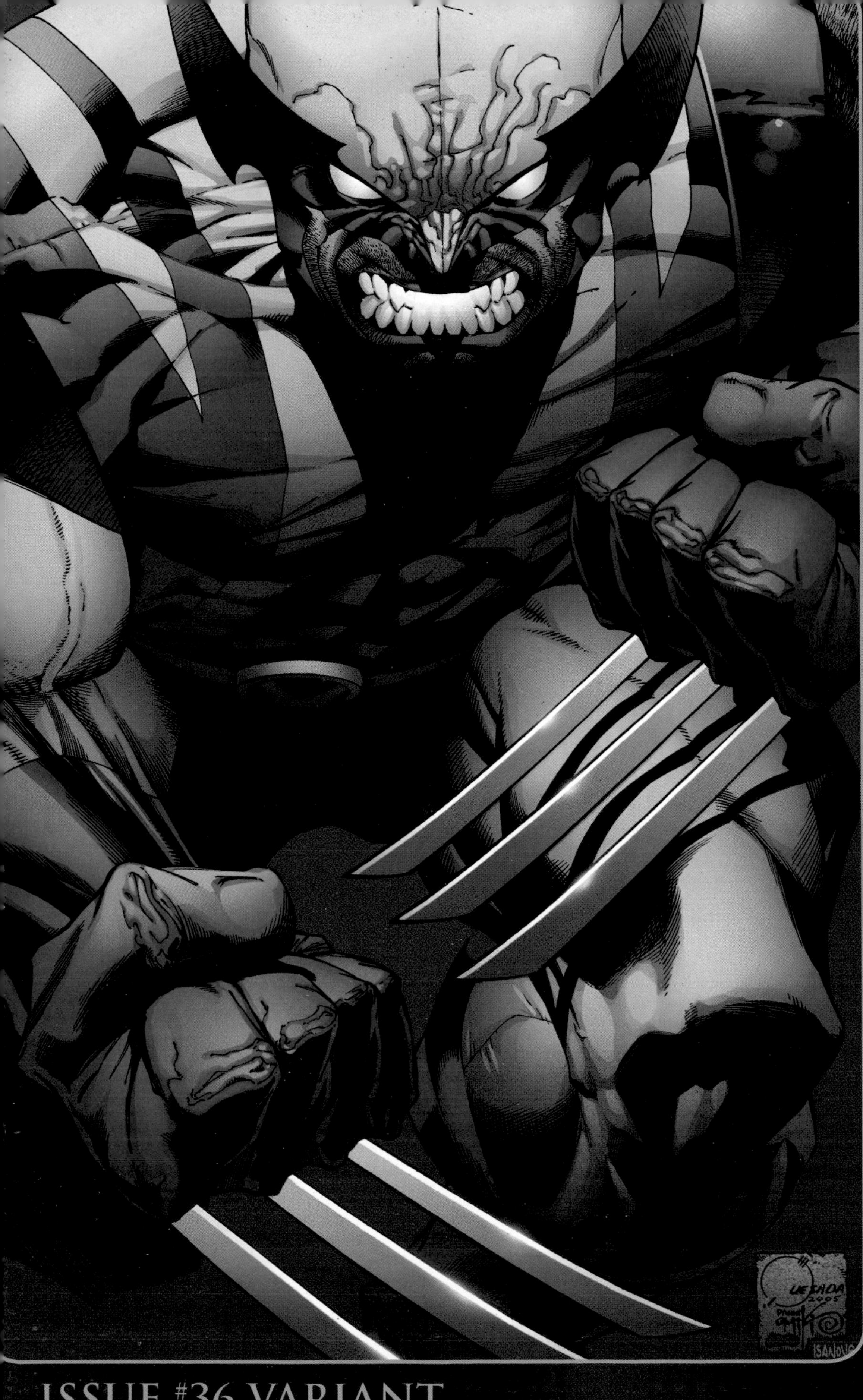

ISSUE #36 VARIANT

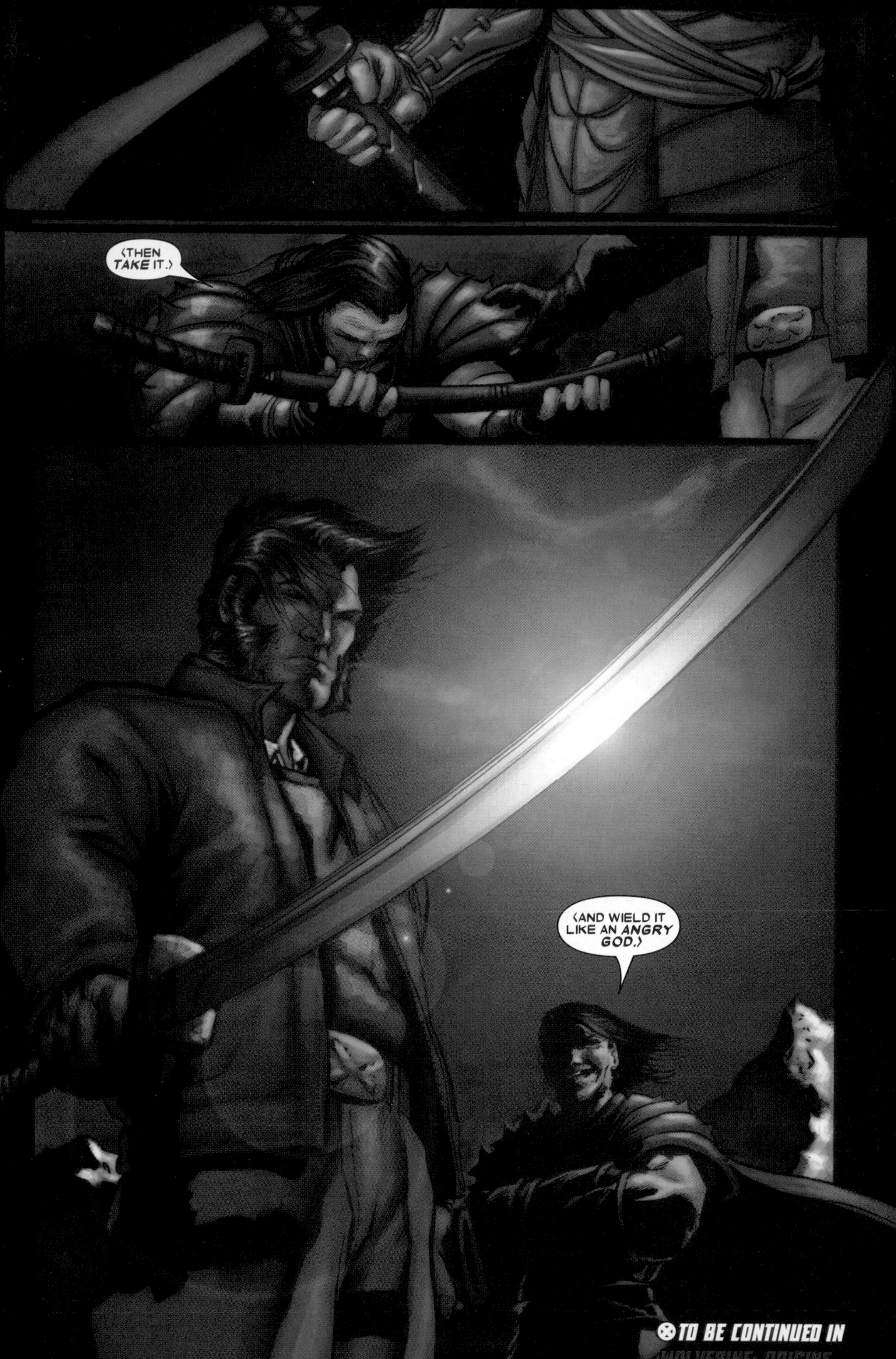

⟨THEN TAKE IT.⟩
⟨AND WIELD IT LIKE AN ANGRY GOD.⟩
TO BE CONTINUED IN
WOLVERINE: ORIGINS